The Falklands War

A Day-by-Day Account from Invasion to Victory

Foreword by Simon Weston OBE

Marshall Cavendish
Editions

Copyright © 2007 Marshall Cavendish Partworks Ltd

First published in 1983 as *The Falklands War* in 14 weekly parts
by Marshall Cavendish Partworks Ltd

First published in 2007 by:

Marshall Cavendish Limited
119 Wardour Street
London W1F 0UW
United Kingdom
T: +44 (0)20 7565 6000
F: +44 (0)20 7734 6221
E: sales@marshallcavendish.co.uk
www.marshallcavendish.co.uk

A CIP record for this book is available from the British Library

ISBN-13 978-0-462-09909-5
ISBN-10 0-462-09909-1

Page viii: © Crown copyright material is reproduced
with the permission of the Controller of HMSO

Designed and typeset by Phoenix Photosetting,
Lordswood, Chatham, Kent

Printed and bound in Great Britain by
TJ International Ltd, Padstow, Cornwall

Contents

Contents

Foreword

As a young, boisterous and over-energetic 20-year-old in 1982, my thoughts as we prepared to ship out to the Falklands were not of fear and dread, but more of excitement and uncertainty. We were all young super-men with everything to live for, and we had been training for action since the very first moment we joined up. The Falklands was a popular conflict unlike the current situations in Iraq and Afghanistan and we were comforted and reassured by the support of the British public.

We boarded the *QE2* at Southampton, and as we climbed onto the decks we were amazed by the size of the crowd that had come to see us off. Amongst the huge throng of parents, wives, girlfriends, children and friends was a certain young lady, who will I'm sure be remembered by all who watched her. This rather lovely girl stripped off her bra and top and flashed her (not unimpressive) breasts to approximately 2000, hormonal troops. The cheers went up and she received a very appreciative response to her selfless act. For us lads it was a little bit of titillation and fun to start us on our great adventure!

Our journey took us to Freetown in Africa, where in sharp contrast to the scene at our departure, we were greeted by the poor coming out to meet the ship in canoes and small boats, selling their goods to raise money. Poverty for these people was clearly appalling and disturbing for us to see, but I have to say it didn't stop us showing our wicked side. Some of us would heat coins up with our lighters and chuck them overboard onto the docks below. The youngsters would jump around and fight to catch or grab the money only for them to end up throwing the hot metal around until it cooled. Looking back, it was not my proudest moment.

As we continued southward we started to pass huge icebergs, and we were told that without sonar there was no doubt that we would have sunk. Suddenly, the fate of the *Titanic* took on a new meaning! At last we arrived at South Georgia, and I remember my revulsion at seeing the injured Argentine soldiers, who appeared to me to be no more than children ... I can picture the sunken submarine and the destroyed helicopter. I think at that point, war started to become a reality, whereas up until then it had just been something we had trained for and heard stories about. Today, soldiers know more about the reality of war because they can look back on the Falklands, the Gulf Wars, Afghanistan and Bosnia. All we had was heroic tales of daring from the First and Second World Wars. Even our exploits and struggles in Northern Ireland did nothing to prepare us for the life-changing experiences to come.

I can recall the day that changed my life with acute clarity – the air raid taking place, the sights, the sounds, my friends, the adrenaline rush to get out of there – and, of course, the pain. That single moment changed everything and it took me years to come to terms with the loss of my second family, the lads. I couldn't have stopped the missile that blew up the *Sir Galahad*, but at least I now know that I have been given the rare chance to become useful in a different way, by using the experience to benefit others.

I left the army with no skills on which to build my life, and very soon came to realize that I needed to grab any and all offers that came my way till I found something I could do. Having been singled out as one of the worst injured it took a long time to regain my self-confidence and reassert my identity. I just got on with it and can truthfully say I do not regret a single moment of the last 25 years.

Looking back it is clear to me that we didn't win the war by tactics, but by the incredible skills, tenacity and amazing talent of our soldiers. We had to interpret situations in the field and subsequently deal with the threat. As a 20-year-old I did not have the desire or inclination to try to analyze the situation – my job was to obey orders. In retrospect I feel sad that the situation need not have escalated to the extent it did, but as a soldier it is not our job to be political, it is our duty to protect, obey and fight for what is right.

What has also become abundantly clear to me, over the years, is that war cannot be won on the cheap. Our services need both money and equipment if victory is to be achievable – and more importantly – our soldiers must join up of their own free will, without conscription. As we sailed through the British Navy in 1982, we saw ships of all shapes and sizes for miles and miles: it was just phenomenal! The quality and quantity of the British Naval Fleet was eerily spectacular, and as trite as this may sound, the sight filled me with so much pride. Today, with the current political climate, it is both tragic and almost a betrayal that our ships are being decommissioned or simply not replaced. Our soldiers willingly put their lives on the line in the most treacherous places, so surely it is only right that we give them everything they need to make survival and victory a real possibility.

Of all the books and reports that I have read about the Falkland's war, this book is by far the most accurate account. For instance, Surgeon Commander Rick Jolly portrayed the Welsh Guards as being unfit and unprepared for battle … what a load of absolute rubbish – we were as fit as we could possibly be! We had endured intensive training and were ready for combat anywhere in the world. This book presents the reality of the conflict and dispels any inaccuracies and over-exaggerations published at the time.

Having said my bit, I encourage you to read this book and relive the personal experiences and fascinating stories of the Falklands War 25 years on.

Simon Weston OBE, March 2007

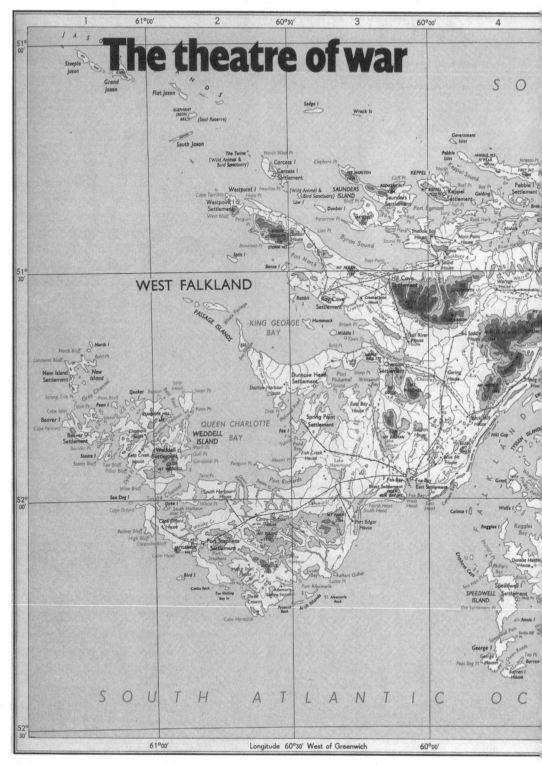

The theatre of war

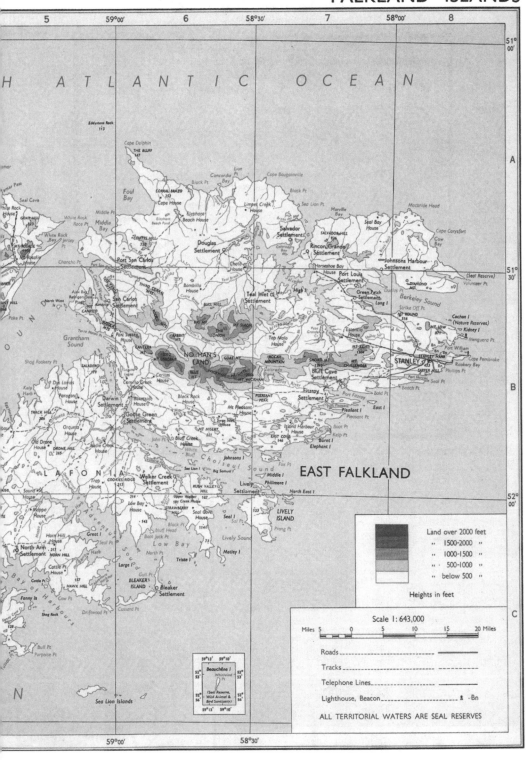

The General War Zone

© Martin Streetly

Location of the Falklands Islands

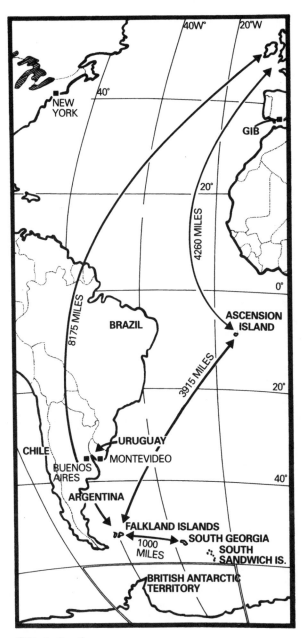

© Martin Streetly

Key Dates in a Long Dispute

1493 Pope Alexander VI grants New World territorial rights to the Spanish Crown.

1494 By the Treaty of Tordesillas Spain and Portugal divide up the American continent.

1502 Amerigo Vespucci may have been driven by gales to within sight of the islands.

1592 Capt John Davis is also driven by fierce storms 'in among certain isles never before discovered'.

1690 First recorded landing by Capt John Strong, who names the 'Falkland Sound' after the Treasurer of the British Navy.
   Over a period of years many French ships visit the islands, which they call Les Iles Malouines after the French port of St Malo. This becomes Las Malvinas in Spanish.

1764 Louis Antoine de Bougainville establishes the first settlement at Port Louis on East Falkland.

1765 Capt John Byron plants a vegetable garden on Saunders Island off West Falkland, and calls the bay Port Egmont after the First Lord of the Admiralty.

1766 The French claim is sold to the Spanish Crown.

1770 Five Spanish ships force the British settlers (who had come in 1766 to build the Port Egmont settlement) to quit.

1771 After negotiations to avoid war, Port Egmont is restored to the British, though Spain makes it clear that sovereignty has not been yielded.

1774 The British pull out of Port Egmont, leaving a lead plaque as a token of ownership of 'Falkland's Island'.

1816 A group of disaffected colonies in South America splits away from Spain's authority, claiming all Spanish property previously controlled from Buenos Aires, including the Falklands. This group will become the new Republic of Argentina.

1820 The new state formally takes over the Falklands, sending a frigate to Port Louis.

1826 Louis Vernet and 90 Argentine colonists re-establish the Port Louis settlement.

1828 Vernet is appointed governor.

1831 Vernet seizes US sealing schooners. In retaliation, the US corvette *Lexington* destroys the fort at Port Louis, imprisons the inhabitants and declares that the islands are free of all government. A new governor set up by the Argentines to build a penal colony is murdered by the prisoners.

1833 The British sloop *Clio* takes over Port Louis, sends the Argentine colonists to Buenos Aires, and claims the Falklands for Britain.

1910 Foreign Office research comes to the surprising conclusion that British actions in the past may have been high-handed, and that there may be some substance in the Argentines' claims.

After World War 1, such doubts are banished by recourse to the new international doctrine of 'prescription', in effect a justification of squatters' rights, whatever the rights and wrongs of occupation.

Argentina also believes its own case to be less than watertight—but extends its claim to embrace the dependencies, South Georgia, the South Sandwich Islands and the British Antarctic Territory.

Before and after World War 2 both sides discuss 'leaseback' by which Britain might concede sovereignty in return for a lengthy lease.

1965 As a result of lobbying at the United Nations, the Assembly passes Resolution 2065, reminding members that the end of all forms of colonialism is a pledge of the organization, and categorizing the Malvinas as a colonial problem.

1967 George Brown assures Nicanor Costa Mendez that sovereignty is negotiable and talks are opened between the countries in New York. The British Government seems keen to rid itself finally of the Falklands problem.

1968 The Falkland Islands Emergency Committee is set up to thwart these tendencies through the 'Falklands lobby', and in April the Foreign Secretary assures the House that the interests of the islanders are paramount in any discussions.

1970 The Conservatives regain power, and encourage the Argentines to employ 'seduction rather than rape'—in other words to win the hearts of the islanders by good deeds.

1971 A delegation of islanders accompanies David Scott of the Foreign Office to Buenos Aires, and takes part in an agreement whereby Argentina starts up a regular air service to replace the supply ship *Darwin* which was being withdrawn.

The air service is instituted, and eventually increases with the building of a temporary landing strip at Stanley.

1974 Argentina, still wooing the islanders, agrees to supply them with cheap fuel, but the islanders instruct James Callaghan, the current Foreign Secretary, to pull out of talks.

1975 After Argentine hostility, British officials are instructed to hold up further talks without seeming to do so.

1976 The military government takes power in Argentina.

1977 Talks about 'economic cooperation' get nowhere with islanders or Argentines. An intelligence report speaks of a possible attempted intervention in South Georgia. The Cabinet decides to send two frigates and a submarine. Nothing happens.

1980 Nicholas Ridley fails to sell 'leaseback' to the islanders and on his return is savaged by all sides of the House for trying. The islanders dig in their heels in the face of all blandishments and threats.

1981 Galtieri takes over from Viola as President of Argentina.

1982 Argentine Special Forces land at Mullet Creek, three miles to the south-west of the Falklands' capital, Port Stanley, thus signalling the Argentine take-over of the Falkland Islands ...

'We have lots of new friends'

With these words, Port Stanley's telex operator broke the news of the invasion to a stunned and disbelieving Britain.

IT WAS 0430 HOURS on 2 April 1982 when 150 men of the *Buzo Tactico*—the Argentine Special Forces—landed by helicopter at Mullet Creek, a small inlet some three miles to the south-west of the Falklands' capital, Port Stanley. This was the beginning of the Argentine take-over of the Falkland Islands, and was followed up by the landing of over 1000 more special troops and marines. By 0930—five hours after the first Argentine soldier landed—the small, 80-man garrison of Royal Marines and others had surrendered.

Just before noon the next day, 3 April, the even smaller Royal Marine force on South Georgia—some 800 miles east of Port Stanley—surrendered after one of the epic David and Goliath battles of our time. The shooting war had started.

The garrison of Royal Marines on the Falkland Islands was known as Naval Party 8901, and at 0900 on 1 April (another grim coincidence) Major Mike Norman RM—in command of the 1982/3 Detachment—formally took over from Major Gary Noott RM and the 1981/2 troops the job of defending the seat of government. His job was to last for exactly 24 hours. At 1530 that day the two majors were sent for by the Governor of the Falkland Islands, Mr Rex Hunt, who showed them a signal from London.

The message read, 'An Argentine invasion fleet will be off Cape Pembroke at the first light tomorrow. It is highly likely they will invade. You are to make the appropriate dispositions.' The Government in London had been receiving reports from intelligence sources that Argentine naval forces conducted exercises at sea between 23 and 28 March, which included a joint anti-submarine operation with the Uruguayan Navy in the

River Plate estuary. Later reports showed that the fleet had sailed south from the main Argentine naval base at Puerto Belgrano on 28 March with marines, soldiers and live ammunition on board. On 29 March it was known to be some 900 miles north of Port Stanley, and consisted of an air-craft carrier, four destroyers and an amphibious landing ship.

Forcing the issue

The Argentine Junta wanted to bully Britain into conceding sovereignty over the islands in the South Atlantic. They needed something to restore their fast-deteriorating popularity at home, and violent demonstrations in Buenos Aires on the night of 30 March showed just how bad things were for them. By milking the diplomatic incident that had blown up over the landing of a party of scrap metal merchants at an old whaling station in South Georgia for all that it was worth, the Argentines had hoped to force concessions from the British government at the Falkland sovereignty nego-tiations in New York. While blowing up the scrap-metal merchant incident, the Junta also strengthened their hand militarily by despatching warships to South Georgian waters and later by putting their task force to sea, equipped to invade the Falkland Islands themselves.

The Junta had been badly briefed. They thought that Britain would back down, rather than risk a war. They also thought that the British would give in, when faced with superior numbers.

It seems that the actual orders to invade were sent to the task force com-mander quite late on—only one or two days before 2 April. The ease with which they were carried out shows that the Argentines must have rehearsed the action in advance, and had worked out very detailed plans. Admiral Carlos Busser was there to command the 4500 invasion troops.

Holding out

The thankless task of defending the islands against this overwhelming force was Mike Norman's. To help him, he had just 43 men from the 'new' NP 8901, 25 from the 'old' party, and 12 sailors from the ice patrol ship HMS *Endurance*. Nine men from the 'old' party had been sent with Lieutenant Keith Mills to South Georgia, there to impose the will of Her Majesty's Government on the scrap dealers.

Norman had an impossible job, and he knew it. The task he set himself, therefore, was to hold out for as long as possible. Norman reasoned that the enemy would go for Port Stanley and neutralize the defences there so that forces could be landed on the airstrip and in the harbour. Accordingly, he organized his defences around the airfield and to the east of Stanley itself. His first priority was to make sure the runway could not be used; he ordered vehicles to be parked on it, with a single small section of men (No 5) covering the obstacles from the south. An OP (observation post) was set up to the east of Yorke Point, and a machine gun crew was to be positioned overlooking part of Yorke Bay—one possible landing site—which was also obstructed by coils of barbed wire. The machine gunners were given two motorcycles for a quick getaway, and a canoe was also hidden as part of an emergency escape plan.

Just south of No 5 Section's position the road from the airfield to Port Stanley makes a right-angled turn at Hooker's Point. It was here that No 1 Section was placed. To the west of them, at the old airstrip, was No 2 Section. Their firepower was to be increased by the addition of an 84mm Carl Gustav anti-tank weapon and its two-man crew. They were also to have light 66mm anti-tank missiles. Farther west still were the VOR directional beacons for the airfield's approaches. No 3 Section was positioned nearby; their task would be to delay the enemy for as long as possible before withdrawing.

Across Port Stanley Bay, at Navy Point, was No 4 Section's location. They were to have the other 84mm Carl Gustav MAW, and were given the thankless task of engaging any enemy landing craft or shipping which tried to get through the narrows. They had a Gemini inflatable boat for a quick return to Government House if they were needed there.

To the south of Port Stanley, on Murray Heights, No 6 Section was placed to give early warning of any Argentines approaching from the south of the town. Another OP was to be located to the west of No 6 Section's position on Sapper Hill and the sole marine manning it, Mike Berry, was to be equipped with a third motorcycle. The main headquarters was to be at Government House with Major Noott acting as the Governor's adviser. Major Norman was to be at Look Out Rocks, on the edge of the town to the south-east, commanding the troops on the ground. The motor vessel MV *Forrest* was sent to sea to keep a radar watch in the waters off Port William to the north. Unfortunately, the party's 81mm mortar was damaged and so couldn't be used, but an extra machine gun was given to No 2 Section at Hooker's Point.

During the night, the garrison was joined by two islanders, Jim Fairfield—a former Royal Marines Corporal—and Bill Curtiss. The marines' barracks at Moody Brook Camp were vacated by 0200 on the morning of 2 April and all positions were occupied. The light was switched off at Pembroke Point lighthouse, and Bill Curtiss put the VOR beacon out of action. The tiny British force was as ready as it could be to receive the Argentine invaders.

All that remained was for the 37 Argentines on the island to be rounded up and placed under guard.

0230. 'Contact!' It was *Forrest*—the enemy were on their way. An hour later, at 0330, it was clear that a large fleet was manoeuvering off Cape Pembroke. There was not a man in the defending force who did not feel the strain of waiting, but they knew they wouldn't have to wait for long. Norman had concluded his final briefing with the words: 'Remember, you're not fighting for the Falklands. This time you're fighting for yourselves.'

0430. 'Contact!' It was the OP on Sapper Hill. Helicopters near Mullet Creek in the general direction of Port Harriet. What were they doing there? The answer came at 0615 when firing and explosions were heard from the direction of Moody Brook. It was the *Buzo Tactico*, shooting up the marines' barrack block there. The Argentines went in hard with sub-machine guns and fragmentation and phosphorus grenades in an attempt to catch the marines in bed—which made a mockery of subsequent claims that the Argentines had been trying to spare British servicemen. What immediately appalled Major Norman, however, was that he had been 'wrong footed'. They were coming from the west, and all his forces were spread out to the east.

Numbers 1 and 5 Sections were immediately ordered to make for Government House, and Major Norman returned there himself post haste. The first attack against the headquarters came in at 0615 and the Argentines managed to get very close to the house—indeed three of them got into the maids' quarters where they hid in the loft—but the attack was beaten off by rifle and machine gun fire.

About a quarter of an hour later—at 0630—the OP at Yorke Point and No 2 Section at the airstrip reported that craft were landing at Yorke Bay. Some minutes later they radioed that about 18 armoured personnel carriers (APCs) were ashore and advancing towards Port Stanley. These were American-made LVTP-7 'Amtracks', equipped with .30in calibre machine guns. As they advanced down the airport road, they were engaged by No 2 Section under Lieutenant Bill Trollope RM. The leading vehicle was stopped by a 66mm LAW (light anti-armour weapon) missile fired by the armourer, Marine Gibbs, which hit the passenger compartment. An 84mm MAW round fired by Marines Brown and Best exploded against the front of the Amtrack. No one got out. The other vehicles deployed their troops and opened fire with their machine guns.

Sniping contest

Beating a prudent retreat, the marines made their way back to Government House where a fierce battle had been raging for some hours as the *Buzo Tactico* tried to storm it. During the heat of the fighting, a radio message was received from No 4 Section near Navy Point saying that it had three targets to engage and what were the priorities. 'What are the targets?' asked Norman. 'Target No 1 is an aircraft carrier; Target No 2 is a cruiser; Target ...' The radio went dead. The section made good its escape in the Gemini inflatable, however, and remained undetected for four days after the surrender.

The battle had, by this stage, turned into a sniping contest. It was now daybreak and more than one marine reckoned that they could hold out against the 600 or so men surrounding Government House. But as Governor Rex Hunt telephoned around Port Stanley to check with the inhabitants on the progress of the Argentine advance, the unwelcome news arrived that the Amtracks were on their way. They could sit well out of range of marines' fire and, if they wanted, raze Government House to the ground. Norman knew that there was no longer any chance of a breakout, so he suggested that Hunt talk to the Argentines. The Governor agreed reluctantly, but did not intend to surrender to the Argentines. He had no choice, however. Vice-Commodore Hector Gilobert, an Argentine who ran LADE, the civil airline supplying the Falklands, was contacted at his home in Stanley (there hadn't been enough time to arrest him) and he agreed to act as go-between.

At this moment, the three Argentine commandos who had been hiding in the maid's bedroom decided it was time to make a move. Crawling cautiously from under the bed, they moved towards the door. In the room directly underneath was Gary Noott. Without a moment's hesitation he fired a burst from his self-loading rifle (SLR) through the ceiling followed, when he heard the men crying out in shocked surprise, by another. Ten seconds later the commandos tumbled down the stairs, unhurt, with their arms in the air, begging to be taken prisoner.

When Hunt met with Admiral Busser at Government House, he told the Argentine that he was unwelcome, and invited him to leave. The Admiral politely declined, pointing out that he had some 2800 men ashore and 2000 more on the ships. The logic was inescapable. At 0925 Hunt ordered the marines to lay down their arms. It was now the turn of South Georgia.

The scrap at South Georgia

Eight hundred miles of ocean separate South Georgia from East Falkland. Though not much further south than the Falklands, South Georgia is a far tougher environment. Soaring mountains are covered in snow and ice 12 months a year, and the glaciers reach down to the sea. Captain James Cook made the first landing in 1775, and the island became a centre for sealing until the numbers began to run out in the early 19th century. Whaling became the major industry at the beginning of the 20th century, and South Georgia had shore factories at no fewer than six sites, including Grytviken and Leith Harbour. When the industry became monopolized by modern factory ships with no need of shore facilities, the stations began to die out. The industry finally failed altogether on South Georgia in 1965, leaving the wreckage and debris of over half a century rotting on the shore and in the shallows where abandoned whaling ships listed and collapsed like so many beached whales.

On 19 March an Argentine scrap-metal merchant with the improbable name of Costantino Sergio Davidoff came ashore at Leith. With 39 work-men he was there, so he stoutly maintains to this day, for the sole purpose of dismantling the forlorn whaling station.

Perhaps Davidoff's glib explanation can be taken near enough at face value, although by running up an Argentine flag he was at the very least being carelessly provocative. The flag soon came down in response to strong British protests, but, for whatever reason, Davidoff stubbornly refused to comply with repeated formal demands that he present himself before the commander of the British Antarctic Survey team, in order to receive proper authorization for his enterprise.

The upshot was a week and more of wrangling between the British Embassy in Buenos Aires and the Argentine Foreign Ministry, and what in retrospect looks like a deliberate orchestration—however improvised—by the Junta of the ultimate crisis in the Falklands.

On orders from London, HMS *Endurance* promptly left Port Stanley for Grytviken, with two dozen marines, there to await developments. Buenos Aires countered by removing all but a handful of the workers, only to replace them with a marine detachment, put ashore by an armed survey ship. The marines' ostensible purpose was to protect the workers. There were further British protests, and then on Saturday 27 March Argentina turned yet another screw—her invasion plans for the Falklands now complete. Two missile corvettes were dispatched to Grytviken in support of the Argentine forces already there, while over-flights of Port Stanley were stepped up. What had seemed during the preceding week as a rather farcical footnote to the long-drawn-out dispute over the Falklands had in fact set the stage for an armed showdown.

The Naval Party on board HMS *Endurance* had been beefed up with nine members of the old Detachment of NP 8901 from Port Stanley, and dispatched to Grytviken in South Georgia. It was commanded by Lieutenant Keith Mills RM—who was subsequently awarded the Distinguished Service Cross for his part in the heroic action they fought. His brief from Captain Nick Barker of HMS *Endurance* was to put up a token defence. He replied, that he was going to 'make their eyes water'.

Mills' Marauders

The Marines—later to be nicknamed 'Mills' Marauders'—were able to hear some of the radio traffic coming out of Port Stanley before and during the fighting, and so they prepared their positions at King Edward Point—the site of the British Antarctic Survey—as being the most likely place for an Argentine landing. The jetty there was wired with a booby trap by Marine Les Daniels who thought it more likely the jetty would go out to meet the Argentines than they come to it!

Just after 1030 on 3 April the Argentine corvette ARA *Guerrico* and the ice patrol ship ARA *Bahia Paraiso* entered the bay. Mills informed them briskly that there was a British military presence on the island and that any attempt to land would be strongly resisted. After ensuring that the staff of the British Antarctic Survey were safe in Grytviken's white wood church, Mills walked down the jetty. He was expecting *Bahia Paraiso* to lower a boat with someone aboard it to negotiate with him; he wasn't expecting the Puma helicopter which landed just 50 yards away from him, disgorging Argentine marines. Mills tried to attract their attention—and succeeded: one of them aimed his rifle at the young officer. As he sprinted back to his defensive position, the Argentines opened fire, while more helicopters tried to land troops. On the far side of King Edward Cove a second Puma dropped more troops, tried to take off, and was hit by machine gun and rifle fire. It landed again—heavily—and no one else got out. There were also two smaller Allouette helicopters in the area, one of which received the full attention of the platoon's firepower and suffered the same fate as the Puma.

The corvette *Guerrico* now entered the fray; it steamed back into the cove and started to open fire with one of its 40mm guns. The marines held their fire until it was in range, and then gave it everything they had: Marine Dave Coombes opened fire with the platoon's sole Carl Gustav and holed the ship below the water line; one more shot and she would have sunk. That shot never came. Instead Coombes fired again and hit the ship's gun; she spent the rest of the engagement firing over the marine's heads, to their relief and amusement. Meanwhile, several 66mm rockets and over 1000 rifle and machine gun rounds had peppered her superstructure and hull, so her skipper withdrew to a tactful distance.

Mills and his men were by this time surrounded and under heavy small arms fire from all sides. Their withdrawal route had been cut, and Corporal Nigel Peters had been wounded in the upper arm. Lt Mills realized that if they waited until dark to effect a withdrawal, they would sustain many more casualties. Having achieved his aims of making the Argentines use military force and of causing them considerable damage, he decided to surrender.

Mills' Marauders had more than made the Argentines' eyes water: they had carried through an amazing feat of arms which, had the invaders but known, was a warning of what was to come. More important, there was no sign of HMS *Endurance*. For her the Admiralty had something else in mind.

The storm breaks in Britain

Front page news around the world, the crisis confronted Britain with some urgent and dangerous options, and not since the Suez crisis had Westminster resounded to such a fierce debate. Meanwhile, the British nation steadied itself for the coming war.

ON WEDNESDAY 31 MARCH, intelligence and embassy reports confirmed to John Nott, British Defence Minister, that almost the entire Argentine fleet was at sea, and that the invasion of the Falklands was set for the early morning of Friday 2 April. There could be no doubt about the quality of this intelligence: it came from interception of Argentine fleet signals and electronic code breaking via the secret establishment at Cheltenham.

John Nott at once called the Prime Minister and a meeting was promptly arranged at her office in the House of Commons, attended also by Mr Atkins and Mr Luce from the Foreign Office, as well as by defence officials and Sir Henry Leach, the First Sea Lord. Margaret Thatcher was clearly impressed by the Admiral's calm assurance that HMS *Hermes* and HMS *Invincible* could sail from Portsmouth on the morning tide the following Monday. These two aircraft carriers would form the backbone of the Task Force.

Mrs Thatcher's first diplomatic move was to draft a message to President Reagan, requesting that he should get on to President Galtieri and ask him for an assurance that he would not authorize a landing or begin hostilities. He could also inform Galtieri that Britain would not escalate the dispute.

Sir Nicholas Henderson, Britain's accomplished Ambassador in Washington, was soon on his way to see Alexander Haig, the US Secretary of State, a known friend of Britain from his time as Supreme Allied

Commander of NATO forces in Europe. He had already received a request from Foreign Secretary Lord Carrington to help in cooling down the Argentines.

Meanwhile, in London, Mrs Thatcher summoned another ministerial meeting on Thursday evening. She ordered that troops should be put on immediate alert for deployment to the South Atlantic. The Task Force was on four hours' notice to sail within 48 hours. Warships from Gibraltar were already sailing south, ready to join forces with the main fleet.

The mood of the nation

The gravity of the news created a mood of shocked disbelief and quiet anger in Britain. Feelings ran stronger than at any time since World War 2. This was so clearly an act of naked aggression; Argentine troops had landed on and seized British territory, island territory moreover, which reminded people at home that they, too, were islanders.

The headlines of popular newpapers screamed 'Shamed!'; but behind such melodrama was the quieter feeling of the majority that things should be put to rights in the Falklands. There was a consciousness that warlike people had taken advantage of unpreparedness, and that this could not be tolerated. 'If Argentina can shove us around, who cannot push us over?' asked one columnist.

Never in recent foreign affairs crises had faraway events produced such a spontaneous feeling of national solidarity. In Buenos Aires the crowds were marching and flag-waving in a display of old-fashioned jingoism. In the pale April sunshine of London there were no marchers, but even the peace lobby on the left were more than half inclined to agree that such an obviously fascist military dictatorship as Argentina's should not be left to have things their own way.

The next morning, Saturday 3 April, members of parliament assembled to hear a statement from the Prime Minister and then hold an emergency debate. At the same time a long, well-ordered queue built up for places in the public galleries of the House of Commons. This was the first great parliamentary occasion in a big international crisis concerning Britain directly since the BBC had started parliamentary broadcasting. It was possible therefore for the population to eavesdrop on the statements and on the debate. The fact that Ministers and MPs were aware that for once the nation was listening to them had a sobering effect.

Mrs Thatcher began by reading in unemotional tones from a carefully prepared brief. Although she knew that it would not be long before the critics began demanding resignations, she went on with mounting confidence and received loyal cheers as she condemned 'this unprovoked aggression' which had 'not a thread of justification, or a scrap of legality!' It was the objective of the government to see that the islands were freed from occupation and returned to British administration at the earliest possible moment.

Although the House approved her firm conclusion that the right of Falkland Islanders to remain British must be upheld, it did not prevent them from blaming her government for allowing the invasion to happen, and there were many cries of 'Resign!'

The search for scapegoats

After Argentina herself, the politicians had three main targets: the Foreign Office, Mr Nott and the intelligence service for failing to give advance warning of Argentine intentions. Poor Mr Nott was howled down when he denied that the government had been taken by surprise and that it would have been wrong to take military action earlier.

John Nott and Lord Carrington remained at their desks in a state of gloom after the Saturday debate, cheered only by the news from New York, where Lord Carrington's man Sir Anthony Parsons was scoring a diplomatic victory which went some way to restore the tarnished reputation of the Foreign Office.

Lord Carrington and Mr Nott offered their resignations over that weekend, as did Humphrey Atkins, and another Foreign Office Minister, Richard Luce. Mrs Thatcher, harrassed and under fire from her own party as well as from the Opposition, tried hard on the Sunday to persuade her senior colleagues to stay on. In the case of John Nott she succeeded, on the grounds that this was no time to appoint a new man to the ministry so busy preparing a difficult campaign faraway in the South Atlantic. She wrote to him saying: 'The Ministry of Defence is not the department responsible for policy towards the Falklands.'

With Lord Carrington, a highly successful Foreign Secretary well respected internationally and a senior party man, it was a different matter. Although he was convinced that a good deal of the criticism of the Foreign Office was unfounded, he insisted that as he had been responsible for the conduct of foreign affairs he thought it right that he should resign. 'The fact remains that the invasion of the Falkland Islands has been a humiliating affront to this country,' he wrote in his letter of resignation.

Playing the American card

At first it looked as if popular support for Britain would not be so easy to establish in the United States. President Reagan had shown himself well-disposed from the start, but roars of laughter greeted the first mention of the Argentine invasion at a White House briefing on Monday 5 April. To the sophisticates, it all seemed too absurd to worry about: an affair with Latin American gauchos in uniform invading an island with a governor who wore a plumed hat, a grand uniform and rode about in a London taxi. The fact that the laughter soon stopped was largely the work of Sir Nicholas Henderson, British Ambassador in Washington.

He launched a powerful propaganda campaign, spearheaded by himself in numerous appearances on American TV and radio, where he soon won star status as a 'natural'. By appealing to the American people, the natural allies of the British, he hoped to work up the vital American national support.

Both the senior British diplomats across the Atlantic had their suspicions about the helpfulness of Mrs Jeane Kirkpatrick, the US ambassador to the UN, a determined lady who seemed intent on cosying up to the Argentines. Sir Nicholas sharply reproached her for attending an Argentine banquet on the night of the invasion of the Falklands. It was, he said, as though he had accepted hospitality at the Iranian Embassy on the day American hostages were seized in Teheran.

To make matters worse, Mrs Kirkpatrick declared: 'If the Argentines owned the Falklands, the moving in of troops is not armed aggression.'

The Haig shuttle

The British placed their hopes on Alexander Meigs Haig, the sprightly 58-year-old retired political general with a distinguished military record and long experience of government, who was President Reagan's Secretary of State. In his telephone conversation with Galtieri, President Reagan had already suggested that he might send as a mediator Vice-President Bush, or 'somebody like that'.

Now it was Al Haig who could clearly see the dangers of the situation for the US in its relations with Latin America. He was keen to try his hand at shuttle diplomacy and put himself forward for the job of go-between. So began the Haig mission, during which the Secretary of State clocked up some 26,000 miles flying between Washington, London and Buenos Aires as the British Task Force steamed slowly into the South Atlantic.

Shortly before Al Haig, in trench coat and Irish tweed hat, flew into London on Thursday 8 April, news came that John Nott had announced a maritime blockade in a 200-mile area around the Falklands. Over dinner at 10 Downing Street, Haig outlined what his mission would try to do. He made it clear from the start that the US agreed with the British in principle even though they hoped that a peaceful solution might be found.

On course for collision

Mrs Thatcher remained sceptical and made it clear that unless the Argentines withdrew their troops the British fleet would not turn round. This was the message which the American mediator and his team had to bear to Galtieri in Buenos Aires. Arriving there the following day, Haig found the Argentine Junta in a fighting mood.

In Britain, people recovered from the shock of the invasion to find themselves reassured that the country still had a powerful navy and armed forces, ready to translate ideals into action. In the dockyards, men worked all hours to make the ships ready; customary union restrictions on who should do which jobs were forgotten. Cartoonists worldwide would have a few field days left them, to crack jokes at the expense of Britain's 'mothballed' navy and its unlikely mission. Those who knew the real merits of the ships and planes involved got on with the task in hand.

The task force gets going

'Now listen in, men. The good news: there isn't any. The bad news: Argentina has invaded the Falklands. Everyone has been recalled. Your leave has hereby been cancelled.' X-Ray Company Commander 45 Commando.

WHEN THE DECISION to assemble a task force was taken, on the evening of 31 March, Admiral of the Fleet Sir Terence Lewin was in New Zealand on an official visit. Roughly half the Royal Navy and Marines had either gone on Easter leave or were looking forward to it. Admiral Sir John Fieldhouse, C-in-C Fleet, had only just flown back from Gibraltar and the NATO exercise 'Spring Train'.

Much later—after the Union Jack was flying above Port Stanley again—an official statement summed up the state of affairs with admirable candour: 'There were no contingency plans on the shelf. We had to improvise.' They succeeded, and brilliantly.

In fact, the earliest that any kind of naval activity can be detected is 29 March, when the Prime Minister and Foreign Secretary decided to send a nuclear submarine to the South Atlantic. That same day Commodore Sam Dunlop in the Straits of Gibraltar informed the crew of his Royal Fleet Auxiliary flagship *Fort Austin* that they were being diverted to the Falklands to resupply the ice patrol ship *Endurance*. This 23,600-ton replenishment ship was in support of no fewer than seven frigates and destroyers quite fortuitously in the midst of 'Spring Train', and these too were put on the alert. At home the ageing carrier *Hermes* was in Portsmouth about to begin a refit, while the newer *Invincible* had just returned from Arctic warfare exercises off Norway.

'Those people down south'

Admiral Sir Henry Leach, First Sea Lord, attended the crucial five-hour meeting of 31 March, held in the Prime Minister's room at the Commons, and assured her that the big ships could sail on the morning tide of 5 April. At the same meeting the unsuspecting liner *Canberra*, at that moment approaching Gibraltar at the end of a world cruise, was nominated as principal troop ship. And a second nuclear submarine would also head south.

It was not until the next evening (1 April) that the Cabinet agreed to put troops on immediate notice. Brigadier Julian Thompson of 3 Commando Brigade spent most of April Fool's Day at his Plymouth HQ in an atmosphere of order, counter-order and disorder. Decision came at 3.15 on the 2nd, still five hours before the Argentine landings, when Thompson picked up his phone to hear Major-General Jeremy Moore: 'You know those people down south. They are going to be attacked.' Forty-five minutes later the Royal Marine Landing Craft Base at Poole was on standby. Thompson began ringing Denmark to recall his staff from the NATO exercises they were planning.

Lt-Colonel Nicholas Vaux, CO of 42 Commando, set about gathering his men from leave six days old. Twenty-five of them were out of the country, and indeed Intelligence Officer Lt Henk de Jaeger got a recall telegram at his New York wedding reception. Thompson's two other units were also a long way from base—40 Commando in Cheshire and 45 Commando at Arbroath, Scotland. Initial reaction there was 'Get lost, April Fools was yesterday', while one marine, visited at home by a policeman, wondered 'What are the Argies doing in the North of Scotland? They must be after the oil!'

At C-in-C's Fleet London HQ, Moore picked up two other most readily available units, 2nd and 3rd Battalions The Parachute Regiment, both based in Aldershot. They too were mainly on leave—Lt-Colonel Herbert Jones, CO of 2 Para, was skiing in France—and on invasion day every London railway station had posters and loudspeakers recalling the Paras.

Of all the services, the RAF was the first to respond positively. On the afternoon of 1 April seven Hercules transports flew from RAF Lyneham in Wiltshire for Gibraltar and Ascension Island. They carried supplies for the Royal Navy at the Rock, and even more crucially, air traffic controllers with equipment to expand Ascension's Wideawake Airfield into a round-the-clock staging post for the Task Force.

Item: 180,000 eggs

Twenty-four hours later the grim-faced figures of Nott and Carrington were making it public knowledge that a Task Force was preparing, while the Cabinet agreed that it should sail on the morning of Monday the 5th.

At Portsmouth, work was proceeding non-stop under dockyard flood-lights. Robert Fox of BBC Radio, making a casual enquiry about morale of an engine rating from *Hermes*, was staggered by the reply: 'All right, I suppose. It all depends if we get a run ashore tonight. The ship's in a bit of a mess though. Her main boilers were in pieces until four days ago.' *Invincible* had 30 men working 20 hours to provision her with just one item—180,000 eggs.

Inland, things were no less hectic. The first four days saw 3000 lorry loads of military equipment pass through Hampshire to Portsmouth and Southampton. NATO stocks in Germany were ruthlessly annexed for the 'out of area' emergency.

Order-in-council

In one area at least there were established rules—the requisitioning of merchant ships. An order-in-council drawn up ceremoniously by Nott, Pym and Trade Minister John Biffen at Windsor Castle on Sunday 4 April gave legal force to 'the taking up of ships from trade', the first call-up of civilian ships since 1945. Conversion to naval needs meant such changes as the fitting of helipads, extra signals equipment, defensive armament and taking aboard Royal Navy detachments. *Canberra*'s cabins were being measured for troop berths even as she steamed north with her cruise passengers on board.

The sailing of the carrier-led Task Force on Monday 5 April has been indelibly etched on the national consciousness. Equally significant were the sailings on Tuesday the 6th. HMS *Fearless*, the amphibious assault ship, left Portsmouth followed by her eight landing craft. Soon after 5 pm, with *Fearless* well down the Channel, a helicopter deposited Brigadier Thompson, Commodore Michael Clapp (Amphibious Warfare Director) and their staff on the ship's flight deck. With them was a priceless document, carried by Major Ewen Southby-Tailyour, Thompson's newly appointed staff officer without portfolio—a 126-page notebook containing his 1978 yachtsman's survey of the 10,000-mile Falklands coastline.

'As likely as men on Mars'

From Plymouth Sound at the same time came the logistics landing ships *Sir Galahad* and *Sir Geraint* with 105mm guns, trucks and engineering equipment loaded. (*Sir Tristram* would join from Canada.) The frigate HMS *Antelope* sailed from Devonport as their escort, while out ahead in the Channel the carriers were joined by their frigate escorts, *Arrow* and *Plymouth*.

In the surface van of the Task Force bound for Ascension was the County-class guided missile destroyer *Glamorgan*, flagship of Rear-

Admiral John Woodward, the surprise and relatively junior choice for Task Force Commander. Lt David Tinker, the ship's Flight Deck Officer, spoke for many when he wrote to his wife on 7 April: 'We are now actually doing something which we have always thought about as likely as Men on Mars.'

At Bickleigh Barracks, Plymouth, Lt-Colonel Vaux had gathered in 42 Commando by 8 April. The unit paraded before Major-General Moore and Vaux gave the historic order: 'To the South Atlantic, quick march!' The commandos were heading for Southampton and the liner *Canberra*. But all was not as it seemed. One company stayed out of the parade in the unit's gym. Major Guy Sheridan's 110 men were wanted for a special operation—the recapture of South Georgia. They found themselves airborne for Ascension next day, Good Friday, along with 70 men of the SAS and SBS.

The destroyer *Antrim* and RFA tanker *Tidespring* (a sister ship, *Tidepool*, was literally reprieved in mid-voyage from a planned transfer to the Chilean Navy) had already reached Ascension for junction with HMS *Endurance*. Their task was to embark the special forces for South Georgia. The troops came aboard two hours after touching down.

Four thousand miles behind, *Invincible's* Sea Harriers were firing 2in rockets for the first time and HRH Sub-Lt Prince Andrew was dropping a depth charge a mile away from his ship. The Task Force was on its way.

SS *Canberra*: the impossible takes a week

When it all started, she wasn't even at home base. *Canberra*, flagship of the Peninsular and Oriental Steam Navigation Company (P&O), was cruising off Naples on the last leg of a world trip.

The lady, a ripe 21 years old, was still quite a vehicle, at 44,800 Gross Registered Tons the nation's second largest liner. In the seven days that followed the Argentine invasion of the Falklands a great deal was to happen to her.

By 2000 hours on the spring evening of Good Friday, 9 April, this first week was over. At this evening hour, from berth 105 in Southampton's Western Dock 8, *Canberra* freed her mooring lines—and 13 minutes later was under her own steam into the Solent. The gin and tonic set—her regular customers—had been replaced by the troops of 40 and 42 Commando and 3rd Battalion The Parachute Regiment who, with supporting troops from many other units, had arrived just the day before, Thursday.

As *Canberra* sailed, the Band of the 2nd Battalion the Parachute Regiment played. To watch, crowds had gathered further down Southampton Water in a park that edges this historic piece of the coast. They cheered, flashed their car headlights and sounded their horns. In return, the Captain of *Canberra*, Captain Scott-Mason, blew on the ship's siren. Ahead lay the ocean and the long thrust southwards of a powerful ship at 24 knots.

Sun deck to flight deck

'Very professional panic' is the term to describe the transformation that turned a liner into a troopship in those few days.

Canberra was the first requisitioned ship to be fitted with a flight deck. There had been no peacetime contingency plans for this, and the designs worked out were done on the spot with whatever materials were locally available. In Southampton, that meant half-inch mild steel plating and long-stalk mild steel Tee Bars. The main problem with *Canberra*, as it was to be with the other liners, *Uganda* and Cunard's *QE2*, was that their superstructures were largely made of aluminium. Such a structure allows ships a maximum amount of enclosed cabin space for minimum penalty of topweight. But it makes fitting a helicopter flight deck (weighing between 70 and 90 tons) on to the superstructure problematic.

Fortunately, *Canberra* had an excellent spot for a flight deck. The sun deck, behind the bridge and forward of the funnels, offered a large area unobstructed by superstructure or by any other top-hamper. Moreover, the sun deck contained the Bonito Club swimming pool, strong enough to hold between 70 and 100 tons of water. After re-routing some aerials, placing a series of stalks and girders in the pool and (of course) draining it, the positioning of the 70-odd tons of flight deck did not prove too difficult—at least, nothing compared to the problem the fitters had with the second helicopter flight deck. The pool, though empty, later managed to regain some of its former recreational role when Royal Marines draped ropes from the girders and created a kind of adventure playground. Nobody, however, tried this underneath the second flight deck, which could be seen to move a quarter of an inch forwards and backwards during heavy seas whilst making a series of rather distressing noises.

The second pad

It had been decided that the best place for the second helicopter pad was on the fo'c's'le, which in *Canberra* was taken up by the Crow's Nest Bar. It had not been designed with strength in mind. The sides of the bar consisted of a series of glass wind-breaks and in the centre of the bar there was a wide spiral staircase which descended through three decks. In addition, there were ventilation ducts and electrical circuits to be avoided. Finally, the helicopter pad had to be of such a size, 80 ft long by 100 ft wide, that beyond its side edge there was a 60 ft sheer drop to the sea. In short, the fo'c's'le of *Canberra* is not the sort of place which would normally attract one as a natural helicopter landing area. However there was no option and plans were approved by Mr Skinner, the Naval Construction Overseer on Monday morning, 5 April.

So the work to fit *Canberra* with its new equipment went on throughout Wednesday, Thursday and into Good Friday. As the former liner slid towards the Solent, and as friends and relatives waved and wept their farewells, on the ship there was still much to be done. Some 26 men from Vospers were still on board to finish off the work on the helicopter pads.

Retaking South Georgia

It seemed fitting that the glacier-strewn island of South Georgia—where the Argentine flag was first hoisted—should be the Task Force's first target. It would soon be the first place to take the Argentine flag down.

JUST BEFORE 1200 hours on 3 April Lt Keith Mills and his 22 Royal Marines defending South Georgia ended their brave resistance and surrendered to the Argentines. On 7 April, Admiral Sir John Fieldhouse was ordered to plan the island's recapture. It was the logical first step in the controlled escalation of force that was to culminate in the removal of all Argentines, from Britan's South Atlantic dependencies.

Paraquet is a somewhat archaic way of spelling 'parakeet', but that is how it was entered in the list of unused and therefore available code names, for operations. This was the name selected for the repossession of South Georgia, although it was changed unofficially and almost immediately to Operation Paraquat.

The small Argentine force on the island was commanded by a naval engineering officer, of dubious reputation called Lt-Commander Alfredo Astiz. There was no way in which the forces under him could properly occupy and control the whole of the wasteland of the island. They had to be content with keeping small garrisons at Leith and Grytviken. This meant that some members of the British Antarctic Survey (BAS) and the two women—Cindy Buxton and Annie Price—who were making a 'Survival' film for ITV remained at large.

A military presence was also kept in the South Atlantic after the surrender at Grytviken in the shape of the ice patrol vessel HMS *Endurance*. The ship had wanted to join the fight, and was on her way to finish off the Argentine corvette ARA *Guerrico*, when she was ordered to stand some 60 miles out to sea and keep a low profile. She remained in the area monitoring Argentine communications and sending intelligence back to the United Kingdom. She also maintained contact with the two women and members of the BAS. *Endurance* was able to stay out of the Argentines' way and eventually rendezvoused with Task Force 317 on 12 April far to the north.

The troops earmarked for the recapture of the island were from the Special Air Service Regiment, the Special Boat Squadron and the Royal Marines. Mountain and Boat Troops of D Squadron 22SAS and 2SBS—a total of some 60 men—were tasked, along with M Company 42 Commando Royal Marines, and the force was under the tactical command of Major Guy Sheridan RM, second in command of 42 Commando.

When 42 Commando left their barracks at Bickleigh just outside Plymouth on 8 April to sail down to the Falklands on board SS *Canberra*, M Company stayed behind hiding in the gymnasium. They were forbidden to phone their wives, and two days later, on 10 April, they flew from RAF Lyneham to Ascension Island where they joined the troops from D Sqn 22SAS and 2SBS. They all embarked on the destroyer HMS *Antrim* and the Royal Fleet Auxiliary *Tidespring*. Also embarked were two Naval Gun-Fire Support (NGS) parties on *Antrim*. The SAS and SBS, together with some of the force command element, sailed in *Antrim*, and the rest of M Company were in *Tidespring*.

The British SSN HMS *Conqueror* was ordered to patrol off South Georgia to prevent any Argentine reinforcement of the island. The commander of the Task Group allocated to the recapture was *Antrim's* captain, Captain Brian Young DSO RN. The Task Group consisted of HMS *Antrim*, HMS *Plymouth* and RFA *Tidespring*. On 12 April they made a rendezvous with HMS *Endurance* with some members of the BAS team on board. The scientists briefed the troops on the Argentines' strengths and locations.

Pre-strike reconnaissance

On 14 April, Major Sheridan was ordered to plan covert reconnaissance of the Leith and Grytviken areas to determine the exact strengths and dispositions of the Argentine troops. This operation would be carried out by patrols from the SAS and SBS. It was felt that the primary objective would be Grytviken, and Leith would come later. An initial photographic reconnaissance of the island was carried out by an RAF Handley-Page Victor bomber from Ascension.

The small force sailed steadily south. As it became clear that part of Task Force 317 was heading for South Georgia, and that Britain was obviously going to take the much-speculated-about 'South Georgia option', the Argentines sent a strong platoon (some 40 marines) to the island in one of their two ex-US Navy Guppy Class submarines, *Santa Fé*. She managed to slip through the net of maritime surveillance which was mounted by RAF

Nimrods operating from Ascension Island and backed up by Victor K2 tanker aircraft. This operation was carried out between 20 and 25 April to give early warning of hostile naval movements, and swept the area from South Georgia to the Argentine mainland. Before *Santa Fé* could land her troops the British were in South Georgian waters.

The plan for Phase One of the operation was for 15 men of Mountain Troop D Sqn 22SAS, who were now in *Endurance*, to land by helicopter on the Fortuna Glacier to the north of Leith, and move by way of Husvik and Stromness to Leith itself. At the same time, 2SBS on board *Antrim* would land by helicopter or Gemini inflatable assault boat in Hound Bay to the south-east and make their way gradually via Moraine Fjord to Grytviken. The OC (officer commanding) M Company 42 Cdo, Captain Chris Nunn RM, was to form a quick-reaction force (QRF) to land as and where required. Most of M Company were on *Tidespring*. The BAS scientists were not at all happy about putting men onto the Fortuna Glacier in the conditions that were likely to be experienced there at that time of year.

Enemy number one—the weather

A reconnaissance was made of the glacier at first light on 21 April by the radar-equipped Wessex HAS 3 helicopter from HMS *Antrim* and, although there was some wind and driving rain, conditions seemed suitable for the operation. The Wessex 3 returned to pick up four SAS men, and the Wessex 5s from RFA *Tidespring* landed alternately on *Antrim's* deck to embark more. The plan was for the Wessex 3 to lead the 5s up onto the glacier by radar. The operation had to be abandoned after they encountered thick low cloud, driving rain and snow storms in Possession Bay. After some hours the weather improved, and a second attempt was made—the helicopters climbed onto the glacier in swirling low cloud. The visibility and navigation problems were made worse by frequent driving squalls of snow and sudden changes in wind speed and direction. Nevertheless, the three helicopters reached the landing zone (LZ) and deplaned their troops and their equipment. They returned to the ships by way of Possession and Antarctic Bays to avoid being sighted by Argentine observation patrols that might have been around.

During the night of 21 April the barometer fell sharply to 960 millibars and a force 10 snowstorm, which gusted to 70 knots, blew all night. The windchill factor on the glacier was dangerously high. The wind blew away the troops' shelters, and after nearly 24 hours in the blizzard and intense cold, the Mountain Troop men—under Captain John Hamilton of the Green Howards—radioed at 1100 on 22 April that they had been unable to move off the glacier, that they could not survive another 12 hours and that frostbite cases or 'environmental casualties' were imminent.

It was decided to extract them using the same formation as before.

Conditions were much worse than the day before, with swirling low clouds and driving snowstorms sweeping across the glacier. The wind was very changeable, gusting to 70 knots and then dropping unexpectedly to 10, which caused problems of severe mechanical turbulence over the mountains. It was decided to leave the Wessex orbiting in Antarctic Bay while the Wessex 3 tried three times to get onto the glacier. The 5s landed on a spit of land to conserve fuel. In the end, all three helicopters had to return to their mother ships to refuel.

A second attempt was made immediately, and this was successful. The three helicopters climbed the glacier, sighted the smoke ignited by the troops to indicate their position and wind direction, and landed there during a welcome break in the weather. But as the SAS men were being enplaned, the wind blew strongly again and whipped up the snow. One of the *Tidespring's* Wessex 5s, callsign YA, had been the first to load troops and was ready for take-off, and so the pilot decided to lift immediately. As he took off and moved forward, he seemed to lose his bearings in the 'white-out' and crashed, skidding for some 50 yards and ending up on his side. The other two helicopters had now embarked their troops, so they lifted and landed next to the crashed YA where they loaded its aircrew and soldiers. Half were taken onto the other Wessex 5, callsign YF, which dumped fuel to carry the extra load as did the Wessex, which had the other half.

Visibility by this time was practically zero, and the wind and snow had not abated. With the survivors on board, the Wessex 3, callsign 406, took off with YF following astern and they made their way down the glacier. Some seconds later, they traversed a small ridge, YF was seen to flare violently and strike the top. It rolled over onto its side and could not be contacted by radio. The overloaded 406 had to return to the ship some 30 miles away to the north. The passengers were disembarked and medical supplies and blankets were taken on board. The Wessex 3 then flew back towards the glacier, but the foul weather prevented landing. Contact was however made by radio with the crashed YF, and it was confirmed that there were no serious casualties.

The heroic Ian Stanley RN

The Wessex 3 returned to *Antrim* to wait for a break in the weather. About an hour later an opportunity presented itself, and 406 flew back to the glacier and managed to locate the survivors. They were embarked and, somewhat overloaded with 17 passengers and their kit, got back to *Antrim* some 35 minutes later. For these feats of daring airmanship the pilot of 406, Lt Commander Ian Stanley RN, was awarded the Distinguished Service Order.

Hours later another team was ready to be put ashore. This time they were to go in Gemini inflatable rubber assault boats, with their somewhat unreliable 30-kilowatt outboard motors. Using five boats, 15 men of 2SBS and Boat Troop D Sqn 22SAS set out in three-man patrols. Almost as soon as it was launched, the first boat's engine failed and it was swept out to sea. Another suffered the same fate in the Antarctic night. One crew was picked up by helicopter. The other boat managed to make a landfall on the last piece of land before the open sea. They waited for five days before they switched on their Sarbe (search and rescue beacon) in case its signals put the operation in jeopardy.

The other patrols landed successfully earlier on, just after 0000 hours, at the north end of Sirling Valley. They reported just after 1200 that ice from the glacier was being blown into Cumberland East Bay and was puncturing the rubber skins of their Geminis. They were recovered during the night, and the following day were put ashore in Moraine Fjord. During a lull in the blizzard on 23 April, Mountain Troop were landed again on the Fortuna Glacier, and proceeded with their mission.

A submarine contact was made. It was thought that it was on a submerged patrol to attack the ships of the Task Group trying to retake the island, and so they withdrew towards the edge of the Exclusion Zone to the north. They made a rendezvous with HMS *Brilliant* which was equipped with two Sea Lynx helicopters, valuable replacements for the Wessex 5s which had been lost.

During the night of 24 April the warships returned, leaving *Tidespring* to continue her withdrawal outside the Exclusion Zone. An intensive anti-submarine operation was begun to locate the Argentine boat. On Sunday 25 April *Antrim's* Wessex 3 made a radar contact, spotting *Santa Fé* on the surface near Grytviken, which she was leaving having landed her reinforcements. It attacked her with depth charges, which exploded very close to her port casing. It is probable that she did not dive when she spotted the Royal Navy helicopters because she thought that she would stand a better chance on the surface than submerged against the sophisticated ASW weapons that the British have.

Badly damaged, she was forced to turn and head back towards Grytviken.

Plymouth launched her Wasp and *Brilliant's* Sea Lynx was ordered to drop an ASW torpedo if the *Santa Fé* dived. *Antrim's* Wessex opened fire with her GPMG, and the Sea Lynx released the torpedo and closed to harass the submarine with its machine gun. The Wasp from *Plymouth* sped in from 40 nautical miles away under control of the Wessex 3 and fired an AS12 missile, and the Wasps from *Endurance* scored hits with their AS12s on the *Santa Fé's* GRP fin. These missiles did little damage as they punched straight through before exploding. The disabled submarine, leaking oil and streaming smoke, was beached alongside the jetty of the BAS base at King Edward's Point.

This event had shocked and demoralized the Argentine garrison. The original recapture plan had envisaged a set-piece landing by M Company, who were at this time some 200 miles away on board *Tidespring*. The SAS D Squadron commander, Major Cedric Delves DSO, on board *Antrim*, urged that the opportunity presented by the shock and confusion of the attack on the submarine should be seized, and an immediate landing made.

A scratch company hurries into the fray

Endurance was still in Hound Bay, and *Plymouth* was unable to land a Wessex 3 helicopter on her flight deck, so a composite company was hurriedly made up from all the military personnel on board *Antrim*. There were 75 of them in all, being elements of Mountain and Boat Troops (SAS), SBS, headquarters personnel, some M Company marines, members of the Mortar, Administrative Echelon and Recce sections and the ten Royal Marines of *Antrim*'s Detachment. There were also the two NGS parties.

Major Sheridan set H-hour at 1445. At H-30 minutes (1415 pm) a Wasp helicopter lifted an NGSO, Captain Chris Brown RA, from 148 Battery of 29 Commando Regiment Royal Artillery, to a spot where he could observe the Argentines at Grytviken. Major Sheridan and 30 SAS men went ashore and set up the Tactical Headquarters at Hestesletten. The rest of the ad hoc company group followed, and a mortar position was established. While this initial landing was going on, the NGSO called down fire from the 4.5in guns of HMS *Plymouth* and HMS *Antrim*, neutralizing the landing site and the slopes of Brown Mountain, where Argentine troops had been seen.

At this stage in the campaign to regain the South Atlantic dependencies, the emphasis was on limiting casualties. So the 235-round bombardment was made as a demonstration of the superior firepower of the British, and no shells were brought down any closer than 800 yards from identified positions. The shells fell in a controlled pattern around the Argentines: the Royal Navy could have hit them if it wished. After this the NGS was 'on call'.

Major Sheridan's party made their way along the steep slopes of Brown Mountain, and by 1700 they were within 1000 yards of King Edward's Point. He ordered the landing of more troops from *Endurance* and *Plymouth* onto Bore Valley Pass, and asked the ships of the Task Group to show themselves by sailing into Cumberland East Bay. As he was doing this, the Argentines raised three large white flags in King Edward's Point settlement.

They had been persuaded that the game was up by some SAS men arriving in their position by walking through a minefield and running a Union Jack up the pole. The astounded Argentine officer in charge could only protest: 'You have just run through a minefield!' A few minutes later, HMS *Antrim* appeared around Sappho Point, and the landings at Bore Valley Pass were cancelled. Major Sheridan flew across King Edward's Cove by helicopter and the Grytviken garrison surrendered at 1715.

The next day, 26 April, the 16 Argentines at Leith were invited to surrender by radio, but they refused. A personal visit from the SAS and Royal Marines, however, convinced them that they should do so without a fight. The intimidating presence of HMS *Plymouth* and *Endurance* helped with the persuasion.

'Shot dead in error'

Among the first troops into the settlement at King Edward's Point were the medical officer and his team from *Antrim* and *Brilliant*. They attended to an injured sailor from *Sante Fé* who was seriously wounded, and had to amputate a leg. He survived his injury. The only fatality was an Argentine petty officer who was shot dead in error while the submarine was being moved under supervision. A skeleton crew of Argentines had been on board, each member with a Royal Marine guard who had instructions to prevent the boat being scuttled. Commands were to be passed down in both Spanish and English so that both could understand. The particular order to blow tanks reached the petty officer and his guard only in Spanish. As the Argentine sailor complied with the command, the Royal Marine thought that he was about to scuttle the boat and so he shot him. Booby traps and mines which the enemy had laid were removed by them under the watchful eyes of the British troops.

The Argentine prisoners, numbering 156 marines and Navy personnel and 38 civilians, were segregated and kept in Shackleton House until they were shipped out to Montevideo in Uruguay on 30 April on board RFA *Tidespring*. The Argentine force commander, Lt-Commander Alfredo Astiz, signed a formal document of surrender on 26 April in the wardroom of HMS *Antrim* in the presence of Captain Brian Young of *Antrim*, Captain Nick Barker CBE RN of *Endurance*, Major Guy Sheridan and the SAS squadron commander.

Major Sheridan, Arctic explorer and ski racing champion, signalled to his Commanding Officer, Lt-Colonel Nick Vaux DSO RM, on board SS *Canberra*, 'Our unit flag flies high over Grytviken.' Colonel Vaux replied, 'When we have sorted out the rest of the South Atlantic we look forward to a spectacular reunion. Did you have the right wax?' M Company remained on South Georgia, setting up OPs and guarding against another Argentine attempt to capture it. The island was once again in British hands, 23 days after Lt Keith Mills' gallant fight.

The long run south

This was no cruise. As the armada rolled south, men got themselves and their weapons to combat-readiness. Few yet believed that the fleet would be going all the way. But the odds were shortening fast as April sped by.

IN APRIL 1982 soldiers and journalists found themselves sailing towards an unexpected war. What happened on the long run south towards it was as remarkable as any part of the whole story.

The mood among the Task Force personnel was summed up the night before *Canberra* left port. Journalists held a sweepstake on how long *Canberra* would be at sea. Some said a week. Others, less optimistic, suggested 'back in Southampton by 27 May'. No one reckoned on a mission beyond Ascension Island. Once aboard, people started relaxing: the soldiers after frantic days assembling and loading men and equipment, the journalists after some bitter disputes with the Ministry of Defence and Royal Navy in the struggle to get a place on board. The press contingent objected to the MoD 'minders' aboard: public relations officers tasked to keep a paternalistic eye on them. They were even more unhappy with the senior naval officer, Captain Chris Burne, whose attitude to the press was, initially, cool. In time, the press and military developed cautious respect, even mutual liking. The minders stayed universally disliked throughout.

For the soldiers, training began almost at once. The units embarked on *Canberra* (40 and 42 Commandos, Zulu Company 45 Commando and 3 Para) share an obsession with military and physical efficiency. From the very start, the men were doing PT on the decks and running around the ship in an attempt to maintain their fitness. It was soon discovered that six laps of the promenade deck was about a mile in distance, and it was henceforth a daily routine to be woken at dawn by the sound of the paras and marines pounding round the ship. Others were not so fortunate in their ambition for exercise. The rest of 45 Commando were embarked aboard the RFA *Stromness*. There, the available deck space was minimal, so the marines had to make do with calisthenics and PT 'circuits'. Those marines aboard HMS *Hermes* were in similar straits: despite the vast exercise area offered by her flight deck, aircraft and helicopter traffic was so heavy that only one hour's exercise a day could be allowed.

For the helicopter pilots and their crews the training was more practical. Along with Sea Harrier aircrews they were practising troop carrying, anti-submarine warfare (ASW), and (in the case of the Sea Harriers) air-to-air fighting and ground attack. All the while, stores were being ferried back and forth between the ships as unit quartermasters put their act together, and mail and supplies were being exchanged with the British mainland.

The pilots soon discovered that *Canberra* presented them with some problems; the 'midships' helicopter deck was mounted over the Bonito Club swimming pool between the foremast and the twin funnels at the stern. The wind there was, as one said, 'about as reliable as when you're taking a goal kick at Twickenham'. Most preferred to land on the forward helipad where, even if the wind was strong, at least it only blew one way.

Aboard *Canberra*, as the great ship plunged south of the Bay of Biscay, the troops got down to the serious business of preparing for war. Weapons training and lectures were daily. All ranks practised stripping and reassembling rifles and machine guns blindfold. They honed their marksmanship and handling skills: practising the loading of rifle magazines and the feeding of machine gun belts into the weapons' breeches.

For the first time, in many cases, there was a feeling of real urgency among the men. Almost all had served in Northern Ireland, but a counter-terrorist campaign requires a different type of weapon-handling skill, that of restraint. Few of them had served in campaigns in Aden or Borneo; fewer at Suez (the last time any of the units concerned had fought the kind of action where the skills they were practising would be at a real premium). Pressmen, naturally, took a keen interest. Videotape and TV film were ferried back to England, all of it showing the men going through their weapon drills, firing over the sterns of various ships, and going through their arduous fitness routines. One of the most intriguing activities was anti-tank training; all units were armed with an as-yet untried weapon, the Milan wire-guided missile. This is a deceptively simple weapon which requires that the operator keep the cross-hairs of his telescopic sight on a moving target—the missile will automatically follow his line of sight and strike the target about 18 inches below the centre of the graticule. Men from 3 Para's anti-tank platoon were seen practising on *Canberra* using little clockwork tanks as a target, with an Argentine flag stuck in the turret to remind the gunners just who they were up against. Some viewers of this game, back home, wrongly concluded that the boys were playing games. In the event,

Milan proved to be devastatingly effective, but not against tanks. The Argentines kept their armour in Port Stanley, so the British troops used the anti-tank weapons against Argentine bunkers. At £20,000 a shot this may not have been very cost-effective, but this form of trench-clearing proved very efficient, particularly in the savage fight at Goose Green.

All the way down to Ascension Island, the pattern changed little: weapon training, fitness, and lectures. Some of the ships stopped to refuel and replenish in Freetown, Sierra Leone, but the men weren't allowed ashore. This was probably a good thing—3000 men, cooped up on a ship like *Canberra* with little to do, can generate a quite remarkable amount of physical frustration. Two tanned English girls who appeared on the quayside to wave them off were maybe wise to stay ashore.

By the time *Canberra* arrived at Ascension on Tuesday 20 April everyone aboard had got to know his fellows. For the journalists it was a surprisingly pleasant experience. The army and marine units aboard *Canberra* had long experience of dealing with the press in Ulster, and put their experience to good use; each unit appointed a public relations officer (PRO) whose job it was to get as much sympathetic publicity for his men as possible. Few failed.

Pressmen were fascinated by the fighting men. As they began to probe beneath the uniforms and red and green berets, they found complex, thoughtful, intelligent people. The soldiers were young. Many had little secondary education. But they knew the issue at stake, they knew what they were there for (even if they didn't necessarily approve) and, for one reason or another, had settled to their task. Most of the men were proud of their élite status as commandos or paratroopers. They accepted that, if one had to go to war, the way of handling it was to go in hard and to win, as quickly as possible. There was a certain prejudice against 'craphats', the ordinary line infantry who couldn't or wouldn't make the effort to become members of an élite. Arrogant? Yes, and violent with it too, but as Major Chris Keeble, the second-in-command of 2 Para remarked: 'A unit's success in action depends on its capacity to generate violence.'

And the paras had a tremendous capacity for violence. So did the marines, but there was almost no violence between the two traditionally antagonistic units—with a common foe to prepare for, the red and green berets closed ranks.

The officers were a surprise as well—intelligent, well-read and not at all aloof. Unlike certain foreign armies where the ranks are distinguished by the quality of their food and equipment and the amount of hard physical work to be done, para and marine units extend few of the courtesies of life towards their officers—at least not in the field. Officers carried the same loads as their men, ran the same distances, but faster, ate the same food in the field and were capable of doing anything they asked of their men. On a long march the colonel's feet bled as freely as the men's.

The chance to march came once the men got ashore on Ascension Island. The RAF and army teams on the island had built seven shooting ranges on the island, five of them inside the perimeter at Wideawake Airfield. There all four battalions (the three commandos and 3 Para) were able to zero their rifles and machine guns. There, too, they were able to fire their heavy weapons: the 120mm Wombat anti-tank guns, the 81mm mortars, Milan and the 105mm light field guns. To get to the ranges the men were landed at Wideawake by helicopter. And then marched. The term 'march' is inadequate to describe the activity. To cover seven miles from range to helicopter would take just over an hour, the men running most of the way carrying their weapons and ammunition—a total load of about 45lb. For the marines and paras Ascension was a bonus as far as PT was concerned. As one of them said: '*Canberra's* OK but it's nice and flat and there are no hills. This is the real thing.' He didn't add that *Canberra's* wooden decks were starting to break up under the incessant pounding of boots.

Canberra stayed at Ascension for nearly two weeks. After the first couple of days it became routine for her to slip out of the anchorage at night to cruise elsewhere. An Argentine Air Force Boeing 707 had been seen skulking around nearby; then an Argentine freighter, *Rio dela Plata*, appeared. Argentina's recent interest in underwater warfare suddenly seemed ominous—it was believed she had tried to buy some miniature submarines from Italy. Accordingly, HMS *Antelope* started carrying anti-submarine 'sweeps' to make sure no one was below her.

There were false alarms. On one occasion some of *Elk's* derelict containers were heaved overboard—and mistaken for a hostile submarine. Later, there were contacts with whales—so many that the standing joke became, 'It's all over, lads. The whales have surrendered!' More ominous were regular sightings of Russian spy trawlers and the occasional spy plane that flew over from Conakry in Guinea, West Africa, or from Cuba. As no one knew how much the Russians were helping Argentina, these sightings were the cause of concern. Once the Task Force went south, the Argentine Boeing returned, so maritime reconnaissance Nimrods flying out of Wideawake were fitted with sidewinder air-to-air missiles, thus becoming temporarily the largest fighters in the world.

May Day began with the landing at Ascension of a Vulcan. Almost before it had stopped, the BBC World Service was announcing its successful raid on Port Stanley Airfield that morning. The following day it announced that the Argentine cruiser *General Belgrano* had been torpedoed. Initial reactions were euphoric; but the mood changed drastically when it became known that hundreds had died. The feeling was, 'It could have been us.' Everybody felt vulnerable, and sympathy for the dead and wounded became surprisingly (to some) strong. It added some salt to the mood expressed by Admiral 'Sandy' Woodward after the retaking of South

Georgia: 'This is the run up to the big match which should, in my opinion, be a walkover.'

Wideawake on Ascension

Without Ascension Island as a staging point for the RAF's extraordinary airlift to the South Atlantic, the odds against Britain's regaining the Falklands would have been enormous. 'Operation Corporate', as the whole task was code-named, stands out as one of the most amazing feats of military organization in recent history.

Ascension Island is a British possession about 1200 miles from the west coast of Africa, 4250 miles from the United Kingdom and 3800 miles from Port Stanley. It is a roughly circular volcanic outcrop about 62 square miles in area, dominated by the 2700ft Green Mountain which sports about the only natural vegetation on the island. The rest is described as 'a lump of clinker', though it is a noted breeding ground of the sooty tern, or 'wideawake', after which the island's airfield is named.

The air routes to the island were activated on 2 April while the fighting was still going on against the Argentine invaders, and the first people to be flown in were the Naval Party whose job it was to provide the vital logistical support to the fleet.

The essential features of the island were the good anchorage in the roads off Georgetown (the capital) and the enormously long airstrip at Wideawake Airfield. This had been built under licence by the US for their satellite tracking station, and is normally operated by a small staff from Pan American Airways including only two air traffic controllers. It usually handles some three aircraft movements a week. At the height of the conflict, this increased to 400 movements a day.

To achieve that sort of turnaround, it was necessary to move in to the island a large tri-service force: the British Forces Support Unit Ascension Island—BFSUAI for short. At the same time, it was essential that the limited resources of the island were not overstrained. By strict control of personnel on the island, for example putting visitors on the next flight out, the BFSUAI just managed to keep the numbers down to the normal figure of 1000, but there were times when this went up unavoidably to some 1500. Personnel embarked on Task Force ships lived on board, coming ashore by day only.

The commander of BFSUAI was Captain McQueen RN, and in addition to supporting the Task Force his responsibilities included working Wideawake Airfield along with its normal staff and defending the island base.

As materials, men and equipment built up, the base became an increasingly attractive target for the Argentines to attack. To counter this, as the military personnel there were already fully committed to other tasks, No 3

RAF Regiment Wing Headquarters and a detachment from No 15 Field Squadron were flown down (arriving 6 May) to provide ground defence against possible Argentine sea-borne attacks or raiding parties. An Argentine-registered freighter was sighted lurking in the area in early May, and the risk of parties of swimmers being sent on sabotage ships and installations was judged to be significant enough to warrant taking precautions.

The air defence of the base was provided initially by hijacking three out of the eight Harrier GR3s which arrived on 5 May. These were en route to the Task Force, and eventually flew down to the Falkland Island area using in-flight refuelling from the tankers based at Ascension Island. The GR3s were each armed with two AIM9 Sidewinder missiles and twin 30mm Aden cannon. On 10 May a mobile early-warning radar was set up on the top of Green Mountain giving a terminal control area out to 230 miles. The radar was a Marconi Martello S259 transportable 3D system, and was manned by the RAF. On 24 May, three Phantom FGR2 interceptors from 29 Squadron RAF arrived to take over air defence duties, and the Harriers were able to leave for their rendezvous with the Task Force.

The long distances involved in flying to and from the United Kingdom and the Falkland Islands meant that aircraft had to be adapted to carry more fuel, and to refuel in fight. This in itself was a major technological feat.

On 16 April, RAF Lynehams's Engineering Wing were tasked with devising an auxiliary fuel tank installation in the Hercules, mainstay of the transport fleet. An extra pair of tanks built into the cargo hold was sufficient to give the Hercules a further three to four hours' endurance. Similarly, a four-tank installation was also devised, but this reduced the Hercules' maximum payload by 75 per cent. These latter modifications were known as LR4s and the former as LR2s. The LR4 Hercules were eventually only used for high-priority drops to the Task Force at extreme range.

Even with the long-range modifications, accomplished initially within the remarkable space of five days, it became clear that effectively supporting the Task force around the Total Exclusion Zone, and any subsequent land operations, would require air-to-air refuelling (AAR) capability in the Hercules. Another rush job was in prospect.

The modifications

Marshall of Cambridge (Engineering) Ltd had been the technical centre for the RAF's Hercules fleet since 1966, as well as the Lockhead service centre since 1975. The firm was the obvious candidate to handle the work. On 15 April, late in the afternoon, Marshalls were tasked with installing a flight-refuelling probe to a Hercules C1 XV200 which had arrived at Cambridge for a major service. It was a technically daunting assignment; far out over the Atlantic, there would be little or no margin for error.

The probe was mounted on the upper forward fuselage, offset to starboard, with an external fuel pipe running along the upper fuselage surface as far as the trailing edge fairing, where the wing joins the fuselage. There it was routed into the ground refuelling pipe. A non-return valve was placed in the 'Y' junction of the pipe at this point. The controls were positioned above the navigator's station on the flight deck, and two floodlights were positioned to the side of the co-pilot's panel, so as to illuminate the probe at night. It took Marshalls just ten days to complete the installation.

On 30 April, the second modification was called for: the installation of Omega navigation equipment as an additional safety precaution. The second PLR2, XV179, became the 'prototype' of this installation.

On the same day as the Omega installation was requested, Marshalls were also asked to prepare a trial installation for a Hercules Tanker variant, using a Mk17B hose drum unit (HDU) produced by Flight Refuelling, but held in stock for use on the VC10 tanker conversions. The next day, Hercules C1 LR4, XV296, arrived at Cambridge for modifications, which was also to include a probe to enable it to act as a receiver/tanker.

Next, aircrews had to train to take fuel on board, while airborne, from the Victor tankers. Two of the unit's instructors were hurriedly qualified as air-to-air refuelling instructors, and after receipt of the first C1 PLR2 at Lyneham, the work began in earnest. Formation flying was the first requirement. The basic technique was for the captain to fly in formation, lining his aircraft up on special markings carried by the tanker, while the co-pilot gave instructors to enable the probe to enter the 'basket' on the end of the drogue. The system worked.

Getting a Victor to join up with a Hercules in mid-air was much more difficult. The Victor's minimum cruising speed was some 230 knots, while the Hercules' fastest safe speed was 210 knots at 23,100 ft. The solution, in the best traditions of the RAF, was simple. The Victor would approach the Hercules from above and behind, calling for the Hercules to begin a descent of 500 ft/min when visual contact was made—usually at about one mile. The Victor then overtook the Hercules and the Hercules moved neatly into line astern to make its prod. The descent was continued for about 15 minutes, at a speed of between 230 and 240 knots. This technique was swiftly dubbed 'tobogganing'.

It was not long before Ascension Island became a vast ammunition dump of missiles, bombs, grenades and gun ammunition of various types, together with the fuses and propellant charges to go with them. There were also thousands of tons of stores and spare parts to be fed down to the Task Force once it had staged at Ascension and moved on towards the Falkland Islands.

Sometimes, urgently required items were air-dropped to ships in the sea train. The bulk of this material was loaded on to the STUFT (ships taken up from trade) anchored off Ascension. This was done by the helicopters based at Wideawake, and sometimes supplemented by the helicopters carried on board the ships themselves. That left 24 and 30 Sqns to concentrate on keeping the UK–Wideawake supply line open. Later they were also to deal with the Hercules tanker operations.

Throughout April the Hercules flights were building up. By 17 April the daily average of flights to and from Wideawake passed 20 a day. Two more support teams were deployed to Ascension, and the Hercules flights were supplemented by the RAF's VC10s and some 20 sorties by Belfasts belonging to Heavylift, a civil cargo airline. Additionally, there were two Boeing 707 charter flights to Wideawake performed by civil firms.

Cross-decking

In the earlier stages of the conflict, as the various ships of the Task Force made their way down to their rendezvous in the South Atlantic, many had to leave in such a hurry that there was not sufficient time for them to be properly loaded and provisioned in Britain. The necessary stores were flown ahead of them to Ascension Island, and were ferried out to them by helicopter. While staging at the island, a lot of cross-decking was done so that a correct mix of stores, equipment and ammunition was held on the ships that would be directly involved in supporting the landings. Cross-decking was the name given to the tedious task of sorting out stores on board.

Some of the ships on the way down did not stop at Ascension Island, but were replenished at sea by helicopters from Wideawake. It was by this means of 'vertrepping' (vertical replenishment) that the QE2 was supplied as she sailed past, 50 miles out from the island, with troops of 5 Infantry Brigade on board. She was on her way to South Georgia, where she handed them over to *Canberra* for the dangerous task of landing them at San Carlos.

The helicopters initially in use at Ascension Island were two Wessex HU5s and two Royal Navy Sea Kings. In early May, *Atlantic Conveyor* was to disembark a Chinook HCI (call sign 'Bravo Papa') which contributed much to the re-storing operations. Later an RAF Sea King HAR3 of 202 Squadron arrived to help and also provided SAR (search and rescue) cover for any aircraft unfortunate enough to come down in the sea.

Preparing loads for the helicopters was punishing work as there was a shortage of lifting gear and underslung cargo nets. Altered requirements sometimes meant that the whole load had to be disassembled and packed again. The Joint Helicopter Support Unit prepared over 2000 loads. In one day 40 Sea King, 40 Chinook and 138 Wessex loads were carried. Maintenance of the various aircraft was well done, and a very high rate of operational serviceability was achieved on fixed and rotary wing machines. The Chinook never once went out of service. Turn-arounds were a high priority, especially for the helicopters. These were refuelled 'hot', the engines still running.

As the Total Exclusion Zone (TEZ) was applied around the Falkland Islands and South Georgia (and, later, after the landings at the San Carlos beach-head) a considerable traffic of supply shipping developed. These ships plied between the TRALA (towing, repair and logistics area) situated well out to sea from the Falkland Islands, and Britain or Ascension Island. To provision this traffic a system of 'motorway stations' was established, where vessels could collect stores. Requests were radioed ahead and the rendezvous was made at sea. These motorway stations were at Ascension Island itself and at Latitudes 20°S and 40°S, and were kept supplied from Ascension.

Role of honour

There was to be further exceptional strain on the facilities at Ascension when the 'Black Buck' raids by Vulcans were mounted. Each mission involved two Vulcans and 11 Victors taking off one after the other. These raids and the other in-flight refuelling missions had put a tremendous strain on the normal system of supplying the airfield with aviation fuel. This was done in normal circumstances by fuel bowser trucks plying the 3¾-mile run from the storage tank farm to the airfield. To supply 24 bays for four-engined-wing aircraft and up to 30 or more helicopters, the Royal Engineers laid a temporary pipeline. The storage farm was kept supplied by tanker ships from the American Military Sealift Command, standing off-shore and pumping in fuel. Apart from fuelling up the bombers and their tankers, the RAF ground crew were faced with the task of aircraft maintenance and loading up with a total of 42 1000lb bombs – 21 into each of two Vulcan B2s—for each of three raids. The other two Black Buck missions involved dropping ARM45 Shrike missiles against radars.

By the time that Port Stanley was recaptured from the Argentines, a total of 535 air movements into the island airfield from Britain had taken place, including flights by RAF Hercules and VC10s, Belfasts chartered from HeavyliftAir Cargo, and Boeing 707s chartered from British Airways and Tradewinds. These aircraft had delivered to Wideawake Airfield 23 helicopters, 5242 passengers and nearly 6000 tons of freight. The ground support personnel, including the original Pan Am staff, worked a small miracle in handling all this traffic, together with all aircraft operating to the south in support of the Task Force. Nimrod Maritime Surveillance aircraft flew 111 sorties from the island; C130 Hercules made 44 airdrops of essential equipment, weapons and personnel to the Fleet; and the Victor K2 tankers supported 67 missions by flying 375 sorties to refuel in flight. Ground crews were able to keep these 20-year-old aircraft 100 per cent serviceable at all times—a remarkable achievement.

In addition to all this, Ascension Island had to act as a post office, handling all mail to and from the UK. In ten weeks, some 19,000 mail bags passed through the island as well as welfare parcels and newspapers. Ascension Island had won a new degree of respect, if not affection, from the serving men who made it the half-way house of the Falklands war.

The political and diplomatic front

The Falklands invasion trapped the Americans within a dilemma of their own making. Like the British, they had become accustomed to the *macho* posturings of the Junta and had not anticipated an invasion of the islands as an immediate threat. It was recognized that the Junta was a weak government afflicted by a declining economy and a low degree of popular approval, but the intelligence reports reaching Washington, such as they were, did not include signs of a military adventure in the making. The Falklands were not, in any case, 'our piece of real estate', as General Alexander Haig, the then Secretary of State, noted later.

The United States' main concern, in Latin American affairs, was Central America, an area of infinite problems right on her own doorstep. In the fight against the spread of left-wing regimes the Argentines were useful allies—fiercely anti-communist, Spanish-speaking and able to provide troops for such tasks as training the Honduras-based opposition to the Sandinistas in Nicaragua.

Argentina's powerful 'friend'

On coming to office at the beginning of 1981, the Reagan administration had jettisoned its predecessor's human rights criteria for political respectability among its friends. Argentina was welcomed back into the fold. A two-way traffic in generals and other dignitaries began: Galtieri paid two visits to Washington; General Vernon Walters, the President's 'troubleshooter', General David Meyer, Army Chief of Staff and Mrs Jeane Kirkpatrick, UN Ambassador, went to Buenos Aires. Another notable visitor, shortly before the invasion, was Thomas Enders, the Assistant Secretary of State for Latin American Affairs. He met Galtieri and Dr Costa Mendez, the Foreign Minister, and was briefed on the Falklands negotiations, but how far he passed on a British appeal for the situation to be kept cool while negotiations continued remains unclear. He told the British Ambassador later that the Argentines had been somewhat non-committal, but had not given him the impression they intended to do anything drastic.

When Sir Nicholas Henderson, the British Ambassador to Washington, told Haig on the evening of 31 March that an invasion was imminent, it came as something more than a surprise. It was a shock with the potential to cause serious damage to the new Latin American relationship. If it came to war the US might have to choose between their Latin American friends and their most reliable allies in Europe, the British. The Argentines had clearly broken the rule of law and the Junta was an exceptionally nasty regime that had murdered thousands of its own citizens, but nevertheless the Argentine cause was enmeshed in the whole complex issue of Latin American national identity and self-respect.

The first American move was an attempt at intercession. At the request of Mrs Thatcher, Reagan phoned Galtieri and warned him that the consequences of invasion would be disastrous. It was too late. Then, as later, Galtieri found it impossible to step back from the brink. The Argentine political machinery possessed only forward drive, and even the threat of losing American support could not change that inexorable movement.

For several days the Washington policy-making machinery was in a state of some disarray. There was powerful opposition from the Latin Americanists, such as Mrs Kirkpatrick and Enders, to taking sides against the Argentines. Both had caused British anger by dining with the Argentine Ambassador to Washington on the night of the invasion. After a visit to Buenos Aires by Vice-President George Bush had been considered, Haig decided on a diplomatic technique he had learned while working as Henry Kissinger's assistant: the shuttle. He would use American influence in an attempt at even-handed mediation. Only he had the necessary weight and experience to make it effective. Reagan agreed, and Haig flew to London with his team, arriving on 8 April. From the beginning until the very end of all negotiations (at the UN in May, well after Haig had given up) the negotiating document remained basically the same. It consisted of three points: **1** Withdrawal by both sides from the islands and their vicinity, which would have meant the British Task Force keeping its distance; **2** The establishment of an interim authority on the islands; **3** Negotiation of the status of the islands by a date to be fixed.

Restore British rule

The British position stated by Mrs Thatcher in Parliament was that British rule must be restored, the Argentine forces withdrawn and the islanders allowed to exercise their right of self-determination. The major part of the Task Force, with two aircraft carriers, had already sailed from Portsmouth. Despite a British willingness to accept US mediation, the reception at No 10 had a slight frost to it. A British official had already made it known to American correspondents in London that the government was appalled that the Reagan administration should choose neutrality in a fight between its closest ally and a fascist dictatorship.

Mrs Thatcher recognized Haig as a friend, albeit one she constantly admonished—'Don't be so woolly, Al'—as she went backwards and forwards over the American plan with him. She wanted the islands back under British rule and she was prepared to go to war to achieve that goal. That, as both Haig and she knew, was partly a negotiating position. The first objective was an Argentine withdrawal and the pressure for that would increase as the fleet, ploughing slowly towards the southern ocean via Ascension Island, came nearer to its destination.

Haig flew off to Buenos Aires on 9 April with the message that Britain would indeed go to war and the Task Force was not a bluff. Even before he had arrived in London the British had declared a 200-mile exclusion zone around the islands, in which they would regard themselves free to sink Argentine ships and intercept aircraft. They had forces which could defeat Argentina, he told the generals, and if the Junta did not agree to withdraw, the Americans would come down on the side of the British. The proposals he brought were intended to help the Junta and prevent it from the certain overthrow that would follow defeat. But Galtieri had got it firmly in his mind that the British would not take action. They had no real commitment to the Falklands and their fleet would not be able to fight at such a distance from its base. It was hardly conducive to quiet diplomacy that the Argentine President had to address a crowd of 100,000 outside the Casa Rosada halfway through the meeting.

The hard men of the Junta

A major influence on the General's rather incoherent mind was undoubtedly the naval C-in-C, Admiral Jorge Anaya. He believed the British were so wrapped up in economic problems that they would sooner negotiate than go to the expense of trying to retrieve the islands. Foreign Minister Costa Mendez, the wiliest and most experienced member of the government, seemed as inflexible as Anaya.

The mood as the American team flew back to London on Easter Sunday, 11 April, was gloomy. But Haig, though weary, was not ready to give up. The inevitable juggling with the formula took place. How could they balance an Argentine demand of free right of access to the islands for its citizens against the British insistence that the islanders should be allowed to determine their future? How could they surmount the obstacle presented by the sovereignty question?

After 18 hours of sleep and discussion aboard the Boeing 707, no one had reached any conclusions that carried much conviction. The London talks failed to break the deadlock, although the British indicated willingness to continue by providing an amended text of the proposals. Haig and Francis Pym, the Foreign Secretary, looked grave as they stood outside No 10 afterwards. He was no more hopeful as a result of his talks, said Haig: 'Time is slipping away from us.'

Confused messages arrived from Buenos Aires. Costa Mendez indicated in a telephone call that the Junta's position had hardened since Haig had left Buenos Aires. It looked for a while as if the shuttle would be called off, but then it was announced that the Argentine Foreign Minister had produced some 'new ideas'. They appear to have been little more than a willingness to continue talking, which always remained the Argentine position.

Haig went back to Washington to reflect with his team before flying to Buenos Aires. The British position by then had shifted on the question of the return of the islands to British administration. There was willingness to consider an interim administration. There was also some hope on the American side that the question of sovereignty would be fudged by avoiding the use of the word.

The shuttle grinds to a halt

The second visit to Buenos Aires on 18 April followed the switchback course that was to become all too familiar to those engaged in negotiations with the Argentines. Galtieri indicated that important concessions were in the making and he would announce them before Haig departed next day. In the event he had no announcement to make. At Francis Pym's cabled suggestion, what would have been the third visit to London was called off.

Pym, after a trip to Brussels to express appreciation for EEC support, flew to Washington on 22 April as desultory attempts at negotiation, involving Peru, continued. He had given an outline of the British position in the House on the previous day. It amounted to a two-part proposal for proceeding with a settlement. The first covered arrangements for an Argentine withdrawal; the second concerned 'the nature of an interim administration of the islands, and the framework for the negotiations on the long-term solution to the dispute for which the United Nations resolution calls'.

Resolution 502

Sir Anthony Parsons, Britain's Ambassador at the United Nations, swung into action as soon as it was clear that Argentina intended to invade. His first initiative was to alert the UN Secretary General, Javier Perez de Cuellar, himself a Latin American. De Cuellar's response was a public appeal that the differences should be settled diplomatically.

The UN's diplomatic machinery is designed for defusing potentially explosive confrontations between member nations; making the machine work well requires a combination of enormous energy and saintly patience.

Sir Anthony Parsons (in fact on the eve of retirement) had both qualities, and he knew his UN well. He had an enviable reputation there as a man with many friends, who despite his relaxed manner was a tough negotiator. He rightly decided that his best chance of success lay in the Security Council, the top layer at the UN, which is composed of 15 members. Of these, the 'Big Five', Britain, the US, France, China and Russia are permanent. The Council's role in an international crisis is to issue resolutions, summing up the viewpoint of its members. Every resolution is subject to a vote; a majority enables the resolution to be passed, although the permanent members hold the right of veto.

On the evening of Thursday 1 April, Sir Anthony took the matter to the Council saying, 'We call on the Security Council to take immediate action in order to prevent an invasion.' Foreign Minister Kamanda of Zaire (now the Democratic Republic of Congo), who was in the chair, was authorized to issue an important statement urging both sides to restrain from the use of force, a formula which allowed those not involved, directly or indirectly, to concentrate their thoughts on peace, rather than anti-colonialism.

This was important, because although Britain was in this case certainly the victim of aggression, former colonial countries were likely to be influenced by the fact that Britain was the greatest colonizer in world history. The Falklands were and are a British colony; the fact that its inhabitants wished to remain that way tended not to weigh much with the more militant black nations.

Argentina told to withdraw

The next day, the now famous Resolution 502 was formally introduced after the invasion had taken place. It demanded an immediate withdrawal of Argentine forces and called upon both sides to refrain from using force to seek a diplomatic solution. At the request of Argentina, there was then a delay so that Foreign Minister Costa Mendez could get to New York before a vote was taken. When he did arrive, his hectoring instructions on how to vote alienated the representatives of non-aligned nations.

The British delegation was also at work canvassing for votes. In this they were greatly helped by the French, who won over the Togo delegation to Britain's side. A minimum of ten votes were needed to ensure success.

The voting took place on 3 April, and its pattern was encouraging. Ten Security Council states supported Britain, and only one, Panama, with natural Latin American sympathies, voted against. Four members abstained: the USSR, Poland, China and Spain. Spain's abstention was understandable, since it has strong ethnic links with Argentina.

The ten supporters of the resolution, representing a wide spectrum of world opinion, gave great strength to the British case. Resolution 502 became the bedrock of international approval for all further action, diplomatic and military. Even the Soviet Union had not used its veto. The UN had recognized Britain's right to self-defence, and this opened up the way for diplomats to request support for an economic blockade of Argentina, together with denial of arms and other assistance to Argentina from the US, the EEC and the Commonwealth.

The European Community was an important potential ally, and on 6 April

Mrs Thatcher sent a personal letter to all EEC heads of government. Soon various countries started banning arms exports to Argentina. Greece quickly came forward to announce a comprehensive ban on imports from Argentina.

It was on Good Friday, the 9th, that the EEC political committee, in emergency session at the Egmont Palace in Brussels, issued a strong statement of solidarity with Britain. They did so with a warmth which surprised even British diplomats, and formally announced a ban on all imports of Argentine goods. In practical terms, such a ban could have only limited effects, but the unanimous support of the Europeans at a critical moment greatly cheered the British government.

At the end of week one of the Falklands crisis, Mrs Thatcher, at the head of a small crisis committee or 'war cabinet', was recovering from the first shock of the invasion. President Galtieri and his Junta, so confident at the beginning, were soon to realize how badly they had misjudged the strength of the reaction from London and the rest of the world.

The Junta digs in

Galtieri, Costa Mendez, Lami Dozo, Admiral Anaya—names obscure to the British public until their fateful deed catapulted them into a brief, harsh limelight. But what had led them to take such a rash political gamble?

TWO DAYS BEFORE Argentine forces occupied the Falklands, 10,000 irate citizens took to the streets of Buenos Aires to demonstrate against the highly unpopular Junta and its leader, General Leopoldo Galtieri. Four days after the occupation Buenos Aires resounded to the massed fervour of 250,000 voices—roaring their approval of his great act of national vindication. It was the Junta's finest hour, and Galtieri savoured his triumph greedily. With a single bold stroke he had, apparently, silenced his critics, won over the populace and diverted attention from the murderous brutality and blustering incompetence of his shabby regime.

In the political turbulence of South America, the coup, the counter-coup and the Junta—simply a clique of officers whose hold on political power rests on their control of the armed forces—are inescapable facts of life. Argentina's modern history is littered with political disasters of this sort, although the particular group of officers who led their nation to war with Britain in 1982 had only very recently come to the fore. Six years earlier they had first glimpsed the prospect of power when a military coup toppled a woeful civilian government, but it was not until the final days of 1981 that Galtieri finally manoeuvred himself into the top job, the presidency.

Dictator though he was, however, Galtieri was by no means in sole command of Argentina's destiny, and the blame for the Falklands debacle rests with others as well—most notably his two fellow service chiefs, Admiral Jorge Anaya of the navy and Brigadier Basilio Lami Dozo of the air force, and Nicanor Costa Mendez, the Foreign Minister. All three were committed to 'regaining' the Malvinas sooner rather than later, and they did not flinch from the use of force—with Anaya being particularly hawkish (ironic when one considers the lacklustre performance of the Argentine

Navy when it really came to blows). Having said that, Galtieri was the man of the moment, the idol of the mob and the one with most to gain (or lose) from the great gamble. Who was this bluff, burly man with a mission, and what drove him on his calamitous course?

Soldier of fortune

General Leopoldo Fortunato Galtieri (1926–2003) was the son of Italian immigrants to Argentina. Top brass in Argentina are traditionally Italian, and Galtieri was typical of those from a modest family who sought fame and fortune in the army. Because of his technical aptitude, he gained entrance to the Argentine Military College to specialize in engineering. As a military engineer, the army sent him on a course in the USA.

He took to the Americans at once. They liked him for his rugged appearance—he could almost be mistaken for a Texan, broad-shouldered and well over six feet tall. During his stay he adopted as his military hero none other than General George Patton, the famous 'blood and guts' US commander in World War 2, to whom he bore a physical resemblance.

He was already coaching himself to take over as head of the military Junta when in the summer of 1981 he paid a ten-day visit to Washington. Once again, he made a good impression on the Americans as a 'tough guy' with a mane of white hair who talked about the need for the Americans to work with reliable anti-Marxist people such as the Argentines. By the time he returned home, this soldier's soldier was convinced that he had made powerful friends who would be only too pleased to see him take over the reins of government.

Galtieri's visit had been at the invitation of the American General Meyer, and he followed it up a few months later by attending an inter-American conference of Army Commanders-in-Chief. It seemed that relations with the great North American power were rapidly improving and General Galtieri appears to have conceived the ill-founded opinion that Washington would be ready to back his claims to the Falklands.

It was just before Christmas 1981 that he was able to seize power as head of the military Junta while at the same time retaining his command over the army. He was determined to recover the Malvinas for Argentina before the 150th anniversary of the British occupation—which was to fall in January 1983. And so he did, although of course by the time that anniversary came round it was Mrs Thatcher who was inspecting the troops, not General Galtieri.

The Argentines consolidate

What is taken by force has to be kept by force. The Argentines did not expect Britain to try to regain the Falklands—at least not in the immediate future. But Port Stanley was nonetheless rapidly converted into something resembling a military fortress after the invasion. In days, Argentine troops were to outnumber the islanders by more than six to one.

The 5th Marine Infantry Battalion and elements of the Amphibious Reconnaissance Group occupied Port Stanley after the invasion on 2 April, to be reinforced during the first 24 hours by the 2nd Airborne Infantry Regiment, the 8th and 25th Infantry Regiments and 9th Engineer Company.

A permanent naval presence was also established with armed naval tugs, and at least two of the 81-ton Z28 class patrol vessels of the *Prefectura Naval* coastguard force, all based at the newly established Apostadero Naval Malvinas (Falklands Naval Station) at Port Stanley, which had now been rechristened Puerto Argentino.

As early as 4 April, the second full day of Argentine occupation, flight elements of the 1st and 4th Naval Attack Squadrons with four MB339, and a similar number of Beech T34C trainer/light strike aircraft, were also deployed to Stanley Airport which was now known as the Base Aéreo Militar Malvinas (Falklands Military Air Base). These were in turn joined by 24IA58 Pucará ground attack aircraft from the Air Force's 2nd and 3rd Attack and Reconnaissance Squadrons, both forming part of the 3rd Air Brigade on the Falklands.

Several Skyvan light transports arrived as well, with three Puma helicopters of the *Prefectura Naval*, plus over 30 Chinook, Puma, Bell UHIH and Agusta A109 helicopters of the Army's 601st Aviation Battalion. Half of the Pucarás and several of the helicopters were re-deployed to the grass airstrips at Goose Green and Pebble Island, each of which was staffed by about 200 Air Force personnel.

Most of the combat elements of the Argentine Air Force were also re-deployed to bases well south on the mainland of Argentina.

Menendez' plan

Throughout the three weeks which elapsed between the initial invasion and the appearance of the first units of the British Task Force in the area, and despite the British declaration of a Total Exclusion Zone, reinforcements and supplies continued to pour into the islands by sea and air from 12 April. These included the 3rd, 6th and 7th Infantry Regiments and 10th Engineer Company from the 10th Motorized Infantry Brigade; the three infantry regiments (4th, 5th and 12th) of the 3rd Mechanized Infantry Brigade together with the 3rd Artillery Group from the same unit; the 11th Artillery Group from the new 11th Motorized Infantry Brigade, still in process of formation; and elements of the 601st Anti-aircraft Artillery Group and the 601st Engineer Battalion, the last two both army headquarters units.

A Tigercat missile unit of the 1st Marine Anti-aircraft Regiment was also deployed to the islands, as was a twin Roland SAM launcher together with a number of twin Exocet surface-to-surface missile launchers.

Total Argentine military personnel in the Falklands now stood at about 12,000, under the command of Major General Mario Benjamin Menendez, who had made his reputation as a hardliner in counter-insurgency operations near the Bolivian frontier but who, like the rest of the Argentine officer corps, lacked conventional combat experience.

Recognizing that Port Stanley was the major strategic target in the islands, General Menendez deployed some 70 per cent of his total available troops in the vicinity and also his own HQ.

The joint forces totalled five infantry regiments. They were the three regiments (3rd, 6th and 7th) of the 10th Brigade, under their brigade commander General Joffre; the 4th Regiment, from the 3rd Brigade, many of whose members were already suffering from the effects of their sudden transition from the sub-tropical climate of their normal station to the near-Antarctic conditions of the Falklands in winter; and the 25th Regiment, from the 9th Brigade, together with the 5th Marine Battalion. They were the only Argentine troops present who were acclimatized to the prevailing weather conditions, both being normally stationed in southern Patagonia. There were also two Marine Commando units, the 601st and 302nd, both of which had participated in the initial assault, and elements of the Marine Amphibious Reconnaissance Group with 12 brand-new Panhard AML 245H90 armoured cars and 15 Mowag Roland wheeled armoured patrol cars.

The Exocets on the islands

Artillery support was provided by the 3rd Artillery Group, with one battery of four 155mm howitzers and two batteries, each with six Italian Oto Melara Model 56 105mm pack howitzers; and the 11th Artillery Group, equipped with 18 Oto Melara 105s, in three batteries. There was also at least one pair of trailer-mounted Exocet launchers.

Air defence was provided by a battery of Oerlikon twin 35mm K63 anti-aircraft guns and two of twin-mounted 20mm Rheinmetall RH202 and single 30mm Oerlikon pieces from the 601st Anti-aircraft Defence Group; a Tigercat SAM battery and the solitary Roland SAM unit of the Marine 1st Anti-aircraft Regiment. The infantry also had British Blowpipe, man-portable SAM launchers, ironically of newer type than those used by the British forces.

Finally, and apart from logistic support and medical units, there were the 9th and 10th Motorized Engineer Companies, from the 9th and 10th Brigades respectively, and a company from the 601st Construction Engineer Battalion, together with a detachment from the 181st Military Police Intelligence Battalion. The latter were something like a Gestapo unit, commanded by the sinister and violently Anglophobic Major Patricio Dowling.

Menendez deployed two of his weaker units, the 4th and 12th Infantry, many of whom were by now suffering from respiratory ailments, on Two Sisters Ridge, Mount Harriet and Mount Kent, to the west of Stanley. This was considered fairly safe as the approaches on three sides lay through almost impassable country. The 7th Infantry, reinforced by one of the Marine Special Forces units, held Mount Longdon and Wireless Ridge to the north, whilst the 5th Marine Infantry Battalion and the other Marine Commando unit were responsible for the defence of Tumbledown, Mount William and Sapper Hill.

A company of the 2nd Airborne Infantry Regiment, the bulk of which was at Goose Green, occupied the low ground between Wireless Ridge and Moody Brook, whilst the 25th Infantry held Stanley Airport and the beaches to the south-east, considered the most likely sites for British landings. The 3rd and 6th Infantry Regiments manned a second line of defence behind these forward positions. Behind these were the 105mm howitzer batteries, whilst the armoured vehicles and heavy artillery were held in reserve in the town itself. The bulk of the 11th Artillery Group was stationed to the north of Stanley, with one battery sharing Stanley Racecourse with a 105mm battery of the 3rd Artillery. Another of the 3rd Artillery's units was based at Moody Brook Barracks.

The Argentines do not appear to have considered the possibility of hauling artillery on to the heights commanding the approaches to Stanley.

In addition to the 12 Pucará ground attack aircraft of the air force's 2nd and 3rd Attack and Reconnaissance Squadrons, and the four Aermacchi 339s of the 1st Naval Attack Squadron, plus the four rather useless Beech T340s of the 4th Naval Attack Squadron, based at Stanley Airport, the army had a Chinook, three Puma, three Agusta A109 and 16 Bell UH1H and D helicopters, whilst the navy had two Pumas and the air force a single Chinook, a Puma and two Bell 212s.

Outside Port Stanley

After Stanley, the main concentration of Argentine forces was at Goose Green. Here was the main body of the 2nd Airborne Infantry Regiment, subsequently to be reinforced by the 12th Infantry and a portion of the 602nd Special Forces Group, together with 200 air force personnel and six Pucarás. Other points on East Falkland were covered by small platoon-strength outposts or by patrols.

Next in importance, though not in actual strength of troop deployment, was Pebble Island, where the grass air strip was also occupied by half a dozen Pucarás together with a Skyvan light transport and two Pumas. Incredibly, no ground troops were deployed to protect this important installation which was to be the first to experience an attack by British ground forces in the re-conquest of the islands.

West Falkland was lightly garrisoned by only two infantry regiments, the 5th at Port Howard and the 8th at Fox Bay. The 9th Motorized Engineer Company was split between these two centres whilst the entire Argentine garrison of the west island was commanded by Brigadier General Parala of the 3rd Brigade. His HQ was at Port Howard. As in the case of East Falkland, no major troop concentrations occurred outside these two centres, the remainder of the island being covered by desultory patrols.

No Argentine aircraft appear to have been based on West Falkland, nor were there any artillery or air defence units.

Although some minor re-deployments of troops and equipment took place after the British landings, these dispositions remained more or less the same until the Argentine surrender on 14 June.

First strike: Vulcan and Harriers hit Stanley

The bomber pilot's endurance and cool; the fighter pilot's lightning reflexes and aggression; the virtuosity of British aircraft designers and technicians: all three tested to the limits in the grey, early hours of 1 May.

JUST BEFORE 0000 hours on 30 April 1982, there was an apocalyptic roar on a tiny volcanic island in the middle of nowhere: the roar of two RAF Vulcan bombers taking off at 103 per cent thrust.

In each of their bomb bays, arranged in three rows of seven, were 21 1000lb conventional bombs: a total of more than nine tons of high explosive, enough to flatten a small town. Each aircraft was more than 2½ tons 'overweight'.

In minutes, the 'prime' aircraft, or mission leader, announced over the radio that a mechanical failure had made his aircraft unserviceable. He immediately turned back to the base, which was, of course, Ascension Island.

The captain of the back-up aircraft, Flight Lt Martin Withers, simply announced to his five-man crew: 'Looks like we've got a job of work.'

If Withers had been asked to imagine the most unlikely job of work he and his Vulcan could be asked to undertake that night, he might well have suggested exactly what he was now doing. It wasn't just that he was on a conventional bombing mission to the Falkland Islands, when his aircraft had been designed specifically to deliver nuclear bombs over Eastern Europe; or even that neither he nor his fellow pilots ever believed they would fly live missions anyway, for in two months, all the RAF's Vulcans were destined for the military scrap heap—outdated after 25 years' service.

What was most bizarre—and dangerous—about this mission, code-named Black Buck, was that it involved flying some 3900 miles over the South Atlantic, to find and bomb a single runway, when the normal range of the aircraft was just 1700 miles; and with not one alternative airfield available for emergency landings or refuelling, except possibly Rio de Janeiro in Brazil.

The problem of range was to be overcome by refuelling in flight. Vulcans had to be hastily readapted for flight refuelling with a makeshift probe, and with just two weeks' practice behind them, Withers and his crew now faced a mission which required this delicate, often risky operation to be undertaken 17 times.

Close to Withers in his Vulcan (number XM607) were the airborne fuel stations on which the operation would depend: no less than 11 gigantic Victor tankers. Their height for flying was 40,000 ft. The optimum height for refuelling was around 27,000 ft, aircraft being more manoeuvrable in the denser air at this level; but both Vulcans and Victors compromised at 31,000 ft.

At every refuelling 'bracket' or scheduled fuelling interlude, the Vulcan would approach a Victor, edge up to the drogue which it trailed on the end of a hose, and painstakingly edge his probe into place. Precise formation flying then had to be maintained throughout the flow of fuel, despite turbulence. The technique is aptly named 'prodding'.

The Victors were split into three waves, and as they flew south, some refuelled others. 'Empty' tankers then headed back to Ascension, finally leaving just two, and XM607.

It was then that the second major hang-up occured. One of the Victors took a prod at his companion, as planned, but flew into turbulence and lost contact. Trying to re-connect, the drogue broke the receiver's probe; again, turbulence was to blame. The receiver was therefore obliged to return directly to Ascension, but not before reversing roles and giving back fuel to its partner.

The remaining Victor—K2 SL189 of 57 Squadron—was flown by Squadron Leader Bob Tuxford. Tuxford was anxious to discover if his drogue still worked after the brush with the other Victor's probe, so he asked the Vulcan to come alongside and inspect. A torch was shone through a window, but to no avail; it was not clear whether the drogue was damaged or not. There was nothing for it but to test it physically. To everyone's relief, the transfer went off properly.

This was, in fact, an unscheduled 'prod'. The final top-up for the Vulcan was to be further towards the Falklands.

The spadework

Before the Vulcan's tanks were full, Tuxford had to signal to Withers to move away—by flashing his lights. Worrying for Withers; but if he had known what had actually gone on inside the Victor, he would have been more worried still. Tuxford and his crew had decided to give the Vulcan more than just what they had to spare: they actually ate into the fuel that was to have taken them back to Ascension. It was vital that the Vulcan mission should not be jeopardized, and they knew that if met by another tanker and given more fuel sometime before reaching a point 450 miles out from Ascension, their Victor would make it home. However, there was no question of signalling back instructions yet: strict radio silence had to be observed until the mission was complete.

XM609 now closed in on the Falklands. Soon it descended to 300 ft above the sea in order to reduce the risk of detection by radar. Forty nautical miles away from the target, the Vulcan climbed to 10,000 ft for the bombing run. Its navigational system proved to have put the aircraft precisely on track. Withers turned on to a heading of 235°—pointing across the runway—and commenced the straight run-in. Releasing the 21 bombs took only five seconds; to the crew it seemed forever. They were three miles out from Stanley; their bombs sailed on; they pulled away, tensely awaiting an Argentine response.

There was no anti-aircraft fire to meet them, only an indication on their detection equipment that ground radar had found them. The electronic counter-measures (for jamming enemy radar) were activated, and the enemy radar went out. To this day no one knows whether it was the ECM or an Argentine, deliberately or inadvertently, switching it off.

One bomb hit the runway at its midway point; the rest fell to one side and caused heavy damage among parked aircraft and stores. It is assumed the run was made 'across' the runway to ensure that at least one would hit the paved area.

After dropping the bombs, the Vulcan ought to have flown down at 300 ft again to escape radar detection. But to save fuel, Withers immediately climbed to economic cruising level, delicately adjusting the throttles in order to achieve the best consumption.

When at last the Vulcan could transmit the codeword for a successful operation, Tuxford and his crew sighed with relief and promptly signalled to Ascension for the life-saving tanker rendezvous. The Vulcan's home run went as planned, and XM607 touched down at Ascension at the end of an astonishing 15¾ hours in the air.

For their extraordinary, record-breaking mission, Flt Lt Withers and Sqn Ldr Tuxford were awarded the Distinguished Flying Cross and the Air Force Cross respectively.

Exactly a month had elapsed between the invasion of the islands on

2 April and the first Black Buck mission. In that time, the Argentine invaders did nothing to extend or improve that vital runway, just 4100 ft long, but they did bring in some hefty anti-aircraft weapons consisting of both guns and missiles.

Denying the use of the runway to Argentine transport planes and combat aircraft was a major strategic necessity at the time. The fact that the cratered runway was soon repaired, and that supply flights came in and out regularly, did not emerge in full until after the surrender.

So it was that on 9 April, a round-the-clock effort was put in hand to prepare the RAF's Vulcans for Black Buck missions. Aircraft were completely refurbished and overhauled. The refuelling probes were sought as far afield as Catterick, Woodford, Goose Bay in Labrador and Wright-Patterson Air Force Base in Ohio. The internal refuelling systems were largely re-manufactured, engines turned back to give full thrust on take-off and bomb bays and crew stations converted to the carriage of conventional 'iron bombs'.

Air-refuelling practice began as early as 14 April, but ten days later, as the five combat-ready Vulcans were about to depart, the order came to fit electronic counter-measures (ECM). Westinghouse ALQ101(V) pods were borrowed from 208 Squadron Buccaneers, while a frantic search finally discovered structural hardpoints and cooling pipes originally intended for the defunct Skybolt missile. Waddington designed, built, fitted and tested a completely new under-wing pylon for the pod, balancing it with a second pylon under the left wing, which after severe difficulties was cleared to fire the AS37 anti-radar Martel missile. Subsequently this was replaced by the AGM 45A Shrike, and later by a pair of Shrikes.

The Harriers go in

As dawn broke on an extremely untidy Stanley airfield on 1 May, Harrier pilots prepared for their first day of action. A few hours after the first Black Buck attack, a force of Sea Harriers, unmodified except for a low-visibility all-grey paint scheme, screamed over the airfields at Stanley and Goose Green, dropping air-burst, delayed-action 1000lb bombs or BL755s. Ground fire was intense: one Sea Harrier pilot said it looked like a child's sparkler on Guy Fawkes night. Another commented: 'They were hosing it around all over the place.' But there was only one hit, a shell of 20mm calibre through the fin of an aircraft flown by Flt Lt David Morgan, which was patched with a bolted aluminium plate.

Throughout the campaign, the basic simplicity of all types of Harriers proved of great value. Aboard *Hermes* just 140 men, plus 20 RAF NCOs, kept a minimum of 20 aircraft serviceable round the clock. Battle damage was in almost every case repaired overnight, often using Speedtape—adhesive aluminium tape. One aircraft took a direct hit in the high-pressure air pipe to the tail reaction-control jets, but the pilot knew nothing until he was back on deck.

The attacks of 1 May took place at dawn to make incoming aircraft difficult to see against the sunrise. As in subsequent attacks, the only hits on the British aircraft were the result of repeated exposure at low level to intense ground fire. No missiles are believed to have been launched on 1 May, but fire from guns of all calibres up to 45mm was considerable. Air-to-ground weapon delivery was visual.

The Sea Harriers operated in pairs, (leader and wing-man) and all recoveries were vertical, landings being made on any suitable deck space 60ft across. Aircraft flew straight back to their ship from all directions and transitioned to the hover, with the wind coming from any direction and the deck heaving up and down as much as 30ft. After the landing, aircraft would taxi forward to be lashed.

Later on 1 May, at least 12 Argentine aircraft, including Mirages (or Daggers) and Canberras, approached the Task Force at high level. Sea Harriers on Combat Air Patrol (CAP) went to intercept, and the hostile forces withdrew as they approached. There is evidence that one Mirage was shot down on this occasion by Argentine fire from near Port Stanley. In all, Argentine ground fire certainly brought down four and probably six of their own aircraft, suggesting a faulty IFF—identification friend or foe—system.

A Harrier dies

The first Task Force air combat kill was gained on Sunday 2 May. Flt Lt Paul Barton, on exchange posting to 801 Sqn, was on CAP in his Sea Harrier when his Blue Foe radar detected two unidentified aircraft at a distance of about 20 miles, closing rapidly. (Ships of the Task Force had closed in from the east and used their guns to bombard Port Stanley Airport.) This presumably had goaded the FAA (Fuerza Aerea Argentina) into retaliating. The hostile aircraft came in at high level doing about 550mph at 1915 local time. Initial closure was head-on, but Barton and his wing-man pulled round and were soon within both gun and Sidewinder parameters astern of the Mirages. Barton let go a brief burst of gunfire from 800 yards, but as a missile had locked on, he fired it. The Mirage exploded instantly into a fireball.

This was the first of 27 firings of the AIM9L, which in sharp contrast to the Americans' experiences with air-to-air missiles in Vietnam, proved reliable and effective, scoring a success rate of around 90 per cent. The final, carefully cross-checked initial tally was 21 confirmed kills, plus three more almost certain. Seven further confirmed kills were gained with Aden guns.

On the same day, Flt Lt Penfold, operating from *Hermes*, suddenly found himself in a brief dogfight with Mirages. One of the enemy fired an AIM9B Sidewinder at Penfold's wing-man who managed to dodge it. Meanwhile Penfold quickly got into AIM9L parameters, listened for the growl in his headset, and fired. Again the Mirage fireballed.

Later the same evening, three of the FAA Canberra bombers were picked up by Task Force radars, coming in at medium level, around 15,000 ft. They dived to low level, but the Task Force controllers directed or 'vectored' CAP Sea Harriers accurately for interception. The bombers fled at full throttle, but not before one had been destroyed by an AIM9L. This was the only Canberra to be intercepted and destroyed during the conflict.

This day, 2 May, had shown beyond doubt that the whole RN air-combat system not only worked but worked magnificently. Sea Harriers serviceability, reliability and the all-round ability of RAF and RN pilots to 'hack it' had been demonstrated in the most convincing way.

Nevertheless, the Harrier was not to have everything its own way. The first loss was two days later during an attack by Sea Harriers of 800 Sqn (from *Hermes*) against the airfield and installations at Goose Green. Lt-Commander Nick Taylor was heavily hit by gunfire (almost certainly from batteries of twin 35mm Oerlikon guns which were later to be captured) and crashed fatally. Taylor was the only pilot of a Harrier or Sea Harrier killed in action by enemy fire.

Sinking the *Belgrano*

Within ten minutes of the torpedoes striking home, she had shipped enough water to give her a list to port of 15°. An hour later, at 1700 on Sunday 2 May, she rolled over and sank, leaving about 350 dead and some 650 survivors in the water.

ON 26 APRIL, the Argentine cruiser *General Belgrano*, under the command of Commandant Hector Bonzo, and escorted by the destroyers *Hipolito Bouchard* and *Piedra Buena*, put to sea from Ushuaia, Argentina's southernmost port. At about the same date the carrier *Veinticinco de Mayo*, probably escorted by a Type 42 destroyer and a submarine (possibly the Type 209, *Galta*) also left one of the mainland bases, probably Comodoro Rivadavia. Subsequently it appeared that a third group, probably escort vessels, also put to sea.

Both the carrier (which took part in the initial invasion of the Falklands) and the cruiser were in a poor state of repair, the former suffering from trouble to one of her shafts and the cruiser from, according to American intelligence sources, poor maintenance which necessitated her spending long periods in dry dock. Consequently both ships were unable to reach anywhere near their normal quoted maximum speed. In the case of the carrier, this would have seriously affected aircraft operations. Indeed, they may have been impossible for other reasons too. However, *Belgrano's* escorts, though ex-US 'Alan M. Sumner' class destroyers, were armed with Exocets, helicopters and sonar.

What orders were given to these ships remains a question of conjecture, but the purpose of a combined sortie such as this, involving nearly all the operational units of the Argentine Navy, seemed obvious to the British Task Force Commander, who was patrolling with the Task force to the north-west of the Falklands. The Argentines were behaving as if they planned to carry out some sort of attack on the Task Force, with the object of seriously damaging or sinking units, presumably the carriers. Success could have spelt disaster for the British: the withdrawal of the Task Force, the end of the blockade of the islands and the postponement of the invasion of the Falklands. One possibility is that the Argentines wanted to attempt some sort of pincer movement: the carrier and its group closing in from the north of the Falklands (the carrier remaining within Argentine-based air cover) and the cruiser group, plus the third group, moving in from the south and west on the Task Force.

Unfortunately for the Argentines, news of the cruiser sailing from Ushuaia was passed to the British by the Chileans, and there was plenty of time for one of the nuclear submarines in the area to position herself ready to intercept *General Belgrano*.

Conqueror, under command of Commander Chris Wreford-Brown (his first submarine command), had sailed for the South Atlantic from her Scottish base, Faslane, on 4 April. During the two-week journey south her crew had constantly practised carrying out attacks, and were well prepared for action when they commenced their patrolling duties in the Total Exclusion Zone set up around the islands. The only reference material on the Argentine Navy available for *Conqueror* before she left was photographs of Argentine warships copied and enlarged from the current Jane's *Fighting Ships*. It was, however, sufficient for identifying *General Belgrano* when *Conqueror* intercepted her about 28 April. For the next few days, *Conqueror* shadowed the cruiser and its escorts as they zig-zagged eastwards and westwards along the edge of the Total Exclusion Zone.

Conqueror continued to shadow them, her crew on six-hour watches reporting movements to the Task Force Commander until, in the words of the crew, the routine abruptly changed 'at least 24 hours' before 1600 (local time) on 2 May. 'Change of routine' implies that *Conqueror's* crew went to a higher state of readiness; the timing of the change was significant, for Saturday 1 May was a day of intense activity around the Falkland Islands.

At about 0400 on that Saturday morning, an RAF Vulcan bomber had raided Stanley airfield, followed later in the morning at 0820 by every Sea Harrier in the Task Force, while SAS and SBS units landed by helicopter and from the submarine *Onyx* on both East and West Falkland under cover of bombardment by *Glamorgan, Arrow* and *Alacrity* at 1500. It may also have been the day the Argentines had designated for their major naval attack. Air raids on the Task Force soon commenced. At 1600 two Argentine Air Force Mirages were shot down, followed an hour later by the shooting down of an Argentine Canberra bomber and the damaging of another. Although it appeared as though these ineffectual raids were being set up in retaliation for the earlier British raids, they may have been planned to co-ordinate with raids from the Argentine Navy. In the event, the carrier was not in position and was unable to operate her aircraft. Neither was *Belgrano* in position to attack the Task Force from the opposite direction, if that was indeed the plan. Indeed, the only Argentine Navy element immediately available to attack was the submarine, which herself was attacked by British Sea King helicopters during the afternoon.

While the intense activity continued north of the Falklands, *Conqueror*, to the south, closed on the cruiser in order to keep a close eye on her movements. Sunday 2 May, it seemed, might be another day of action, for by then, all three Argentine naval groups would be in a position potentially very threatening to the Task Force.

With the SAS and SBS units ashore, the Task Force ships could afford to stand off, and *Glamorgan, Alacrity* and *Arrow* went back under cover of *Hermes'* air defence umbrella.

By this time, the cruiser was rapidly closing on an area known as the Burdwood Bank, where the depth of water was considered insufficient for *Conqueror* to enter with safety. In such a shallow area, she would run a serious risk of being detected and be unable to retain full manoeuvrability so essential under attack. In the circumstances, there was a serious possibility that *Conqueror* might lose sight of the cruiser at a particularly vital moment.

Signals passed hurriedly between the submarine's CO and the Task Force commander. Meanwhile, the threat from the other Argentine units was growing. The Task Force commander signalled to Admiral Sir John Fieldhouse, C-in-C at Northwood in the UK, for instructions.

Such was the importance attached to the threat that the Chief of the Defence Staff, Sir Terence Lewin, appraised the Prime Minister of the situation just before lunchtime on Sunday 2 May (about 0900 local Falklands time). An impromptu meeting of the War Cabinet then took place at Chequers (the Prime Minister's official country residence). It was decided that such was the gravity of the situation facing the Task Force that it was necessary to take immediate action to foil the impending attack. An order was formulated enabling the Task Force to attack the Argentine units closest to the Total Exclusion Zone. Thus *Conqueror* was ordered to attack *Belgrano*, at that time about six hours away from the Task force.

The *Belgrano* and her escorts were still pursuing an irregular zig-zag course as the *Conqueror* commenced her attack.

The kill

The *Conqueror* closed with the cruiser and fired two, possibly three, Mk 8 torpedoes. As she fired, the *Belgrano* altered to 280°, on a course taking her north-west towards the main Task Force which was in a position off the cruiser's starboard bow. As she was in the act of turning, two of the torpedoes struck home, one in the bow, and some three seconds later one towards the stern. There has been some debate as to why *Conqueror* used old Mk 8 straight-running torpedoes (a weapon designed in World War 2) with a limited range of 5000 yards instead of the Mk 24 wire-guided, self-homing Tigerfish torpedoes with an estimated range of 20–30 miles. The reason may well have been the urgency of the situation and *Belgrano*'s position, for with the cruiser about to enter the shoal water, zig-zagging and possibly within Exocet range, it was essential that she be stopped at the earliest possible opportunity.

Fired at a range of less than three miles, at 1600 local time, the first torpedo hit the cruiser in the port bow, killing eight to ten men there. The bow section collapsed as far back as the fo'c's'le break, just in front of 'A' turret.

The second torpedo struck the cruiser towards the stern in the area of the after machinery room, wrecking the steering and killing or trapping about 250 men, most of whom were either in their bunks or in the ship's canteen. The generally poor state of the cruiser, poor damage control (it is possible that many of the watertight doors were not shut) and the fact that some 300 of her crew of about 1000 were raw recruits with an average age of 18 could only increase the casualties. Later, the CO claimed that all internal and external communications were lost in the explosions. Within ten minutes of the torpedoes striking home, *Belgrano* was listing 15°.

Ten minutes later, the list had increased to 21° and the CO had decided he had no option but to give the order 'Abandon ship'. It was passed around the crew by word of mouth. A total of 70 self-inflating rafts, each capable of holding 20 men, were launched.

Adrift

An hour after being struck, at 1700 local time, *Belgrano* did roll over—and sink—in position 55° 27'S, 61° 24' W; the wind force was 3–4. According to the Argentine Joint Services Headquarters communiqué, she sank in 55° 24'S, 61° 32'W, south-east of the Isle de los Estados and 35 miles south of Burdwood Bank.

After dark, the wind began to rise, and with it the sea; gusts to 60mph and waves up to 18ft high. Occupants of the rafts described the experience as 'similar to tossing about on a trampoline'. Some of the rafts had turned out to be unserviceable because of damage in the torpedo attacks. Many of the sound ones were therefore overcrowded with up to 30 men. Some were suffering from terrible burns; no one had been wearing anti-flash masks or gloves. Life rafts afford scant comfort in such conditions—at least one blew over, with the loss of all aboard.

At the time it was thought up to 900 men died that night; in fact, the toll was substantially less. In total, 770 survivors were rescued by a combination of ARA destroyers and Chilean vessels, probably with the aid of flood-lights.

Precise figures are debatable, but the number of dead is officially reckoned to be 323, either in the attack itself or subsequently.

During the rescue operation, two armed tugs, *Alferez Sobral* and *Comodoro Somellera*, were looking for survivors when a Sea King heli-copter from *Hermes* flew into the vicinity. The tugs were 90 miles or so inside the Total Exclusion Zone, and they made the mistake of firing on the Sea King with a heavy machine gun. The pilot summoned two Lynx heli-copters from nearby frigates. These were armed with Sea Skua anti-ship missiles; *Comodoro Somellera* was sunk, and *Alferez Sobral* badly dam-aged. Her captain and seven crew were killed.

The shock wave of war

Suddenly, the war took on a new dimension. When *Belgrano* went down, the shock wave of real warfare was felt around the world. With 368 sailors dead it was no longer possible to characterize the quarrel over the Falklands as music-hall melodrama.

ON MONDAY 3 MAY, the day after the nuclear submarine HMS *Conqueror* had sunk the ARA *General Belgrano*, the world woke up to the fact that there was a real war going on in the South Atlantic. While in the UK, the *Sun's* 'Gotcha!' headline was quickly changed to the less offensive 'Did 1200 Argies drown?', the world's press was beginning to reflect the fact that the destruction of the ageing Argentine cruiser had shaken many governments awake to the realities of conflict. It was no longer possible to chacterize the quarrel as music-hall melodrama.

If the world of politics and the media awoke to reality, the man in the street awoke to horror. There is nothing like the loss of a ship for bringing the violence of war alive to the imagination. Ships, like big villages, are complete communities. On ships of the British Task Force, news of the sinking was often greeted by subdued silence.

In Argentina, the news was shattering; nowhere more so than the city of Punta Alta, a southern coastal town of about 50,000 inhabitants where lived many of the families of *Belgrano's* crew. A cloud of misery hung over the place for days after the Junta finally admitted the sinking. People spoke in whispers, and waited in stricken tension as the business of counting and identifying dead and wounded dragged on. One housewife ruefully admitted to a reporter that she had never believed a shooting war would start, nor indeed that the British ships would dare come to the South Atlantic. And a man in Comodoro Rivadavia expressed the new mood of national despair when he said he would commit suicide 'if we pull out of the Malvinas'.

Distressed

In the US news of the sinking came just two days after the decision formally to back the British cause. *Belgrano* had once been a ship of the US Navy, too. Commissioned as *Phoenix* in 1939, she was, in fact, no less than a survivor of the Japanese bombing of Pearl Harbor. Now an ally, Britain, had sunk her; and along with her, American diplomats thought it likely they had sunk the possibility of a strong and unified anti-communist coalition in Latin America. 'Events around the Falkland Islands could scarcely be more distressing', noted the *Wall Street Journal*. 'British and Argentine seamen in watery graves; ships and planes being destroyed that better could be deployed against the Soviet Union...'

The Soviet Union was keeping a close watch on the developing situation in the South Atlantic with the aid of half a dozen spy satellites, and had predictably taken an anti-British stance. As soon as news of the sinking broke, the TASS news agency blamed the US for giving Britain the go-ahead. The US's satellites, like the Russians', were busy over the region, feeding information to the British fleet. 'Needless to say all this fits perfectly into Washington's global imperialist line', observed the TASS analyst from Moscow.

US opinion was quite sharply divided. The 'doves' called for UN negotiations and a peaceful settlement. The 'hawks' claimed that the US should have sent an aircraft carrier to support Britain at the onset of the conflict, settling the matter swiftly and decisively.

Criticism

The British government hardened its resolve to fight rather than negotiate, and much international reaction was hostile to Britain. A new Peruvian peace plan foundered. In Dublin the Irish government suspended economic sanctions which had been imposed by all EEC members against Argentina, and called for an immediate meeting of the UN Security Council, labelling Britain as the new aggressor. In Rome, government officials called for a compromise, while the Swedes said that 'this British action is out of all proportion to the situation.'

West Germany called for a cease-fire, and Chancellor Schmidt and the visiting Portuguese Prime Minister expressed their joint dismay. 'Further loss of life must be avoided. Both parties must put prestige aside and concentrate on a negotiated solution', echoed Foreign Minister Kjeld Olesen of Denmark. The French leader, François Mitterand, expressed 'consternation' at the intensifying hostilities. But in the event, Britain succeeded in retaining the vital support of all of her allies in NATO at a subsequent top-level meeting of the alliance's defence ministers.

Meanwhile in Argentina, euphoria had vanished and a grim assessment of the real costs of war began. With the economy already in tatters, the government devalued the peso by over 14 per cent, to help pay for the war by promoting exports. At the same time, gasoline prices were raised 30 per cent, and new taxes were imposed on tobacco and liquor. At the chic end of Buenos Aires, on the trendy Lavalle Street where fashionable young Argentines hang around the boutiques, fast food joints and cinemas, the Film Classification Board hurriedly closed down a number of foreign films. Among them were *Coming Home* (the Jane Fonda anti-Vietnam war film), *Z* (the Costa-Gavras indictment of the Greek Colonels' Junta) and even the most popular film of the day—ironically, the British *Chariots of Fire*.

In Britain, Defence Minister John Nott agreed in answer to press questioning that although Britain was technically only 'engaged in hostilities', 'most laymen would say that Britain and Argentina were now at war.'

The shattering blow

HMS *Sheffield* was the first of a new breed of modern, compact destroyers. But she was taken out by a single sea-skimming missile fired from over the horizon. The question now: is any of the Task Force safe from Exocet attack?

THE LAST CHAPTER in the story of *Sheffield* began innocently enough, with no hint of the tragedy that lay ahead. In March 1982 she had taken part in the NATO 'Spring Train' exercise and had returned to Gibraltar to replenish stores and ammunition. It was then that a strange episode hit the headlines: a group of Argentine scrap-merchants had landed illegally on South Georgia.

As the spectre of armed conflict drew closer, *Sheffield* and the other escorts at Gibraltar were among the first to join the Task Force sailing out of Portsmouth on 5 April. She had a new Captain, 42-year-old James 'Sam' Salt. By coincidence, the Task Force Commander, Rear Admiral 'Sandy' Woodward, was one of her former captains.

Her main role with the Task Force was to screen the two carriers, the flagship *Hermes* and *Invincible*, and on that fateful Tuesday 4 May she was stationed about 20 miles ahead of *Hermes*. It was a comparatively calm, clear but cold day somewhere close to the Islands. The ship was at 'defence stations', the second state of readiness, which allowed the 290 officers and ratings to share six-hour watches, so they could rest from the demanding routine of being closed up and eat a meal or simply catch up on sleep. In fact the blow fell during the navy's traditional 'dinner hour' about 1000 local time, and cooks were about to serve a meal from the galley amidships when danger approached.

The captain was on the bridge and the Operations Room a deck below was fully manned and alert. The ship was transmitting a message from the flagship to Fleet headquarters at Northwood, via the satellite link. To prevent interference from the main surveillance radar and avoid giving away the Task Force's exact position, *Sheffield*'s Type 966 radar—an updated version of the original Type 965—was switched off. To compensate for the gap in radar cover a repeat 'picture' of the radar being received aboard *Hermes* was being transmitted by means of a data-link. The scene was set.

The Exocet strikes

In spite of these precautions something went badly wrong. On board there was some confusion, apparently three hostile aircraft were identified on the main radar plot aboard *Hermes*. In the absence of any positive identification they were assumed to be Mirage III interceptors. Lynx helicopters were aloft, equipped with electronic support measures capable not only of identifying hostile aircraft radars but also the frequency and type of those radars. But the helicopters were too far out and too high to pick up any radar emissions from the Argentine aircraft, which were deliberately flying low and not using their search radars. Nor were they Mirage IIIs but brand-new Super Etendard naval strike aircraft, each equipped with a long-range fuel tank and one AM39 Exocet anti-ship missile. Knowing that the British had good electronic support measures (ESM) equipment the Argentine pilots were under orders not to use their Agave radars until they were close—within 25–30 miles.

Sheffield and the other escorts had their own ESM equipment, but there had been no time to change the computer's memory to show Exocet as a hostile weapon. There was also the problem that a number of friendly radars, such as the surface-warning radars of the Task Force, transmitted on the same frequency as the homing head of the Exocet missile. As a result the ESM equipment did not respond rapidly to the readings until the Exocet was already dangerously close. Captain Salt himself saw the flame and the smoke of its rocket motor through the bridge windows.

There was only time to shout 'Take cover' over the intercom, giving four or five seconds for everyone to throw themselves flat on the deck. The Exocet struck the ship on the starboard side amidships at the level of No 2 Deck, one deck below the fo'c's'le deck. As the angle of impact was about 30° from the centreline the missile entered the forward engine room and travelled aft, going right over the gas turbines and plunging into the aft bulkhead without detonating. To the stunned people on the bridge and in the Operations Room, it sounded like a colossal explosion, but photographs taken later indicated that the 364lb warhead did not detonate, and the noise and shock-effect can be attributed to the impact of 1455lb of missile-body and rocket motor.

Sheffield catches fire

Even without the detonation of the warhead the results were catastrophic. The friction as the Exocet passed through the thin steel plating generated a sheet of flame and the main supply tank immediately behind caught fire, sending dense clouds of white smoke billowing up. Horrified onlookers aboard *Hermes* saw a column of white smoke climbing up from the stricken ship. The fierce heat of the burning fuel then set fire to paint, PVC cable covering, foam cushions and other inflammable materials, filling the passageways with thick clouds of toxic smoke. In the words of Captain Salt: 'I know it sounds incredible, but in 15 to 20 seconds the whole working area of the ship was filled with black, acrid, pungent smoke, mainly from the cable-runs and paint. Then of course it caught on fuel and other combustibles.'

The men manning the Damage Control Centre and the Mechanical Control Room were the only ones who could get the ship working again. The loss of electrical power had put all weapon systems, pumping and auxiliary units out of action. The main officers and ratings manning these two nerve-centres volunteered to try to get systems working again, but the smoke and toxic fumes asphyxiated them. They, and the cooks in the nearby galley, formed the majority of the 20 officers and ratings who died.

The impact of the missile had knocked out the main generator in the aft (stern) engine room, and the other main generator in the forward engine room inexplicably refused to start. *Sheffield* had two standby generators, one at each end of the ship, but here again a jinx seemed to be at work. The forward generator had been stripped for repair and was awaiting spare parts, and the aft generator now proved defective. Without power, there was no way of even ventilating the ship to clear the central part of smoke, and fire-fighting parties found themselves cut off from the areas on fire. Even an auxiliary turbine-driven fire pump refused to start, and meanwhile the fire was gaining the upper hand.

The personal fire-fighting equipment proved hopeless. Carbon dioxide fire extinguishers were carried but there was no way of replenishing them when the carbon dioxide was used up. As only five sets of Survival Support Devices (breathing apparatus) were carried only a handful of men could operate in smoke. Each SSD carries only ten minutes' supply of air, so until more sets could be flown across from the other ships the fire-fighting effort had to rely on five men working for ten minutes each. It was an exhausting and unequal contest.

Two ships, the frigates *Yarmouth* and *Arrow*, came alongside to take off injured men and play fire hoses on the burning hull. Helicopters ferried spare sets of breathing apparatus and fire-fighting gear from other ships, but it was too late. The decks became so hot that shoes began to burn through the soles. The plating glowed white-hot in places. It was an impossible predicament, despite the efforts of the fire-fighters. After about five gru-elling hours Captain Salt ordered his men to abandon the struggle. There were still 22 Sea Dart missiles and their warheads in the forward magazine, in addition to some 120 4.5in shells, torpedo warheads, depth-charges and chaff rockets.

The injured had already been evacuated, and TV cameramen were on hand to record the scene as dazed, badly burned men were carried by medics to the sick bay aboard *Hermes*. Nobody who saw those films can erase the memory of their injuries, but what made them worse was the effect of polyester clothing. Man-made fibres in navy-issue shirts and trousers had melted and stuck to the burns, complicating them hideously and making plastic surgery necessary. Aboard *Sheffield* the fire-fighters had already been ordered to change into No 6 rig, tropical gear, but for many the order came too late to save them from disfiguring burns.

Abandon ship

Admiral Woodward agreed with the decision to abandon *Sheffield*. But to everyone's surprise the gutted hulk refused to sink, so the salvage tug *Irishman* was ordered to take her in tow. If it was at all possible to get the ship to South Georgia or Ascension Island then the navy's technical experts would learn a lot from examining the structure. As things turned out, pho-tographs were taken of damaged bulkheads and any portable equipment was removed for examination. It was careful examination of these photo-graphs that showed that the Exocet warhead had not detonated, for the superstructure remained intact. All previous target-firings of Exocet had left the ships with massive holes in their decks and side plating. But there was no sign of this—only massive fire damage to the central part of the ship.

At first, it looked as if the gamble might succeed but when the weather worsened the task of towing *Sheffield* became harder and harder. As each wave washed against the hole in her side more water found its way below. With many tons of water already on board from the fire hoses she was rap-idly reduced to a waterlogged hulk, wallowing from side to side. On 10 May, six days after being hit, *Sheffield* was sunk in deep water between the Falklands and South Georgia. Perhaps it was a more dignified end than being towed back to England to be dissected by the experts in clinical detail.

Post mortem on the 'Shiny Sheff'

The Type 42 destroyer was born out of the far-reaching consequences of the 1966 decision to phase out the navy's aircraft carriers, which were to have been escorted by four 6000 tonne destroyers. At first the Defence

Minister Denis Healey resisted pressure from the Navy Board to axe all four ships, but subsequently he insisted that a cheaper and smaller type of missile-armed ship be designed. This was how the 3500 tonne Sea Dart-carrying Type 42 guided-missile destroyer replaced the 6000 tonne Type 82 large destroyer.

A simple, brutal, cost-cutting criterion was adopted: everything that could be saved from the Type 82 design would be saved, but the cost would be held to £20 million instead of £30 million. In practice this meant leaving out the Ikara long-range anti-submarine missile system and the elaborate command facilities of the Type 82.

While detailed design was still in progress the first Type 42 was ordered from Vickers Shipbuilders. She was to be called *Sheffield*, commemorating the cruiser of that name which had gone to the breaker's yard in September 1967.

Sheffield completed her final trials at the beginning of 1975 and went south to Portsmouth Naval base for the formal commissioning ceremony on 28 February. By then she had cost £23 million.

As the first of a new class and bearer of an illustrious name, 'Shiny Sheff' attracted a lot of attention. For one thing, she inherited all the traditions of her predecessor, and some material benefits as well, such as the stainless steel wardroom dinner-service presented to the original *Sheffield* by the Master Cutlers of the City of Sheffield. Commentators were impressed by her compact design, although some expressed doubt about the absence of any close-range defence against aircraft and others drew attention to the fact that the hull was tightly packed with equipment. For example, the addition of even the smallest extra weapon could only be achieved by removing the two boats carried amidships.

Everything in the Type 42 design emphasized weight-reduction in order to keep within the arbitrary limit of 3150 tonnes (standard displacement)— one anchor instead of two, one galley instead of two, a manual hoist for the Sea Dart missiles rather than the mechanical system in the Type 82. Even though experience had already shown that a single helicopter had little chance of remaining operational for 50 per cent of the time, a double hangar was ruled out, again on grounds of cost and size.

In short, the Type 42 represented the smallest possible Sea Dart platform that could be built. She was somewhat inferior to ships in the US Navy rated as frigates and hardly merited the designation of destroyer. But she was all that Mr Healey and the Treasury would allow and the design had, at least, the merit of being cheap enough to build in numbers.

Grave weaknesses

Outwardly all seemed well, but the restriction of dimensions resulted in several major handicaps. The most obvious was comparatively poor seakeeping caused by the short fo'c's'le which allowed spray to blanket the bows and the ship to pitch in heavy seas. Every previous class of Royal Navy warship had managed to achieve an improvement in seakeeping on its predecessor. But when it was pointed out that the addition of a mere 30 to 40ft would not only improve seakeeping but also relieve crowding on the mess decks, such an alteration was overruled. The result was that a weakness was perpetuated in order to save one per cent of the total building cost—the cost of the hull being less than ten per cent of the entire ship and the increase in tonnage being only ten per cent of the original displacement.

Internally, the cramped dimensions caused even more headaches, which were ultimately to result in grave military weaknesses. The layout of the Operations Room was particularly awkward, with the various electronic warfare, sonar, radar and communications operators finding difficulty in passing action information and data to one another. This failure to be able to integrate the various functions of the Action Information Organization is now seen by many electronics experts as the real reason why both *Sheffield* and her sister *Coventry* failed to cope with the attacks made on them. The latter was unable to cope with a second wave of A4 Skyhawk aircraft.

The hand-operated hoist for the Sea Dart did not help to provide a sustained rate of launching, but as there were only 22 missiles in the magazine, anything more rapid would simply have emptied the magazine faster. The cramped dimensions did not allow space for an obsolescent defence against aircraft such as the Sea Cat missile system, even if the cost-limit had permitted it. When *Sheffield* was first commissioned a visitor to her was shocked to learn from the captain that any addition to the armament, no matter how small, could only be achieved by removing the boats. This prophecy came true in May 1982 when the surviving Type 42s all had twin 30mm and single 20mm guns added on the upper deck amidships, in the place of the boats. Not only was there insufficient margin of stability to allow the extra topweight, but there was insufficient deck-space as well.

Radar inadequacies

Other problems of the Type 42 design were the result of British industrial and economic weakness, rather than political influences at the design stage. The only surveillance radar available was the venerable Type 965, designed in the early 1950s to cope with Russian bombers flying at medium altitude and a subsonic speed, but it had too slow a data-rate to be able to track supersonic targets, and no ability to pick out low-flying targets.

Nor was the Type 9920 surface warning and target-indication radar any better, and in the Falklands it proved incapable of detecting aircraft flying over land. A belated attempt had been made to remedy the more glaring deficiencies of Type 965 by updating the processing equipment, but an offer by British industry to update the 992Q in similar fashion had been vetoed on financial grounds. In fact, 992Q was more crucial to survival in the Falklands than 965, as it had the vital task of allocating targets to the Sea Dart tracker radars.

After ten ships had been ordered the seakeeping problem was tackled by 'stretching' the hull. In other words, the missing length—almost 40ft—was restored to the forward part of the hull. This relieved crowding in the accommodation spaces and permitted a larger missile magazine, but did very little to provide extra deck-space aft. However, the addition of nearly two feet to the beam has given a bigger margin of stability for additional topweight. In the last four of the original Type 42s (known as Batch 2) the superannuated Type 965 radar was finally replaced by the Anglo-Dutch Type 1022—the antenna British, the processing equipment Dutch. In action, Type 1022 proved vastly superior to its predecessor, and well able to discriminate low-flying targets in conditions which defeated the older radars. This new radar was also fitted in the *Manchester* and her three Batch 3 sisters.

Another important advantage over the Batch 2 ships was that the Batch 2 computer software was modular in design. This meant that it was impossible to incorporate changes very rapidly. Ships like HMS *Exeter* could go straight to Ascension, and there receive a 'package' of modifications to enable her Action Information Organization to cope with the Exocet threat, whereas older ships of the same class would require the entire program to be rewritten.

The weakness of the Type 992Q radar was to have been remedied by fitting a new Surveillance and Target Indicating Radar *(STIR)* to the entire class, replacing both 965 and 992Q. Type 1022 was only intended to be an interim radar, pending the arrival of the Type 1030 *STIR*, but this was cancelled as part of the 1981 defence cuts. The Sea Dart missile and its associated system also had several weaknesses, mainly due to the fact that they were first trialled in 1965. But during the Falklands campaign, *Exeter* shot down at least one aircraft at only 75ft, an altitude previously believed to be outside the missiles' capabilities.

The Task Force's weak spot

The attack which sank *Sheffield* was an extremely skilful and well planned operation. It found the weak spot in the Task Force's defences. The Super Etendards, flown by the cream of the Argentine pilots, flew low and thus avoided early detection. Later the pilots admitted that they had sighted two 'blips' on their radar screen, one large and one small, and had fired two Exocets at these targets. These echoes were presumably *Sheffield* and *Hermes*. About 25 minutes after *Sheffield* was hit a third Exocet was fired at the Task Force. The frigate *Yarmouth* reported sighting this missile. She fired her Corvus chaff-rockets, apparently deflecting it, and spotters aboard *Alacrity* thought they saw the missile fall into the water.

In the final analysis, all warships have to be expendable and escort warships are more expendable than most. HMS *Sheffield*'s primary task was to protect the two carriers, and if her sinking kept the flagship out of harm's way she had achieved that purpose. It also provided the Task Force Commander with a timely reminder of the risk to his proposed amphibious landings. A relative immunity to Exocet attack was the main factor in the choice of San Carlos as the landing site.

The attack on *Sheffield*, coming so soon after the torpedoing of the Argentine cruiser *General Belgrano*, shocked both sides into the belated realization that they had stumbled into a full-scale war. There was a hardening of attitudes on both sides; a new determination in Britain to see the battle convincingly won. Other nations watched, appalled, as a conflict begun in such an unlikely location steadily escalated to a full-scale demonstration of modern warfare. For Exocet salesmen in Paris, it was a field day.

A nation mourns

If there ever was a period of phoney war for the British public it ended abruptly on Tuesday, 4 May. The unthinkable had suddenly happened.

Unlike the decrepit *Belgrano, Sheffield* was a modern warship which had been reduced to a burnt-out hulk by a single missile fired by an Argentine pilot at little risk to himself. The British Fleet was no longer invulnerable. British sailors were dead, though not in the numbers the Argentines had sustained. Others were disfigured by hideous injuries. The Task Force sailed on, but Britain suddenly seemed to be on the brink of a war it could no longer be sure of winning.

At home, as the news came through piece by piece, the British people were overtaken by a terrible sense of bereavement. The relatives and friends of the 20 dead seamen were not the only ones to mourn. The city of Sheffield, which had a special affinity with the ships that bore its name, quietly lamented.

The shock of the loss of the 'Shiny Sheff' was immense. Margaret Thatcher had proclaimed at the start of the campaign – 'Defeat? The possibility does not exist' – and much of her party and the nation believed her. Here was a chilling demonstration that in the age of missile warfare the Task Force, and with it Britain's hopes, might succumb to attack by what some Fleet Street papers had been describing as a pack of comic opera gauchos.

The headline war

The news of the missile strike on *Sheffield* came just as Fleet Street was drawing up battle lines of its own regarding attitudes to the war. The *Sun,* locked in a fierce circulation battle with its mass-circulation rival the *Daily Mirror*, ran a massive front page headline on 5 May – 'British Warship Sunk by Argies' – with an editorial urging greater resolve for a military solution. The *Mirror* recoiled from the shock, called the sinking 'Too High a Price' and exhorted the politicians to find peace through diplomacy. The *Guardian* ran a cartoon by Les Gibbard echoing a famous *Mirror* cartoon of World War 2 showing a torpedoed merchant seaman clinging to a life raft. The 'Price of Sovereignty has been increased – official' ran the 1982 caption.

The British media now turned viciously on itself. The *Sun* accused the *Mirror* of 'treason'; the *Mirror* retorted by calling its rival the 'harlot of Fleet Street'. Conservative MPs sought a scapegoat in the BBC who in some news broadcasts, notably *Newsnight*, had been questioning the accuracy of some official Ministry of Defence announcements. The *Panorama* broadcast of 10 May which voiced some contrary views on government policy caused a real uproar, undoubtedly because the sinking of *Sheffield* and the press reaction had raised the political temperature.

How then did the news come in and how was it handled? *Sheffield* was struck by an air-launched AM39 Exocet shortly after 1400 hours on Tuesday 4 May. Twenty were killed by the initial impact and, after fires gained a hold, the ship's commander Captain Sam Salt gave the order to abandon ship. It was late afternoon in London when the first signals began to arrive at Fleet HQ and the news obviously had a major political dimension. By 1800 hours Margaret Thatcher knew and she convened an emergency meeting at the House of Commons with senior political and military advisers. The meeting decided to announce the news; the BBC had already heard something and were pressing for verification and rumours were sweeping the House that it was *Invincible* that had been sunk. Ian McDonald, the MoD's acting Chief of Public Relations, was summoned to the House, briefed by John Nott and then hastened back to the Ministry's Press Centre, drafting a statement on the way.

The war on TV

McDonald arrived at the packed Press Centre just as the BBC's main evening news was on the air and the programme was dramatically interrupted and went over live to take his statement. The first the British public knew of the loss of *Sheffield* was the pronouncement in Mr McDonald's sombre tones:

> 'In the course of its duties within the Total Exclusion Zone around the Falkland Islands, HMS *Sheffield*, a Type 42 destroyer, was attacked and hit late this afternoon by an Argentine missile. The ship caught fire which spread out of control.'

This was high drama and it was happening live in front of a record audience of 12 million viewers. In the House of Commons, MPs in the middle of a routine debate repeatedly rose to demand a statement until finally John Nott came into the chamber just before 2300. The Minister spoke of 11 casualties, until a note was passed advising him to raise his estimate to 30. The tension rose even more.

In the South Atlantic the press and TV journalists who were actually witnessing the successful rescue operation to pick up *Sheffield*'s crew were unable to file copy or get back TV pictures while the politicians were handling the release of the news in London.

Indeed, when *Sheffield* finally sank, the First Sea Lord instructed Ian McDonald not to announce the fact on TV as the printed media was judged to be more 'discreet'. In fact, TV coverage of *Sheffield*, including an interview with Captain Sam Salt, pictures of survivors and helicopter film of the smouldering hulk taken on 7 May, were not seen on British TV screens until 26–28 May; and by then the war had moved into its land fighting phase.

The House of Commons Defence Committee investigating the handling of press information during the conflict noted the inconsistencies in the way the MoD handled bad news. It conceded that where there were substantial casualties the MoD was under pressure to inform next-of-kin before the press. On the other hand, it was important to announce the loss of a ship because the Argentines would do so anyway. Other than the invasion itself, the loss of *Sheffield*, coupled with the sinking of *General Belgrano*, was the first really big news of the war. The announcement of the loss, live on prime-time TV, plus the frenzied press reaction, made it unforgettable.

Coming home

As *Sheffield* burned, survivors of the *Belgrano* sinking two days previously were on their way home. Their stories horrified a nation that had gone to war confident that the British, 8000 miles away, could be no threat.

A WEEK AFTER THE SINKING of the ageing cruiser *General Belgrano* many of the survivors were back home with their families – and telling of their experiences. The World War 2 warship had been the pride of the Argentine Navy and her sinking dealt a savage blow to the Service's – and the nation's – morale. The loss of life was truly fearful.

It undoubtedly affected the course of the battle for the Falklands. After the loss of *Belgrano*, the Argentine Navy returned to port and stayed there, playing no further part in the fighting.

Her sinking had the most profound effect on those who sailed in her. Here is the story of the sinking and the dramatic rescue as seen through the eyes of ordinary seamen, in the words of those who survived.

'The attack caught us unawares while we were resting,' said Nursing Petty Officer Silverio Octavio Muscardin. 'It did not give us time to prepare ourselves. I was sleeping and I heard this incredible noise. Although I was in the bow of the ship, away from the engine room where the torpedo struck, beneath me was the magazine where the munitions are kept. Luckily, the torpedoes missed the part or it would have been a complete disaster.'

'I was about to have a cup of tea when I heard what sounded like a silenced pistol and the power was cut off,' reported Petty Officer, Operations, Muguel Angel Reynoso. 'The ship stopped and, after a jolt, began to list. I went back to my post, opened my bag, took out a parka and put it on. I fetched a lamp and went to my lifeboat station ready to abandon ship. We began to release the lifeboats and lower them onto the deck and then into the water. It all happened in only 45 minutes.'

'I was in the second dormitory,' recalled 19-year-old conscript Fernando

Argibay. 'We heard two explosions almost one after the other. I grabbed my life jacket and started to run upstairs. Nobody knew what had happened. When I arrived on deck we began to undo the lifeboats and prepare them for launching. There was no time to lose. I jumped 30 feet and when I reached the life raft one of my mates was already there. Our raft broke loose from the ship. It was very stormy and cold. Nobody jumped after I did. Then we saw a colleague floating in the water – his life raft had overturned – and we tried to take him on board. We began to row with arms and oars. We couldn't see very well because of the oil and smoke.'

'There was no panic although many victims came off deck with burns,' continued PO Muscardin. 'Everything was done in an orderly fashion as if it were a routine drill call to action stations. On checking our crew lists, we found some men were missing. These men remained beneath the waves. We all quickly abandoned ship from the same side – that is to windward. *Belgrano* sank in 40 minutes from the port and bow. It was incredible that such a huge mass could be devoured by the water in such a short time. When we saw that *Belgrano* was sinking, we shouted: "Long live the Fatherland." And perhaps through despair and a sense of helplessness, we tried to sing the national anthem.'

'I did not want to see how *Belgrano* sank,' said Corporal Jorge Ricardo Paez. 'I am a sentimental soul and for four years the ship had been my second home. She was something I loved very much in spite of being an old ship.'

'As soon as we had abandoned ship and reached the life rafts, we all introduced ourselves and tried to make friends,' PO Muscardin goes on, 'We knew in that area there were a lot of fishing boats. But we needed to keep cool heads, if we were going to last out. Personally, I felt we would be in the life rafts for five or six days before we were picked up because we were outside the operational zone. But everyone kept themselves under control and there were no scenes of despair or terror as often happens in such circumstances. In my life raft we were all professionals, all ten of us. There weren't any conscripts. We drifted for 32 hours and comforted each other. We talked and prayed together. We organized rations, took turns baling out and re-inflating the raft when necessary. Expecting our rescue to be a few days off, we got the life-saving equipment ready and handed it round. We had sweets, chocolates, chewing gum and flares and a signal lamp.'

'The wind was icy and the waves gigantic,' continues Lieutenant Madero. 'In the life raft we huddled together for warmth and still we could not see any rescue ship nearby. Neither had the search aircraft found us. There were 15 of us in a covered orange life raft. We had some chocolate and blankets to cover us. The temperature felt like 20 below.'

'The current swept us more than 60 miles southwards towards the Antarctic,' reported Fernando Argibay. 'We saw the *Piedra Buena* which signalled to us with green lights – we thought we had been found. But the submarine was still patrolling and we had to get away from it. We went on drifting like that for 28 hours. I only knew the name of one other survivor on the raft – Ricardo – and Pepe, the man we rescued. We three hugged together to keep warm. I felt my legs going numb. We prayed and sang and tried to tell each other jokes. I thought of my dear ones. We were picked up at 8pm on Monday and we greeted and embraced those who had already been rescued. We continued picking people up until 5am on Tuesday.'

'There were 19 of us in the life raft, including several conscripts,' says Corporal Mario Daniel Berdeccia. 'Some were nervous and I remember one of them was rocking about, putting the life raft in danger. We held him down and pacified him. As we moved away from the ship we sang the Naval March and that certainly raised our spirits. Afterwards we fell silent and began to plan our survival.'

'Despite being in the life raft for 36 hours without being able to move, we got over the cold, the anguish and everything straight away,' Corporal Paez said. 'We had a man who was severely burned and as I am a nurse I treated him. I put some ointment on him which I found on deck and gave him a painkiller. Later when we saw things were going well, I put a bandage on his face. As we knew our forces were near, we were not worried. We were sure we would be rescued.'

'I was familiar with the search and rescue procedure so I explained it to the others,' said PO Muscardin. 'I told them that we would be rescued between 8am and noon on the following day. But when midday arrived, the others were disheartened. All night the sea was rough – state seven or eight according to my calculations. At 1pm on the following day I heard the sound of an aircraft. When I saw the plane passing over I gave the order to fire a distress flare. The plane returned and when it was well ahead of us we fired another. The aircraft banked and circled, indicating that we had been spotted. Everyone began shouting – already we were in a whole new situation. At 6pm on Monday 3 May, we caught sight of the rescue ships that were searching for us, and when darkness fell we launched a distress flare. At midnight we set off another and at about 1.30 on Tuesday we were rescued by the *Commandante Piedrabuena*. It is impossible to describe how we were received – there is no way we can thank those people for their reassurance and the faith with which they consoled us.'

'In my life raft there were 17 people and everyone behaved sensibly,' said Romeo Gullino, Chief Petty Officer, engineering. 'Even the conscripts behaved like veterans. We were not afraid but tense, very cold and uncomfortable because of the water that kept coming in. I suffered a lot although I was always confident that we would be saved. I thought about my children, about the really important things in life. In a lifeboat out at sea there is plenty of time to think in spite of the fatigue, the blunting of your feelings and the loss of objectivity. But it was nice to arrive home and wake up and receive so much fondness. I joined the navy in 1966 and I belong to the permanent crew of *Belgrano* – you see I am not used to speaking of her in the past tense. I am not ashamed to say that I cried when I was reunited with my family and when I saw so many of my dependents waiting for me.'

'Engage and stop': the Narwal incident

She was inside the Total Exclusion Zone. She refused to stop. And, unfortunately for one hapless Argentine sailor on board *Narwal*, the Harrier pilots sent out to intercept this possible spy ship were under orders to engage and stop her.

On 9 May, two Sea Harriers of 800 Squadron launched from *Hermes* to carry out a routine combined ground attack/Combat air patrol (CAP) mission. They were armed with two Sidewinder AIM9L air-to-air missiles on the outer wing pylons and a single 1000lb bomb on the centreline fuselage station. They carried the standard two 30mm Aden guns.

The aircraft were flown by Flight Lt David Morgan of the RAF and Lt Commander Gordon Batt of the Royal Navy. The two pilots had been briefed to close on Port Stanley airfield for a bombing mission, after which they were to assume a CAP role with *Coventry* as the control ship. But when the two aircraft reached Stanley, they found that the weather was particularly bad with a very low cloud base—about 300ft. Dropping their bombs indiscriminately through the cloud cover in the hope of hitting the runway or a worthwhile target would also risk hitting civilian targets. And flying below cloud base would invite intensive anti-aircraft gunfire and surface-to-air missiles attack. So the two Sea Harriers broke off and turned to take up their CAP role instead.

Turning away in a south-easterly direction, the two aircraft approached their designated patrol area. Then Flt Lt Morgan picked up a radar contact about 60 miles away on a bearing of 150° and *Coventry* ordered them to investigate. Breaking cloud cover at about 300–400ft, the two pilots suddenly spotted a trawler on a westward heading and manoeuvred to carry out a standard series of passes. One Sea Harrier flew over the ship from the beam, while the second made a pass at 90 degrees to the first, running along the length of the ship.

With both aircraft flying so low, contact with *Coventry* was lost. Flt Lt Morgan peeled off and climbed through the clouds to call the control ship for further instructions. Meanwhile, the second Sea Harrier carried out another pass, this time across the vessel's stern, to identify her. Lt Cdr Batt spotted her name—*Narwal*—and relayed it via Flt Lt Morgan back to *Coventry*. The vessel, which had been behaving suspiciously, was apparently a spy ship, and after a delay of about two minutes, the instructions came back: 'Engage and stop the vessel.'

Flt Lt Morgan dived back through the clouds just as Lt Cdr Batt was carrying out the first straffing run. A quick burst of 30mm fire was laid across the *Narwal's* bow. This was the internationally recognised order to heave-to—or accept engagement. But *Narwal* did not react. She continued on her westward course at about 12–15 knots.

Both Sea Harriers still had their 1000lb bombs, so rather than waste the rest of the 240 rounds of 30mm each aircraft carried, they decided to use the bombs. These would have to be jettisoned before going back to *Hermes*, anyway. They would be delivered at the end of a shallow dive. This would improve the chances of a hit and allow the bombs more chance to arm their fuses which were still set for a high drop. The idea was that a shallow dive would give the bombs a spinning action and as they were also set to arm after a certain number of resolutions the bombs should explode on impact.

Battered but on course

Flt Lt Morgan carried out the first bombing run, but narrowly missed the target—his bomb passed very close behind the *Narwal's* bridge super-structure and hit the sea beyond. It did not explode. The second bomb, dropped by Lt Cdr Batt, made a direct hit on the fo'c's'le and penetrated two or three decks, coming to rest inside the hull. This bomb too failed to explode, but it did cause the only fatality of the action. It hit an Argentine sailor below decks.

In spite of this battering, *Narwal* continued on her course so the two Sea Harriers made another attack with their Aden guns. The aircraft came in from either side of the vessel with one aiming at the bridge and engine room areas and the other aiming along the waterline.

The Aden's heavy 30mm shells punched easily through the vessel's thin outer skin and smashed their way into the *Narwal's* vitals, wreaking havoc along the way—only stopped by a strong bulkhead or heavy piece of machinery. The punishing attack tore chunks off the ship and she finally hove to, turning through 90° and coming to a dead stop facing north. The only movement was that created by the sea's swell.

Riddled by shells

The two Sea Harriers were then instructed to return to their ship as their fuel was by now getting low. A second pair of aircraft was detached from CAP to overfly the area and three Sea Kings were sent out with a boarding party to capture the ship and her crew. *Narwal* was in a very poor state, being riddled along the water line by the 30mm shells. Both Flt Lt David Morgan and Lt Cdr Batt were awarded the Distinguished Service Cross, Lt Cdr Batt posthumously after his Harrier was lost shortly after launching from *Hermes* on 24 May. Their action helped preserve the secrecy of British shipping movements in the Total Exclusion Zone which was vital to the safety of the first reinforcements who could soon be sailing south.

10 MAY 1982

The crucial plan

The decision was agonizing to reach, vital to the whole success of the operation. If the Task Force landed in the wrong place, catastrophe could well be unavoidable. The men who had to work it out were unused to such responsibility.

AS SOME 60 key commanding officers gathered on board *Fearless* on 10 May, everyone knew that the decision they were about to make was the most momentous of the whole war. The seal was set on the Task Force's final destination: the actual site for the landing on the Falklands.

Behind that decision lay weeks of agonized—and sometimes sharp-tempered—debate.

One of the first to mark up his map of the islands—and on the first weekend after the Argentine invasion—was a man with some very special knowledge of the terrain involved. For Major Ewen Southby-Tailyour the distant islands and their rugged coastlines were places etched in detail on his memory and affections. He had commanded NP8901, the Royal Marines garrison of the islands some four years previously, and had spent his leisure hours sailing in coastal waters.

The circle he now made on the map, that first weekend, was round a place named San Carlos. Alongside he wrote: 'sheltered, dominated, good ops. 65 miles to Stanley; 92 by sea.' 'Dominated' means surrounded largely by high ground; 'ops' are observation posts, (ideally sited on hill tops). Southby-Tailyour was quickly taken on as a special advisor to the Task Force. In the next few weeks he was to be deeply involved in the deliberations that led to San Carlos as the final choice—a fateful responsibility which would lie heavily on him.

There was controversy from the start. Early on, Rear Admiral Woodward favoured landing at Port North on West Falkland, 115 miles from Port Stanley and about as far from Argentine ground forces as possible. There would be time, he thought, to build an airstrip there from which Harriers, possibly even Phantoms and Buccaneers, flown down from

Ascension, could operate to take the pressure off his carriers. The Royal Marines involved in the planning, principally the team of senior officers known as 'R' Group, did not like the idea. It disobeyed one of the most basic of all rules of warfare—that forces should be concentrated against the main objective, in this case Port Stanley. As Thompson said, 'It was like landing at Barmouth to attack Cardiff.'

Similar objections could be, and were, made against San Carlos, but it seems to have remained one of the principal alternatives because it was, at least, closer to Stanley than Port North. The planners were well aware how much the politicians needed a quick campaign; they also knew that once the men were landed, their condition would deteriorate rapidly, given near-Antarctic weather and the problems of keeping them supplied.

The third main possibility was a landing close to Stanley. Cow Bay and Uranie Bay, to the north of the capital, were considered specifically. Landing would be followed by an immediate assault on the town itself. Brigadier Thompson was initially attracted by the idea, thinking that the commandos could quickly push up on to the nearby high ground of Mount Estancia, so dominating Stanley to the north. In the event, this was the first option to be ruled out. No one could guarantee getting artillery ashore quickly enough to support the commandos, and the Argentines, with pow-erful helicopter lift at their disposal, could mount a devastating counter-attack. The classic requirement for success in an amphibious assault is superiority of three to one; the British had an inferiority of at least that.

On Ascension, the debate hotted up. Woodward seemed convinced the air threat could be dealt with by the fleet with the help of land-based air power, operating from a strip built by the army. The soldiers felt very strongly that he was mistaken, and that it was vital to select a site where artillery and missiles could be taken ashore easily and set up in effective, protected sites. Some 'R' Group officers actually cabled back to London asking their superiors to fly down to Ascension to help them argue the case. This they did, and seemed to have swayed the Admiral, for after a second day's conference on Ascension, he agreed to drop the West Falklands option.

Helicopter too far

Two daring but lunatic schemes were aired. SAS commanders suggested an Entebbe-style raid on Stanley airport, crack units to land there, then drive into town and gun down the Argentine high command. Practice for this raid is reputed to have been undertaken back in the UK at a remote Scottish airfield, until intelligence started sending back reports on the strength of Argentine defences on the road into Stanley.

Captain Jeremy Larken, in command of the assault ship *Fearless*, pro-posed backing the ship into Stanley harbour, her troops to transfer direct to landing craft and try a frontal attack. Others suggested landing men by heli-copter in large numbers. But it was clear that there were not enough troops to take Stanley frontally, and no one knew whether the harbour was mined.

Discussion continued after 'R' Group had been ordered south from Ascension on 8 May. Ewen Southby-Tailyour's experience proved invalu-able; he had marked his maps with more than 40 possible bays in East and West Falklands.

As the days went by, Southby-Tailyour noticed that his colleagues in 'R' Group kept returning to the San Carlos option. He had told them San Carlos Water was deep enough to allow the big ships to approach; shortly a Task Force frigate navigated Falkland Sound, proving it was not mined. SAS and SBS squadrons had been ashore since the first days of May, and now for the first time reliable intelligence confirmed that there were, to Thompson's amazement and delight, no Argentines in the San Carlos area. This, together with the growing appreciation that Rapier missiles could be effectively sited on the hills surrounding the bay, seems to have clinched the decision. And there was the comforting thought that should *Canberra* be hit, San Carlos Bay was shallow enough for her to rest on the bottom with her top decks above water.

No going back

At the crucial meeting of 10 May, San Carlos appears to have received a broad spectrum of support. The army was relieved that the navy felt able to back the idea; points of agreement had until then been pitifully scarce. Back in London, Downing Street were quick to agree the San Carlos choice, and impressed with the plan as a whole.

Ewen Southby-Tailyour had good reason to congratulate himself, but he was absent from the meeting, suffering an acute crisis of confidence. That night he wrote in his diary: 'The responsibility is beginning to wear me down. I am worried about the accuracy of everything I have told them.'

The Queen is called up

Queen Elizabeth 2, the pride of the Cunard cruise-liner fleet, was going to war. Southampton had not seen a send-off like it for 40 years. No single event in the conflict was destined to bring back such vivid memories of World War 2.

THEY HAD BEEN GIVEN an emotional send-off which brought back memories of World War 2. Family and friends had packed the quayside, cheering the departing liner, and girls who came nearest the side of the ship were greeted with the catcalls and wolfwhistles of the troops who packed the rails of *QE2*. Singing telegram girl, Linda Goodrick, sister of Gunner Alan Goodrick, turned up in her scanties to see her brother on his way; and Lance Corporal Peter Lenman's wife Dawn stripped off her blouse and bra to give her husband and his mates a memorable send off. Cameras covered the event live for national television and pictures were transmitted by satellite live for US breakfast TV.

Left on the quayside was Welsh Guardsman Nigel Warburton who watched frustrated as the luxury troop ship turned in Southampton Water. He was on crutches after being injured in training. Lance Corporal Colin Overton of 1 Scots Guards had actually got on board when he was struck down by appendicitis and was rushed ashore to be whisked away by ambulance.

Southampton had not seen a send-off like this for almost 40 years. In emotion generated, it easily outstripped the departure of the Task Force. The first casualties of the conflict had been seen since then and were fresh wounds in everyone's memory. These men were sailing to a war that all now knew was for real. But as the great roar of cheering died away, the resounding salutes of other ships' sirens fell silent and the huge liner sailed out of earshot, a strange stillness descended on the quayside.

Luxury, and it was all paid for

There are few people who would turn down the chance to sail on one of the world's most famous luxury liners—especially when the ticket is being paid for by the British government. But they might not be so eager if they knew that their destination was the Falklands and, more importantly, if they knew what they were expected to do when they got there.

Those who sailed with the *Queen Elizabeth 2* on the afternoon of 12 May 1982 knew where they were going, though, and expressed no reservations. As the majestic vessel slipped her moorings at 1600 hours most of her passengers still hoped that there would be a diplomatic settlement and that their role in the recapture of the Falklands would be no more nor less than the glorious task of garrison duty.

But in the hot Southampton sunshine, 5 Infantry Brigade were able to bask in one moment of glory, at least, as the *QE2* sailed down the Solent fêted by a retinue of pleasure boats and harbour craft.

The 67,000 ton vessel had been converted from liner to troopship in just 11 days by a team of dockyard fitters from Vospers and service personnel. Some 250 men worked on her around the clock. The plans had been drawn up for *QE2*'s conversion by a party of naval engineers before she had even returned to Southampton at the end of her latest world cruise. The planners were already well versed in this sort of conversion work after their frenetic efforts on the *Canberra* and *Uganda* and smaller merchant ships. In Southampton, steel-works manager of Vosper Repair Ltd Graham Young began again to track down the large amounts of steel plating and bracing that he knew would be needed in the construction of helicopter pads. Both Cunard's and the Navy's offices were in turmoil as plans were made and altered almost every hour to cope with the changing demands. The experience with other ships taken up from trade helped, but the sheer volume of work was overwhelming.

Soldier proofing

As the materials for the conversion work, stores for the voyage and equipment for the armed forces poured into the dockyard, *QE2*'s next passengers were far from the plush berths that awaited them. They were roughing it in the mountains of Wales on a working-up exercise called Welsh Falcon. This exercise was of obvious necessity. Some units of 5 Brigade were fresh from public ceremonial duties, and it gave time for the liner to be 'soldier proofed'. Thousands of yards of chipboard were used to protect the ship's carpets and floors from the impact of 3250 pairs of military feet, even though for most of the journey the troops would be wearing their plimsolls. Everything that was breakable, inflammable and removable was taken out of the ship. As the stores and equipment began to find their places and the conversion work for the three helicopter decks, the replenishment at sea facilities and the new communications equipment neared its end, the ship began to return to some sort of order.

One of the most key men responsible for establishing some semblance of peace was Lance Corporal Peter Allsopp. His diplomatic task was to assign the accommodation for the troops. The ship's crew under the Senior Naval Officer Captain James RN; provisions for Major-General Jeremy Moore and his staff; Brigadier Tony Wilson and his staff of 5 Brigade and the men of 1st Battalion Welsh Guards, 2nd Battalion Scots Guards, and the Gurkhas—over 3000 men in all—had to be found places.

Five-fold protection

En route southwards, *QE2*'s protection was to be guaranteed by five factors: speed, a complement of Sea King anti-submarine helicopters, secrecy as to her movements, a discreet naval escort and a determination to keep the ship away from the main areas of threat, especially out of the range of Argentine strike aircraft. It was widely assumed that *QE2* would stop over at Ascension as *Canberra* and the other units of the amphibious task group had done. In fact, *QE2* sailed straight past Ascension Island without stopping, only passing close enough to allow helicopters to fly to and from the island.

The *QE2*'s final destination was to be Grytviken harbour in South Georgia where she passed her cargo of fighting men to *Canberra* and *Norland* via a flotilla of trawler/minesweepers, tugs and dispatch vessels. In return she took survivors from HMS *Ardent* and other lost ships. But in the end, though *QE2* was the largest ship taken up from trade and certainly the most prestigious, as part of the Task Force she was just another member of a team. That fact was best shown by an incident in Grytviken. A trawler/minesweeper—one of five very similar looking vessels of a little under 1500 tons—came alongside her. Captain Jackson looked down at the boat and asked: 'Which one are you?' The reply came back: 'HMS *Cordella*—which one are *you*?'

14 MAY 1982

SAS hit Pebble Island

Faultlessly, the SAS carried out an operation they had been practising for over 40 years. They left behind 11 wrecked aircraft and opened the way for the Task Force to land at San Carlos. The Argentines never knew what hit them.

ON THE NIGHT OF 14–15 MAY the land battle to regain the Falklands began in earnest when the SAS staged a dramatic raid on the Argentine airfield on Pebble Island. The operation was a brilliant success (a throwback to the very first SAS raids in North Africa in December 1941 when two patrols totalling ten men destroyed 61 German aircraft on the ground).

Pebble Island in peacetime is a farm of some 22,000 acres occupied by thousands of sheep and a holiday lodge. In war it was vital to the Argentines. A long, low outcrop lying off the northern shore of West Falkland, its geological structure made it an ideal site for the creation of a long runway capable of bearing large aircraft. More important, it was 108 miles closer to the Argentine mainland than Port Stanley. With Stanley airfield under constant attack, it was the best point from which to resupply Argentine troops on West Falkland and at Goose Green.

In the weeks before the SAS raid the Argentines stored huge amounts of fuel on Pebble Island and sited a radar station which overlooked the approaches to San Carlos. More ominously, several Pucara and Aermacchi MB 339A and 326 aircraft were based there. Pebble Island—and especially the radar—had to be neutralized. The SAS were ordered to 'take it out'.

An eight-man SAS patrol composed of four-man 'sticks' from Boat Troop D Squadron 22 SAS was landed on West Falkland Island on the night of 11–12 May. Their task was to reconnoitre the settlement and seek out the suspected enemy radar. They were also to pinpoint the ammunition dump, and advise on the best time to attack the most aircraft. It is possible that the patrol was put ashore during a bombardment from one of the Task Force ships. That would have kept the Pebble Island radar operator sufficiently preoccupied.

Having landed on West Falkland, the SAS men carried their canoes across country to a previously selected launching point. They then hid the canoes in a valley, and settled down to observe Pebble Island and confirm that there were no enemy at the proposed canoe landing points. That they were close enough to the island to carry out such a preparatory surveillance suggests that the sight for launching the canoes could have been on Keppel Island.

After sunset on 13 May, the patrol canoed across the water separating them from their objective, avoiding a known tidal rip on the way. Once again they hid their canoes, and two men moved forward to find a suitable observation post (OP). OPs were established on the 960ft First Mount Hill, situated to the north-west of the objective, from where they were able to carry out detailed covert surveillance of the airstrip and Pebble Island settlement, locate the radar and ammunition and aviation fuel dumps, and establish how many aircraft were there.

'Attack tonight'

After last light on 14 May, the patrol radioed to *Hermes* a message for the planned raid: 'Eleven aircraft. Believe real. Attack tonight.' They then marked out a landing zone (LZ) for the incoming helicopters to land 45 further men from D Squadron 22 SAS and a naval gunfire expert on the island. The Naval Gunfire Support Forward Observer (NGSFO) was Captain Chris Brown RA from 148 Battery of 29 Commando Regiment Royal Artillery, who had already played a key role in the recapture of Grytviken in South Georgia. The 4.5in guns of HMS *Glamorgan* were to provide direct support for the raid.

The raiding party was flown to the LZ in Sea King HC4 helicopters, the pilots using passive night goggles to aid their vision. The first man to deplane was the NGSFO. The party split into an assault group and a support group to give covering fire. The first party was to attack the targets (the aircraft, fuel, ammunition and radar) and the second party was to keep the garrison of Argentine naval air personnel occupied. However, the landing was late and a hard cross-country night march to the objective lay ahead of the heavily laden soldiers. The SAS men were burdened with mortar bombs, explosives and detonating equipment, general purpose machine guns (GPMGs) and other small arms—such as the M16 automatic rifle—as well as the disassembled parts of the mortars.

A mortar base plate position was set up, and the mortar bombs were thankfully dumped there. The mortar crews set up their weapons, and the rest of the raiding party continued on their way. Originally there had been a plan to contact the civilians in the little community at Pebble Island set-tlement, but when the soldiers reached their objective, there was no time left to do so. Only half an hour was left for the attack.

One troop covered the settlement while the others went about their busi-ness. Most of the Argentine garrison were pinned down in their trenches by automatic fire from the GPMGs of the covering party and 4.5in shells from *Glamorgan*, called in at a rate of one a minute by the NGSFO. Complete surprise had been achieved. The BBC's reporter with the Task Force ships, Brian Hanrahan, related how orange cordite flashes repeatedly lit up the night sky as the shells were fired, interspersed with the blinding white glare of the starshells fired to illuminate the Argentine position.

Assault group

The assault group, led by Captain John Hamilton, approached their tar-gets—aided by the confusion, glare, noise and missiles. The demolition experts would have been carrying handy sizes of plastic explosive charges with a short length fuse to allow them time to get away from the target. It is probable that they would have aimed to destroy the same piece of each aircraft to prevent the Argentines assembling an operational aircraft by cannibalizing the wrecks.

Eleven aircraft were destroyed in the raid, along with the radar system, the ammunition dump and the store of aviation fuel. Of the aircraft, it is known that six of these were the troublesome Pucarás and one was a Shorts' Skyvan. There was some speculation, and unconfirmed reports, about the nature of the other four, but these were eventually identified as being T-34C Mentors belonging to CANA 4 Esc.

The SAS Squadron began to withdraw at 0745 GMT. While they were pulling out, they were attacked by the Argentine garrison and a brisk fire-fight ensued. This was brought to an abrupt halt when a man who appeared to be an officer, urging the Argentine troops forward, was spotted and shot. The Argentines fell back, and the SAS withdrawal continued unopposed. The squadron marched back to its mortar base plate and the LZ where they were picked up by helicopter and flown back to the Task Force ships. The raid had been a spectacular success: only two of the SAS men had sus-tained minor wounds. These were, according to settlers, caused by a large, remote-controlled mine which the Argentines detonated too late to have much effect.

New twists in the corridors of power

Though Al Haig was back home in Washington, the diplomatic battle to avoid bloodshed was not at an end. New arbiters were found, new peace plans proposed. Could some kind of compromise be found, even at this late hour?

BY APRIL'S END Secretary of State Alexander Haig's gruelling three-way transatlantic shuttle had collapsed and the US decided to back the British. But as the Task Force steamed relentlessly southwards, diplomats continued their desperate search for a solution. Nobody really wanted to instigate a bloodbath, but the problem was to find the formula for an honourable peace which would satisfy two increasingly intransigent opponents. Could a compromise be cobbled together before British Forces actually set foot back on the Falklands? This was the dilemma that packed the diplomats' diaries throughout the early part of May.

On 1 May the so-called Peruvian plan was presented. This was put together by Haig and President Belaúnde of Peru. A rare thing in Latin America, Belaúnde was a mild, democratic head of government. Though Peru was traditionally an ally of Argentina, it was also an ally of the US, and genuinely seems to have sought agreement between the two warring parties. The plan offered a 72-hour truce, a mutual British and Argentine withdrawal from the disputed area and the resumption of negotiations— this time under the auspices of the United Nations—on the future of the Falklands. Meanwhile, British Foreign Secretary Francis Pym returned to Washington, this time as an ally.

Mr Pym travelled on to the UN building in New York on 2 May. But that same day *Belgrano* was sunk—taking, many thought, the Peruvian peace plan down with her. However, that night Mr Pym dined with UN Secretary General Javier Pérez de Cuellar—by coincidence another Peruvian—and

Sir Anthony Parsons, British Ambassador to the UN, and their thoughts turned to mediation by the Secretary-General himself.

On 3 May President Galtieri rejected the Peruvian plan, citing the sinking of *Belgrano*. This incident—and its consequent loss of life—began to turn world opinion against Britain, which was now being seen as the big bully pushing little Argentina around.

On 4 May Ireland went to the Security Council to call for an immediate cessation of hostilities and for the negotiation of a diplomatic settlement under UN auspices. In doing so, she had broken the EEC's united front which had lasted since the invasion. Ireland and Italy also asked the EEC to lift the economic sanctions that it had imposed on Argentina, even though they were not due for renewal until 17 May.

Meanwhile the USSR, which had abstained at the Security Council debate immediately following the invasion, came off the fence on 4 May with President Breshnev describing the British decision to send the Task Force as 'colonial brigandage'. That same day *Sheffield* was hit.

By this time the Junta must have reflected that its position did not look at all bad. The destruction of *Sheffield* did not seem to have won diplomatic sympathy for Britain. Militarily, things were looking good too. The Argentine Air Force had demonstrated that the Task Force was vulnerable to Exocet attack and expected to sink at least one of the British aircraft carriers before any landing could take place on the Falklands. The British attacks on the airfield at Port Stanley had substantially failed. Damage inflicted on the runway was repaired quickly and the British air blockade was being run with impunity. The Argentine troops on the Falklands were well armed, well supplied and well dug in, or so it looked from Buenos Aires. There was certainly no indication that Argentina was contemplating military defeat.

The destruction of *Sheffield* hardened UK opinion behind the Task Force. But the government knew that to placate international opinion it needed to be seen to be continuing negotiations. Thus, at a full meeting of the cabinet of 5 May the Peruvian plan was approved. But on 6 May the Junta rejected the Peruvian peace plan for a second time.

UN steps in

On 7 May UN Secretary-General Pérez de Cuellar moved back into play and began discussions with the representatives of the two sides separately at the UN. His six-point plan asked for an immediate end to hostilities, the withdrawal of the British Fleet, the opening of negotiations on the future of the islands, the ending of all economic sanctions and the establishing of an interim joint administration under the auspices of the UN itself.

From the British point of view, the plan had both possibilities and pitfalls. On the positive side it provided for the withdrawal of forces by Argentina. This had, after all, been demanded by Resolution 502 on

3 April. Once Argentina had begun to withdraw, there would be no objection to the Task Force returning to Portsmouth and the immediate ending of hostilities. Britain was still prepared to negotiate with Argentina about the long-term future of the islands, provided that no pre-conditions were attached. It was recognized that there would be enormous moral pressure on the British government to make real concessions on sovereignty to Argentina. But it was still hoped that some form of power sharing or lease-back agreement could be reached. The interim UN administration would be a bitter pill, but again the British government would be willing to consider this provided that the Falklands were guaranteed substantial self-government.

For Argentina there was less to commend the plan. Their invasion had been a triumph and to withdraw with no guarantees that the 'Malvinas' would eventually be restored to them would be worse than a military defeat. And there were fears within the Argentine military that in any negotiations on sovereignty—under the UN plan or any other—they would be swindled by the greater diplomatic skills of the British and their American friends.

More important, though, was the feeling that the Junta could not withdraw, even if it wanted to. If Galtieri was to order his troops to do so, they might well mutiny and shatter the shaky authority of his weak government. Chaos would follow—an advantage which the British enemy would naturally seize. The Junta was also buoyed up by its own propaganda. They had begun to believe that if war broke out Argentina would win. But it was necessary for them, too, to be seen to negotiate to hold on to the sympathetic world opinion which was still swinging to their side.

Consequently, on 7 May, Secretary General Pérez de Cuellar declared himself 'encouraged' by the preliminary responses to his plan, although on that same day Mr Pym made it clear in the House of Commons that Britain would not accept a ceasefire without a prior Argentine commitment to withdraw.

On 8 May, defence spokesman Ian McDonald announced that the British Fleet would treat as hostile all Argentine ships and aircraft outside a 12-mile coastal strip.

The sovereignty pre-condition

On 9 May, Argentine Foreign Minister Nicanor Costa Mendez said on American TV: 'We want to settle the fundamentals for the acceptance of Argentine sovereignty. We are not saying that Britain must accept at the beginning our sovereignty. We are not putting sovereignty as a pre-condition for our talks.' But at home he was less guarded. On Argentine TV he said: 'Every negotiation must inexorably be conducive to Argentine sovereignty over the Malvinas.'

The Junta mulled over the proposals and sent Deputy Foreign Minister

Enrique Ros back to New York with what he called a 'very interesting answer'.

On 11 May, Pérez de Cuellar indicated that the Argentines had made a dramatic concession—they had not called for the inclusion of sovereignty. The next day the Junta conceded that 'sovereignty was not a pre-condition' to talks.

This was not 'peace in our time', British officials told enquirers, but Parsons talked about 'some very interesting propositions' that had come from Pérez de Cuellar. He was sufficiently encouraged to concede that the islands could be run in the interim period by a UN administrator rather than a British governor. The bare bones of an agreement seemed to be there, even though what would happen in the future was left unclear and some important points (such as South Georgia, which the British had already recaptured) were left hanging.

On 14 May, Parsons and the British Ambassador in Washington, Sir Nicholas Henderson, flew back to London for consultations; and on 16 May they attended a meeting of the inner cabinet at Chequers. The point that Parsons emphasized was that diplomatic ambiguity was useful only up to a point and it was best to have the military aspects of the agreement spelt out in detail.

The final flurry

The document setting out an interim agreement which was handed to Pérez de Cuellar by Parsons when he returned to New York on 17 May was the high water mark of British attempts to reach an agreement. The UN administrator was formally accepted and the question of the islanders' rights to self-determination was dealt with by including article 73 of the UN Charter which sets out the rights of non-self-governing territories. The issue of sovereignty was left open. The interim agreement would remain in force until a 'definitive agreement' on the future of the islands had been reached.

The ball was thrown back into the Argentine court where it was given a leaden reception. And when Parsons went up to Pérez de Cuellar's office on 18 May to look at the Argentine reply, there were few surprises. Their withdrawal terms would have meant the Task Force returning to Portsmouth and a key sentence in the British draft had been struck out. The deleted words read: 'The negotiations shall be initiated without prejudice to the rights, claims and positions of the parties and without prejudgment of the outcome'.

Negotiations were finally at an end. The troops on board the Task Force prepared for invasion.

D Day in San Carlos

The crucial day arrives. At the last moment, the fleet changes course. The destination is San Carlos Water on East Falkland. Men, crowded on the assault ships, check and re-check their weapons. Beneath brilliant stars, the final contest is about to begin.

THE MOST CRITICAL PHASE of the operation had now begun. On the evening of 20 May, shrouded by a thick fog and moving at a speed of 11 knots, the 11 ships of the amphibious force and their escorts moved slowly towards East Falkland. Tension increased on the bridge as regular reports of Argentine air activity came in from British submarines and intelligence teams monitoring air movements on the Argentine mainland. From the bridge of the assault ship *Fearless* came an order from Captain Jeremy Larken for *Canberra* to stop dumping her rubbish in the sea, leaving a tell-tale mark for an enemy reconnaissance aircraft or patrol ship. Incredibly, although the convoy's radar betrayed ample signs of Argentine air activity, the amphibious force was not spotted by any enemy aircraft.

Aboard the assault ships *Intrepid* and *Fearless* there was hardly room to move, as marines and paras took what rest they could in the packed cabins, companionways and store-rooms. On the tank decks marines worked steadily on their vehicles, securing canvases and mounting machine guns. There was time to reflect on what lay ahead and also to digest the grim news of the loss on 18 May of 18 SAS men, drowned when the Sea King helicopter transferring them to *Hermes* was hit by an albatross and plunged into the sea.

The point of no return was reached at 1800 hours on the evening of 20 May. No orders were received from Northwood ordering the amphibious force to turn back and now they were committed to the landing. As darkness fell the greatest danger had passed. Days later, after the Argentine air force had demonstrated the havoc it could cause among the Task Force's ships, it became clear how kindly fortune had smiled on the amphibious force. The lifting of the mist, a concerted Argentine attack and the sinking of one of the troop-carrying ships could have dealt a devastating blow to landing plans.

As H-hour approached a quiet confidence stole over senior officers aboard the assault ships. Jeremy Larken recalled that, 'The atmosphere seemed to be right. The whole thing seemed to be working.' Below decks weapons were obsessively checked, grenades primed, linked-belt ammunition loaded. At 2000 hours the men ate—steak on *Canberra*, stew on the cramped naval ships. As the minutes ticked away, the troops began to pull on their heavy web fighting order and to smear their faces with black camouflage cream.

The route to San Carlos

One of the most unlikely and eccentric figures thrown up by the Falklands War, yachtsman Major Ewen Southby-Tailyour, RM had occupied a tour of duty in the Falklands by exploring and mapping every creek and inlet of the Falkland coastline. The intimate knowledge of the islands booked his passage with the Task Force, and his advice proved invaluable when it came to making a choice of landing site for the reoccupation of the Falklands.

After plans for a direct assault on Port Stanley had been abandoned, and a landing on West Falkland ruled out, confirmation came from Northwood on 8 May that San Carlos Bay, 50 miles east of Port Stanley on the opposite coast of East Falkland, was to be the jumping-off point for 3 Commando Brigade, commanded by Brigadier Julian Thompson.

On 10 May, aboard *Fearless*, Thompson briefed his unit commanders. The beach-head at San Carlos would be established by 2 and 3 Btns Parachute Regiment and 40, 42 and 45 Marine Commandos, supported by Scorpions and Scimitars of the Blues and Royals. A murmur went round the 60-odd naval, Army and Royal Marine officers gathered in *Fearless*'s wardroom when it was revealed that *Canberra* would go all the way into San Carlos Bay. Nevertheless, it was felt that she would be safer in San Carlos water than in the open sea, and she was carrying stores vital to the landing operation. With somewhat brutal realism, it had been calculated that if she was hit and sunk in San Carlos Water, she would settle in the shallows and remain operable.

An amphibious landing is the most risky of all naval operations. The decision on when and where to land will almost certainly involve a compromise between the land, sea and air commanders. The choice of San Carlos proved no exception. Brigadier Julian Thompson later recalled that he was 'never wild about San Carlos. It was too far away from where you had to end up, like attacking Cardiff by way of Barmouth. But no matter how many times you went around it like a dog sniffing a lamp-post, you always came back to it.' Thompson's reservations were understandable—San Carlos was 50 miles away from Port Stanley but only 13 miles away from a strong enemy garrison at Darwin and Goose Green. The beaches were far from ideal for the unloading of large quantities of men, equipment and stores. It was feared that the Argentines might anticipate the British decision, mine the beaches and the sea approaches, and occupy the high ground surrounding San Carlos Water. These drawbacks were outweighed by a number of vital considerations. San Carlos provided a protected anchorage out of range of Argentine artillery and safe from Exocet attack. Once inside the anchorage, the surrounding high ground would provide excellent protection against raids by the Argentine air force. Once they crossed the line of the ridge, their fighter pilots would only have a few seconds in which to select and attack a target. At the same time, they would present targets for the Rapier batteries sited on the hills at points specially chosen by the computers at the radar research establishment at Malvern.

In early May, the build-up to the landings began to gather pace. On 13 May, Julian Thompson gave his confident and eager unit COs the final instructions for Operation Sutton. Two days later, on 15 May, the civilians on board the ships of the amphibious force were read the Declaration of Active Service, which placed them under military discipline. On 18 May the amphibious force rendezvoused with *Hermes*. On the same day vital reinforcements flew aboard the carriers in the form of 12 Harriers transferred from the container ship *Atlantic Conveyor*. Next day four more Harriers (ground attack GR3s) flew in after an epic air-refuelled flight from Britain via Ascension Island.

Admiral Woodward detached seven frigates from his battle squadron for air defence and naval gunfire support during the landing operation. In order to secure maximum protection the convoy closed up as tightly as possible, in a shoebox formation, for the final lap to San Carlos.

Last-minute cross-decking

One further precaution remained to be taken. It would have been an almost suicidal risk to leave the entire brigade on *Canberra*, and it was decided to disperse the units between ships. The cross-decking of 1800 men in an Atlantic gale was a fearful proposition, particularly if it meant a jackstay transfer, one man at a time. Fortunately the weather relented and the operation was accomplished on 19 May in the mildest of swells, allowing the landing craft vehicles (LCVs) to transport troops from *Canberra's* lower port galley doors. There was only one mishap, when a marine mistimed his jump and for two heart-stopping minutes bobbed about between *Canberra* and the LCV before being hauled safely inboard. It was only after the cross-decking had been completed that Brigadier Thompson realized that although the brigade had been successfully dispersed, his entire staff remained together on *Fearless*. Had *Fearless* come to grief, the brigade would have been left leaderless.

With the brigade dispersed, Admiral Woodward received the go-ahead from Northwood to instruct Brigadier Thompson to land in the Falklands at his own discretion. Thus it was that on the evening of 20 May the invasion fleet moved into the Total Exclusion Zone, steering a deliberately deceptive south-westerly course towards Port Stanley. Only at the last possible moment, as the amphibious force approached the coast of East Falkland, had it turned west and made for the Falkland Sound. The die was now cast. As the final night ticked away, men would sense the approach of the islands, and—for most—the first taste of real battle in their professional lives.

Spotted by the Argentines

By now the mist had lifted, giving way to a night of crystal-clear skies and a sea that was almost unnervingly flat and calm. Overhead, the Southern Cross glittered brilliantly and the pin-sharp stars lit up the surrounding hills. At about 1900 hours on the night of the 20 May the fleet had finally been spotted by a high-flying Argentine Canberra which had radioed a report back to Stanley. Soon British signal intelligence was picking up traffic on the Argentine military network as a report went through of a suspected enemy landing a few miles to the north of the settlement at Goose Green.

In *Fearless*'s landing craft the assault troops of 40 Commando had their helmets on. Their heavy webbing was secured and their faces blackened. Their bergen rucksacks were done up tight. Grenades were primed, weapons cocked. But the most important piece of equipment they had with them was their spades. Later that day they'd be digging for their lives in the soggy peat of East Falkland, but there was a long way to go before they'd see the safety of the foxhole. They were about to make a landing in force on an enemy-held shore.

The plan for D Day was simple enough. The landing itself was to be carried out in three phrases. Phase one consisted of 40 Commando going ashore by landing craft and securing the San Carlos settlement. They were to establish a defensive position on the reverse slopes of the coastal hills. 45 Commando were to land and secure the Ajax Bay complex and then take up a defensive position on the reverse slopes of the high ground to the west.

In phase two, 2 Para were to go ashore by landing craft and then move forward to a forming-up point. From there, they were to clear the area up to the Sussex Mountains and establish a defensive point. 3 Para were to land and secure Port San Carlos settlement and prepare a defensive position on the reverse slopes of Settlement Rocks, while 42 Commando were to remain in reserve on board ship in case anything calamitous happened.

The phasing of the initial wave of the landing was necessary because there were not enough landing craft to move more than two battalion-size major units at one go. The Blues and Royals would provide one of the troops of the Medium Recce Squadron in the landing craft with 40 Commando in phase one, and their other troop with 3 Para in phase two, to exploit forward and to give observation and direct fire support as needed, with a Scorpion and a Scimitar in each of two landing craft in the initial wave.

Naval gunfire support was to be provided to the assaulting battalions by four frigates—*Antrim, Ardent, Plymouth* and *Yarmouth. Ardent* was equipped with a single Mk 8 4.5in gun turret, and the three other ships had Mk 6 twin-gun turrets. *Ardent* was also to give naval gunfire support (NGS) to a diversionary operation which was to be mounted in the area of Goose Green and carried out by the Special Air Services. She was to position herself in Grantham Sound, south west of the Sussex Mountains. From there she could provide cover fire for both operations.

In phrase three the beach-head would be built up with the rest of the main force landing. Four field batteries of 105mm light guns (three of them being the field batteries of 29 Commando Regiment Royal Artillery and the other battery from 4 Field Regiment Royal Artillery) were to go ashore as soon after light as possible. The six guns of each battery were to give direct support to one or other of the four assaulting battalions and commandos. Low level air defence for the beach-head was to be provided by Rapier missiles of T Battery (Shah Sujah's Troop) from 12 Air Defence Regiment Royal Artillery. They were to deploy at first light and set up their fire units to cover the whole beach-head. Once the beach-head was secure, the logistics and headquarters units could go ashore and the supporting forces could start on their tasks. Royal Engineers, for example, were to build a foward Harrier base using lengths of interlocking aluminum strips.

H Hour was 0230 on the morning of 21 May. This was to have been the moment that the first landing craft took to the water. But they were delayed. The pump that filled the embarkation dock on board *Fearless* had broken down and Captain Jeremy Larken had to take the considerable risk of flooding the dock by simply opening the gates and letting the sea swamp in. Two landing craft collided, putting one of them out of action, and one man fell and broke his pelvis. This delayed the departure of the assault force by almost an hour.

As 40 Commando set off across the darkness of San Carlos Water, they could not know what to expect. Intelligence reports had told them that their landing would be unopposed. But already a furious firefight was lighting up the sky around Fanning Head behind them. Were there more Argentines dug in around the beach-heads ahead?

Special forces patrols had been operating in the area of San Carlos Water since 1 May watching the Argentines and reporting their strengths and movements to the staff aboard HMS *Fearless*. They had also scouted various landing beaches to see if they were defended. It was intelligence reports from these sources that gave the all-clear for the landing, though they warned of the possibility of a counter-attack from Darwin over the Sussex Mountains. It was only later, the night before the landing, that the Special Boat Services reported the presence of Argentines on Fanning Head.

This was a crucial position. It overlooked both the landing beaches and the entrance to San Carlos Water. As a result, the straightforward plan drawn up on 12–13 May had to be modified. An assault group of the SAS was to take out the Fanning Head position on the night of the landings, prior to the amphibious assault group appearing in range in the Falkland Sound. The SAS was to tie down Darwin garrison and the landing of 2 Para was to be moved up to phase one of the operation.

Salvoes of gunfire

Just after midnight on 21 May, 25 men from 2 SBS and a naval gunfire observation party were helicoptered ashore and landed a short distance from the Argentine position on Fanning Head. They pinpointed the enemy position and at about 0200 brought down salvoes of naval gunfire from HMS *Antrim*'s twin 4.5in guns. The SBS opened fire with machine guns and 60mm mortars and the firefight went on through the night.

At first light, Spanish-speaking Royal Marine officer Captain Rod Bell inched forward with a loudhailer and asked the Argentines to surrender; but the wind was blowing in the wrong direction and the Argentines could not hear properly. Some seemed willing to give in. Others continued firing. General confusion and spasmodic firing went on for another two hours. At the end of that time six Argentines surrendered and led the SBS troops to another three who were wounded. Twelve Argentines lay dead and the remainder—estimated at around 80 Argentines—had withdrawn. The group had been armed with Fabrica Militar Argentina Model 1968 105mm recoilless guns and French Thompson-Brandt 81mm medium mortars trained on the Sound. These armaments could have posed a considerable threat to both the Task Force in the Sound and the assault force on the beaches if they had remained in Argentine hands after sunrise. They also had British-made Shorts Blowpipe shoulder-launched surface-to-air missiles.

To deceive the Argentines about the real invasion plan, many diversionary raids were mounted. The aim was to make them think that Pebble Island-type attacks were to be the British style for a while longer, and the hope was that the actual contact reports from the landing site would sound like just another hit and run raid. This would gain the British valuable time in which to consolidate the beach-head and secure it from Argentine counter-attacks.

To confuse the picture further, shore targets were bombarded by naval gunfire, the airstrips around the islands were bombed by Harriers and special force operations created the diversions. During the night, Task Force warships from the Carrier Battle Group, working in detachments of two or three destroyers and frigates, shelled targets near Bluff Cove, Fitzroy, Port Louis and Port Stanley. RAF Harriers bombed Stanley airport, and the airstrips at Goose Green and Fox Bay.

Noise and confusion

The SAS carried out a diversionary attack on the garrison at Darwin. This raid also had the purpose of keeping the Argentines tied up so that they could not intervene at the landing beaches around San Carlos Water. Though the raid was carried out by only 40 or so men, they used automatic fire from machine guns, anti-tank missiles and mortars to create so much noise and confusion that the garrison thought it was under attack from an infantry battalion. The scene was now set for the invasion to proceed.

In San Carlos Water the landing craft chugged away from *Norland* and *Fearless*. This was the first decisive action of Operation Sutton.

2 Para's landing site was code named 'Blue Beach One' and—across Bonners Bay—40 Cdo's was 'Blue Beach Two'. 3 Para and 42 Cdo landings at Port San Carlos Settlement were to go ashore at 'Green Beach One' and 'Green Beach Two', and 45 Cdo, whose task was the Ajax Bay Settlement, landed at 'Red Beach'. The first troops ashore were to be 2 Para and 40 Cdo (supported by 3 Troop of the Blues and Royals' Medium Recce Squadron). The Scorpion and Scimitar light tanks were to lead the assaulting marines onto the beaches.

So far, so good. But much of the vital equipment was still aboard. And all knew how high the risks were of Argentine retribution.

No resistance on the beaches

The plan was to use the eight large utility landing craft and eight smaller craft from the two assault ships *Fearless* and *Intrepid*—16 in all—lifting the 1,200 men and equipment and ferrying the battalions and commandos in turn to the beaches. The only hitch was that the crew of *Norland* forgot to put out lights in the bow and stern to guide the landing craft. Rigging these lights late had a knock-on effect and meant that 3 Para were an hour late in putting back phase two of the landing.

The first men were ashore at 0400 and the landing at Blue Beaches One and Two of 2 Para and 40 Cdo, led up the gravelly beach by the Blues and

Royals, was complete by 0730. There was no resistance, but the paras were not pleased with the marines who had landed on the shallow shelving middle of the beach. This left the steeper edges to the paras who had to wade ashore waist deep. They stumbled ashore to be greeted by a band of grubby, bearded SBS men who had been camped out on the hillside for several days.

Just after first light, as the dawn came up, 45 Cdo landed at Ajax Bay from *Stromness*. At approximately 0930 3 Para were put ashore from *Intrepid* by the launch craft from *Fearless* together with 4 Troop of the Medium Recce Squadron, Blues and Royals. 42 Cdo stayed in reserve, ready to go into action anywhere they were needed.

Once ashore and off the beach, 2 Para turned south and painfully climbed the 3000ft to secure the ridge line of the Sussex Mountains against the threat of attack from Darwin garrison. When the ridge was secure, the battalion took up its defensive positions on the reverse slopes of the mountain and began to dig in.

40 Cdo moved away from their beach in an easterly direction and climbed up onto the Verde Mountains where they established a reverse slope defensive position. This gave a defensive line close in to the beach against counter attacks from the east and south and, with 45 Cdo's position at Ajax Bay, from an amphibious assault from the west as well.

At Green Beach 1—the landing site chosen for 3 Para—an unforeseen sandbar some 50 yards short of the beach meant that some last-minute improvisations had to be made. B Company, who were the first to land, did in fact, get wet. A Company, who were next, had to cross-deck from their landing craft which had grounded on the obstacle. C Company's craft made a landfall about half a mile short of the beach, and they had to march to the proper landing site with their 50lb bergens and other kit. Their company commander, Major Martin Osborne, reckoned that this 'half mile tab to the mortarline' was a fair exchange for a dry landing in the cold but sunny conditions.

B Company secured the beach-head, and A Company passed through them and into Port San Carlos Settlement. They knocked on doors and quickly discovered that there were no Argentines in the area. The settlers were wide awake, roused by the noise of the approaching landing craft and the naval bombardment.

They had been expecting the British for days. A routine house cleaning operation was soon under way. C Company climbed up to the 600ft ring contour of Settlement Rocks and dug in on the reverse slopes. Over the next few days, 3 Para cleared the area of Fanning Head for Argentine survivors and observation posts. Phase two of Operation Sutton was secured and 42 Cdo were brought ashore from *Canberra* at 1000 and landed at Green Beach 2. When all the infantry were ashore and establishing defensive positions, digging trenches and building sangars, the remainder of the equipment could be passed through the beaches.

The priority was to get the artillery in place. The three field batteries of 29 Cdo Regt RA, with its attached battery from 4 Field Regiment, making four batteries of 105mm Light Guns in all, and the Rapiers of T Battery 12AD Regt RA were brought ashore by helicopters.

Most of the selected sites for the Rapiers had been secured by 0930 but some on the high ground still remained uncleared. Recce parties were ferried to these points by Sea King helicopters, escorted by two Aerospatiale Gazelles from the 3 Commando Brigade Air Squadron with machine guns mounted in their cabins. It was during this operation that two Gazelles were brought down by Argentine fire, killing three Royal Marines. These were the only British casualties of what was otherwise an unopposed landing.

To give local air defence while the Rapier posts were being set up, Blowpipe sections from the Air Defence Troop of the 3 Cdo Bde HQ and Signals Squadron were distributed around the assaulting infantry. Number One section went with 2 Para to the Sussex Mountains, 2 Section landed at Ajax Bay with 45 Cdo, 3 Section went ashore at San Carlos Settlement with 40 Cdo and later was attached to Brigade HQ.

Forward air control was provided during the landing and the later stages of the campaign by attaching Tactical Air Control Parties (TACPs) from HQ & Signals Squadron. 605 TACP went with 42 Cdo, 611 TACP with 45 Cdo and 612 TACP with 3 Para.

A Brigade Maintenance Area (BMA) was to be set up at Ajax Bay. This was a difficult task as the Commando Logistics Regiment responsible was desperately short of personnel and helicopters. A hospital was rapidly set up in the abandoned refrigeration plant at Ajax Bay, and run by Surgeon Commander Rick Jolly. This came to be nicknamed the 'Red and Green Life Support Machine'. It was composed of Royal Navy, Royal Marine and Royal Army Medical Corps personnel, and was later beefed up by men from 16 Field Ambulance RAMC.

From first light onwards, the heli-lift of men and equipment was joined by helicopters from the Naval Task Group. By the end of the day, more than 3000 men and nearly 1000 tons of stores and equipment had been ferried successfully ashore. The Medical Squadron was one of the last units to leave the ships, being disembarked from *Canberra* at 2200 just before she sailed away from the dangerous waters of San Carlos Sound.

AT 0845 there was the first air raid warning of a very hazardous day. Five minutes later a single Pucará counter-insurgency aircraft flew into sight, reconnoitring the Sound. It then proceeded to attack HMS *Argonaut*, firing eight rockets at her which only just missed the target. Then it turned its attention to *Canberra*, firing more rockets at her. Again it missed, but was engaged by some of the 50 machine guns lashed to the cruise liner's rails and by Blowpipe SAMs fired from the decks. The aircraft was eventually brought down by a shell from the 4.5in gun of one of the frigates.

At 0930 just as the troops of 2 Para were going ashore, the first of the airstrikes by Argentine high-performance jets came in. Two Mirages attacked the amphibious assault group. These air attacks increased in intensity throughout the day, and over subsequent days. This was particularly frustrating for the troops on the ground who watched helplessly as the Argentine aeroplanes attacked the ships in San Carlos Water. Eventually the soldiers and marines joined in with defensive fire from their machine guns. Some even used their rifles. 3 Para claim that a Mirage was shot down by a machine gun crew at Fanning Head.

As the Rapier posts became operational, they played an increasingly important role in the air defence battle. The first Rapier kills were credited to the post call sign '33 Charlie', commanded by Sergeant Taff Morgan, which shot down two A4 Skyhawks. At least one of the two or three Pucarás shot down that day was a victim of the General Dynamics Stinger surface-to-air missiles used by the SAS. Initially, there seems to have been some difficulty with the Rapiers, whose delicate electronics had been upset by the long voyage. Royal Engineer fitters soon got to work on them.

To begin with, anti-aircraft fire was haphazard and there seems to have been some difficulty in controlling it. Eventually arcs of fire were allocated and co-ordinated, and aircraft recognition improved. Once controlled fire discipline had been established, it played havoc with the attacking Argentine aircraft, and the better recognition of aircraft allowed Sea Harriers to fly combat air patrols without running the risk of being hit by air defence missiles from the ships in San Carlos Water.

During all this activity in the air, the Task Force helicopters continued to ferry in loads of ammunition, food, petrol in pods and jerrycans, and other stores slung under their fuselage. The landing craft shipped men, equipment and vehicles—including the workhorses of the campaign, the Volvo BV202E Snocats—to the landing beaches, and by the end of the day most of 3 Commando Brigade were ashore.

Stores and equipment continued to be landed over the following days at constant risk from the Argentine air attack. These continued at peak intensity for four days: 21, 23, 25 and 30 May. But by letting the British ashore unopposed, allowing them to secure and develop their beach-head, then letting them break out unopposed, the Argentines had thrown away the land battle.

Overkilling *Ardent*

About half the men were ashore, without opposition: for the land forces of the British Task Force, first light on Friday 21 May brought a sense of achievement and relief. For men left on board ships in San Carlos Water, it brought an eerie feeling of living on borrowed time. Approaching San Carlos in broad daylight the previous day, the convoy, at its most vulnerable, had escaped attack. This had been partly due to murky weather, but today, by contrast, was beautifully clear. It was simply a question of waiting for what everyone dreaded most: Argentine air attacks. Here was the Argentines' best chance of bringing disaster on the British: by mounting air attacks against supply ships now presented 'on a plate'—within the confines of a single bay—they could eliminate the essential back-up for the men ashore, rendering them useless after the few days it would take for their immediate supplies and ammunition to run out.

As expected, the Argentine Air Force inflicted heavy damage on the Task Force that day, but for reasons over which there is still argument, the Skyhawks and Mirages went almost exclusively for the fighting ships. *Argonaut* was to be crippled; *Antrim* was to be damaged by bombs and rockets; *Arrow* was hit by cannon fire, as was *Broadsword*. The troopship *Norland* had several near misses, and *Canberra* survived repeated attacks; how she escaped still remains something of a mystery. But the most notable casualty of that violent day was undoubtedly the frigate *Ardent*, who sank—eventually—after taking the brunt of what the Argentine Air Force had to offer.

On the 'gun line'

Dawn on 21 May saw *Ardent* on the 'gun line' to the south of the screen of fighting ships protecting the landing operations area inside San Carlos Water. She had been ordered to bombard Goose Green with her 4.5in gun, a typical task for a Type 21 frigate. Besides gunfire support, her role was to act as a screen against air attack. 'Screen' in this context is a euphemism, for frigates are, when it comes down to it, expendable. They are positioned on the fringes of an escort group and, if necessary, they are sacrificed to preserve major units. *Ardent* expected a hard time that day.

The first air raid warning at 0700 local time came to nothing. At 0845 there were some relatively low-key attacks from Pucarás and Aermacchis based on the islands, soon followed by Skyhawks and Mirages attacking in earnest. For the next six hours, wave after wave made the 400-mile journey from the mainland. They quickly turned their attention to *Ardent*, almost certainly because her single 4.5in gun was bringing down accurate fire on Argentine Pucarás at Goose Green and on troop positions at Camilla Creek and Port Darwin. It seems *Ardent* destroyed as many as three Pucarás on the Goose Green airstrip, and kept two Argentine battalions pinned down all morning.

The strikes came at roughly half-hourly intervals; in one *Ardent* was straddled, but not damaged by bombs, and she apparently managed to hit a Skyhawk; records do not show whether this was with the 4.5 in gun or the Sea Cat missile system.

Ardent's captain, Commander Alan West, must have felt this was not only a lucky, but a useful morning. By attracting a substantial share of air strikes against herself, *Ardent* relieved the pressure on other ships; and it seems that apart from the one attack on the paras at Sussex Mountains, no further Pucarás were flown against British troop positions ashore on this crucial first day. After the capture of Goose Green it was realized just how valuable *Ardent*'s gunfire support had been, for had the Pucarás flown that day, it could well have been to drop the huge quantities of napalm that were discovered by the paras after they took the airstrip. The results of a napalm attack could have been devastating.

Out of the frying pan

When her gunfire support mission was over, *Ardent* was ordered to take up station further north and right in the centre of Falkland Sound, an extremely exposed position, where it was hoped she would split up enemy air strikes coming in from the south. From then on it was only a matter of time before the Argentine pilots would score a hit.

Soon two Skyhawks attacked together, dropping 500lb bombs on her aft end. Commander West later commented with military sang-froid: 'These caused a large amount of damage aft, writing off our aft missile system. We were on fire and making smoke.' With her aft Sea Cat launcher—her major anti-aircraft weapon—out of action, together with her 4.5in gun, there was little more *Ardent* could do, except steam away to the protection of San Carlos Water.

Her crew had not, however, finished their day's work. A group of five, led by Lt Cdr John Sephton, grabbed small arms, bolted machine guns to the rails, and continued firing at attacking aircraft. Then they were hit again, and Sephton was killed.

Three Skyhawks came in over the stern and accurately placed a trio of 500lb bombs, causing more severe damage.

Then she was hit by no less than ten bombs. Steerage was lost; just one small gun remained in action, manned by the civilian NAAFI manager, 33-year-old John Leake.

Next a wave of five Mirages attacked. As they came in about 30 feet above the water they were pounced on by two Sea Harriers. Two were shot down, and two more sped off trailing black smoke.

One of the Skyhawks fell, amazingly, to John Leake. A former soldier and skill-at-arms instructor, Leake was once an expert with the General Purpose Machine Gun. Now, for probably the first time in his life, he was using one in anger—and to devastating effect. In hindsight he has been credited with one confirmed kill—the Skyhawk—and one probable, maybe one of the two damaged in the same attack. His courage seemed to symbolize the dogged resistance of *Ardent* as she fought for her life out in the Sound.

The final air attack on *Ardent*—the 17th of the day—came from an

Aermacchi. It delivered two 500lb bombs and 14 68mm rockets, the latter blowing a huge hole in her port side.

It was two hours before dusk. The whole ship aft of the funnel was a mass of flames. Twenty-two of her crew were dead. The heat and anger of action had kept the men going; now shock began to take over. There was time to reflect on the unspeakable things bombs had done to friends; there were 30 wounded to be coped with.

Close to tears, West gave the order to abandon the sinking ship. Another frigate, *Yarmouth*, put her stern against *Ardent*'s bows and the survivors simply stepped across. *Yarmouth*'s Wasp helicopters ferried the injured to *Canberra*. *Ardent*'s tangled hulk continued to burn into the night, sinking after a few hours, appropriately enough off a nearby headland named Wreck Point.

In their zeal to finish off this single, lone frigate, Argentine pilots had foregone many of their best chances to sink transport and supply ships inside San Carlos Bay. Not one such vessel went down; and not one soldier was prevented from going ashore.

Battle in Bomb Alley

No one doubted the courage of the Argentine pilots as they attacked the British ships in San Carlos Water. As the Skyhawks and Mirages made their approach, they flew into a curtain of fire that demanded all the guts for which they became world famous.

FRIDAY, 21 MAY 1982 dawned clear and bright over Falkland Sound. The morning light revealed a concentration of shipping gathered to support the British landings which had started shortly after midnight on the 20th.

Aboard the various ships, including the great white shape of *Canberra*, one thought was uppermost: would the Argentine Air Force attack this most choice of military targets, ships landing troops? At around 0850, the question was answered as the first Pucará aircraft appeared over East Falkland and headed for the ships. Thus began the three day, air-to-sea battle of 'Bomb Alley'.

The events of 21–23 May have all been well recorded from the British point of view, but what of that of the Argentine air crew who fought and died over what they came to know as 'Death Valley'? Let the reader try and imagine himself amongst their number with a 'fly on the wall' account of the battle from the cockpit of a Skyhawk.

In the half light of dawn, the Skyhawk pilots of the V. Brigada make last minute visual checks of their aircraft. The Skyhawks sit low on their undercarriages, weighed down under the weight of bombs and fuel tanks hung under their wings. Four hundred miles is a long way for these tiny bombers and the technical people have sweated long hours calculating the optimum fuel/armament ratio to get the planes to the target, attack and return with a safety margin besides.

As events were to show, such calculations proved to be just too tight, especially amongst the Mirage squadrons. Over 'Death Valley' there would only be time for one pass at a target and use of maximum power to avoid missiles, gun fire or Harriers meant an almost certain watery end to the sortie, not a pleasant prospect in the South Atlantic winter.

To say that the Skyhawk is cramped is an understatement. Clad in bulky coveralls, survival vests, life jackets and anti-G corsets and leggings, even a relatively small man is hard put to it to get comfortable. Once strapped in, practised eyes and hands go through the familar starting routine.

Once in the air, the automatic visual 'scan' begins from instruments to outside the cockpit, to behind the cockpit and back, constantly watching for the unusual. Particularly important this morning are speed and fuel consumption; deviation from the flight-plan means the very real possibility of running out of fuel. Outside the glass bubble of the canopy is sea, from horizon to horizon, no reference points for navigation whatsoever. The compass seems to grow visibly as eyes check and recheck headings. How does it compare with the flight notes strapped on to the knee pad? Did the mechanics recheck the settings as they were asked?

Soon the Skyhawk is 250 miles out and it is starting to get very lonely for our pilot. From take-off, radio silence has been maintained and the sense of solitude is now heightened by entering 'Harrier country'. The formation is now in radar range of the Task Force and somewhere out there are the enemy interceptors. To give some measure of protection from radar detection, our pilot pushes the Skvhawk's nose down until it is only a few feet above the waves. What has so far been an almost boring instrument flying exercise now becomes distinctly exciting.

Sluggish under its load of bombs and fuel, the Skyhawk now starts to buck and kick at the controls as it hits the low level turbulence over the sea. Pulse rates shoot up as waves are avoided rather than flown over and eyes bore into the sky looking for the speck on the horizon which will grow into a Harrier. If the grumbling conscript who was made to clean the canopy properly were here now, he would understand why, for it is under these conditions that the merest speck of dirt easily becomes an enemy aircraft to straining eyes.

The first sight of East Falkland is almost a relief. Sight of land momentarily brings back the discomfort of the ejector seat and its harness but this is soon gone as the first British ships flash into view. The briefing called for the attack run to start over the main island so that it should come from out of the sun. Actions in the cockpit become purely automatic; cannon safety—off; gun sight—on; bomb panel—live; harness tightened...

Outside it's a matter of orientation; that's San Carlos Water over to the left so Fanning Head should be somewhere in front ... Down below there are ships, how many? Angry white smoke smudges suddenly appear, the first anti-aircraft fire. Over to the right a plume of white smoke spears upwards—a missile! Red beads lazily arch towards the cockpit to shoot by at extraordinary speed. In amongst these tracer shells are high explosive rounds which, though unseen, can mortally cripple the speeding Skyhawk.

Over the main island now and into a gut-wrenching 180° turn. Vision starts to grey as gravity pulls the blood away from the head and there is the painful bite of the G-suit into the thighs and midriff to prevent a complete blackout. Once level again, select a target; there! The grey superstructure starts to fill the sight, peppered with twinkling muzzle flashes as the crew brings every weapon it can to bear. Bigger and bigger grows the grey shape. Tracers flash past; the pilot's body tenses for the seemingly inevitable thump as a shell hits home. Will they fire the missiles? The ship now fills the whole windscreen. Just a little longer, a little longer … now! The Skyhawk jumps forward, freed of the drag and weight of the bombs. There is a kaleidoscope of images as the plane flashes over the target at mast height, an upturned face here, a spar there, aerial wires dangerously close.

Once over the ship, there is another harsh turn to get away from the bomb blast and a chance for one quick glance back at the ship. In the speed and confusion there really is no way of telling whether or not the target has been hit unless there is a really big explosion. As fast as the fuel state will allow, the Skyhawk heads for home. East Falkland flashes by as quickly as before and the long sea crossing looms ahead.

There are two dangers now: the Harriers and the sudden insistent glare if the fuel warning lights come on. A half-perceived explosion signifies the first of these as a British Sidewinder blows apart a colleague's plane. Who was it? Did he get out? Will the British pick him up? Will *anyone* pick him up?—the thoughts of aircrew at times like these are universal.

As the miles increase, the tension starts to relax a little to be replaced by weariness and a longing to be home. As the coast comes up, anxious eyes peer intently at the fuel gauges; is there enough left to get me home? At last, the familiar landmarks around the airfield crawl into view and tired limbs and minds go into the landing routine. With perhaps a less than stylish landing, the Skyhawk is down.

Leaving our representative Argentine pilot to his debriefing, we will perhaps have gained some insight into the intensity of the fighting in and over Falkland Sound during the period of the British landings. By the end of 21 May, all hilarity about 'bean eating' Argentines had gone. In a few short hours, the Fuerza Aerea had seriously damaged HMS *Argonaut*, sunk *Ardent* and hit *Antrim*, *Brilliant* and *Broadsword* with bombs which fortunately did not explode. Indeed, by Monday 24th, the total of sunk or damaged ships had risen to ten with HMS *Antelope* blowing up in the most spectacular fashion in San Carlos Water. The cost to the Argentine Air Force for this carnage was 26 aircraft.

Argentina's 'finest'

There is no doubt that flying of the nature described takes great courage and skill. It says much for the morale of the Argentine pilots. Journalist Garasino reports that the feeling at bases such as Rio Gallegos during May was not unlike that of the RAF's 'Few' during the Battle of Britain and that the pilots regarded themselves as Argentina's 'finest'. The effect of the losses suffered by the Fuerza Aerea is harder to pin down. The pilots Garasino talked to admitted heavy casualties (as many as 15 in a day) but expressed relief that they were much lower than had been expected. On the other side of the coin, Lieutenant Lucero, who ejected over San Carlos on the 25th and was picked up by *Fearless*, reported that he was 'greatly surprised' by the weight of the defences, having been told they would be minimal.

The British defences during this three-day period comprised 4.5in naval guns, Bofors guns, small arms, Sea Wolf, Sea Dart and Sea Cat missiles and Sea Harriers. (For the sake of total accuracy, Rapier missiles should be added to this list, once they had been taken ashore.) Of these, the Harriers proved to be the most effective. British official figures for the campaign as a whole credit the type with 16 confirmed and one probable missile 'kills' and four confirmed and two probable gun 'kills'.

The three 'Sea' missiles accounted for 21 aircraft between them throughout the campaign and may be regarded as being generally effective, not least in the deterrent effect of their highly visible detonations. The seaborne missiles proved less potent than the Army's Rapier system, which, despite problems, accounted for some 20 aircraft.

The three-day sea—air battle in 'Bomb Alley' dispelled any doubts that the Falklands campaign was going to be a 'walkover' and proved that both sides were going to fight it out with considerable courage. As the British forces pushed inland and the main action shifted away from San Carlos, one interesting little mystery remained: why did the Argentines fail to sink *Canberra* on the first day of the landings? Here was a physically large, ill-armed target which should have been extremely difficult to miss and one which, if sunk or damaged, would have had enormous propaganda potential. No clear answer to this puzzle has yet emerged but it seems likely that the Fuerza Aerea concentrated on hitting the escort ships first before turning their attention to the 'big one'. So successful were they in this regard that *Canberra* was hastily withdrawn on the night of the 21st and was never again left so vulnerable.

Fate of an Amazon

Fire reached *Antelope*'s missile magazines and the darkness of San Carlos Water was lit by the most dramatic explosions of the war. For the thousands of Task Force personnel who were watching, it was surely the lowest moment of all.

ON 22 MAY, the day after the destruction of *Ardent*, the British consolidated their position ashore. The SAS eliminated several Argentine observation posts on the western side of Falkland Sound, and this could have persuaded the Argentine Air Force not to commit aircraft to further attacks that day. Equally, they may have been licking the wounds received the day before. At least 16 aircraft had been lost—no air force can accept a daily casualty rate of that order.

When the Argentines still had not appeared by dark, everyone on and around San Carlos Water sighed with relief. Some vital redeployments could now take place, including the replacement of the damaged *Antrim* and the exit of *Canberra* (all her men now ashore) with a number of supply ships.

Sunday 23 May began quietly, but hopes of a real lull in the air attacks were soon dispelled. Skyhawk and Mirage attacks resumed, probably attracted by the fact that a group of stores ships and escorts were making their way back into San Carlos Water.

Ardent's sister ship *Antelope* was deployed out in Falkland Sound, again providing protection for ships inside the bay, again without the protection of the hills. At about 1400 local time, two Skyhawks appeared from behind the hills of West Falkland, banked steeply over the Sound and tore along some 40 feet above the surface. The first was shot down by a Rapier missile from the hills above San Carlos. The second ditched his bombs short and disappeared.

Almost immediately, the major attack came in. Waves of Mirages and Skyhawks flew over the anchorage and down the Sound, wheeling and diving over the ships, desperately trying to evade the defences. Inevitably, some got through the curtain of fire put up by every available weapon. Four Skyhawks approached *Antelope*, one racing in across the starboard beam at mast-head height. Leading Seaman Jeffrey Warren, manning the starboard 20mm gun, succeeded in pumping shells into it.

Substantial damage

As the aircraft crossed, its belly tore into the main mast, bending it right over. Two 500lb bombs were released; then the aircraft disintegrated.

One bomb started a fire, but the other failed to detonate and lodged in the engine room. Mercifully, there were few casualties: an 18-year-old steward was killed and three others injured.

The fire was soon put out, leaving substantial damage. With the unexploded bomb aboard, *Antelope*'s captain, Commander Nick Tobin, decided to seek safety inside San Carlos Bay. He hoped the calmer conditions there would enable the bomb to be safely defused, and the ship repaired.

Brian Hanrahan, the BBC reporter, described her arrival: 'She came slowly up the bay making smoke, her main mast bent over at an angle. There were holes along her side and she dropped anchor half a mile away.' As she steamed in, crew not required for operating the ship or handling weapons were assembled on the aft flight deck in their orange 'once only' survival suits. *Antelope* dropped anchor.

Third time unlucky

At this stage in the air war, the Argentines were using bombs of World War 2 design. They were fitted with propellers, which rotated in the passing air stream, so that the fuse detonated only after being dropped from a certain height. Because the pilots were flying so low in order to escape radar detection and the British missile systems, their bombs were not being fully armed on the descent. This is why the bomb which entered *Antelope* failed to explode. Later the Argentines realized the mistake and used bombs whose flight was retarded by parachute. The faulty fuses were reported widely in the UK press at this stage of the conflict, much to the fury of service personnel who thought it may have alerted the Argentines to the need for readjustment.

A team of bomb disposal experts led by Sergeant Jim Prescott of the Royal Engineers was taken over to *Antelope* by helicopter. The entire crew was brought up on deck. The ship's Lynx helicopter took off with tools and vital spares—in case there should be nothing else left to salvage.

According to BBC reporter Robert Fox, Prescott actually extracted the bomb's fuse twice, but being unsure of how stable the weapon was without it, put it back each time. All the time he was relaying to members of his team a radio commentary on what he was doing, just in case an accident prevented him from passing on valuable knowledge for future encounters with similar bombs.

It is understood he was extracting the fuse for a third time when the explosive in the bomb overheated and detonated. Prescott was killed instantly. One of the bomb disposal team lost an arm. Most of the ship's crew were thrown to the deck, three sustaining injuries.

The bomb started a series of major fires in the machinery room and adjacent compartments. Fire-fighting teams tried to beat the flames, but power was soon lost, together with water pressure. The fire spread out of control; the aluminium superstructure started to melt, collapsing in on itself. It was now dark.

Tobin was forced to give the order to abandon ship. The ships' boats, with some help from landing craft, carried the whole company, but just in case anyone had been thrown in the water, helicopters quartered the area.

The rest of the ships in San Carlos Water, and thousands of men ashore, had witnessed these events in subdued, fascinated horror. They did not have long to wait before the sensational finale. Just ten minutes after the last man had left her, fire reached *Antelope*'s missile magazine. The night was lit by a brilliant fireball and a series of violent explosions: the ship was opened up like a can. A Press Association photographer, Martin Weaver, was waiting with his camera to take the most dramatic picture of the war.

The fireworks were not yet over. For the rest of the night the ship burned white hot, shooting glowing debris into the air. At dawn the fire had died down somewhat, but the bulk still glowed red hot. The upper deck was a tangled mess of molten metal. The next day *Antelope* broke her back, and the sea put an end to the fire, sending up a funeral pall of white steam. The bows and stern reared up out of the water in a defiant 'V', then slowly sank.

That, according to the weapons officer of one Task Force destroyer, was 'our lowest ebb'. Seeing a ship sink, for the first time, is a sobering experience, and it had thoroughly shaken those thousands of witnesses. They were disturbed by the futility of the ship's loss and the ease with which it was done.

It seemed to them that the Argentines could prise open their vital, outer defensive screen whenever they chose, except perhaps at night. They wondered how much more they could take.

Arguably, many more ships would have followed *Antelope* and *Ardent* had not San Carlos been chosen as the landing site. Both *Antelope* and *Ardent*, out in Falkland Sound, were sitting ducks. Inside San Carlos Water they may well have survived.

This is because a screen of hills overlooks the inlet on three sides. Argentine jets could approach from the land side, but they were left with only seconds to select, and attack, their targets. Mostly this meant attacking the first ship which came into view, and this partly explains why the pilots failed to select strategic targets like supply ships. The planes were operating at the extreme edge of their range, so that after seconds over San Carlos, they had to turn for home—or run out of fuel on the way back. Without these factors working against the Argentines, many feel the landings would have been a disaster.

The Harriers were a potent weapon against the Argentine air attacks, but there were too few of them, and they too operated with a fuel restriction. For safety, the carriers had to operate well out to sea, out of range of the Mirages and Skyhawks. This meant Harrier presence over the operation areas was drastically curtailed. There were gaps in the Harrier cover when aircraft changed 'shifts', and with the sheer numbers of Argentine planes coming in, some had to get through. On 21 May, Harriers more often than not brought down Mirages or Skyhawks *after* they had attacked ships.

The sinking of Coventry and Atlantic Conveyor

During the seemingly interminable day of 25 May HMS *Coventry* fought off Argentine air attacks with immense courage and skill but eventually succumbed to the constant attacks. Next it was *Atlantic Conveyor*'s turn, the victim of a bizarre stroke of fate, when two Exocet missiles were seduced off course by 'chaff' from *Hermes* and tragically re-selected a new target.

IN THE WORDS of Captain David Hart-Dyke RN, 24 May was a 'good day' for *Coventry*. The destroyer's radar enabled the Sea Harrier Combat Air Patrol (CAP) to destroy three aircraft, while the early warning given to ships and Rapier missile batteries in Falkland Sound helped them to destroy another six attackers. But their very success marked *Coventry* and her team mate, the frigate *Broadsword*, down for swift retribution.

Coventry had been built by Cammell Laird at Birkenhead between 1973 and 1978. Like her sister ship *Sheffield* she was a Type 42 guided missile-armed destroyer intended to screen a surface force from air attack. To do this she was equipped with a long-range surveillance radar (Type 965) and Sea Dart semi-active homing missiles.

Front line force

In accordance with her role, *Coventry* and her sisters *Sheffield* and *Glasgow* had formed an advanced air defence screen around the carriers *Invincible* and *Hermes*. This involved tracking and controlling the Sea Harriers, to position them in the right place to intercept Argentine air attacks, a task which *Coventry* performed admirably from 1 May. Apart from the Sea Harriers, the Sea Dart missile offered the only other chance for the Task Force to thin out the Argentines' superiority in the air, and so *Coventry* and *Glasgow* were used on the 'front line' to attack the aircraft which were running supplies into Port Stanley. After *Glasgow* was put out of action by an unexploded bomb on 12 May, *Coventry* was the last air defence ship until reinforcements arrived from the United Kingdom.

HMS *Coventry* had already scored two notable 'firsts'; on 3 May her Lynx helicopter had fired the first Sea Skua missiles at a supply ship off Port Stanley, and on 9 May she fired the first operational Sea Darts, 'splashing' two Skyhawks and a troop-carrying Puma helicopter.

Maximum damage

In the last week *Coventry* was ordered to operate with the Seawolf-armed frigate *Broadsword*, in the hope that the combination of Sea Dart's medium range (25 miles) and Seawolf's precision at short range (5 miles) would inflict maximum damage on the Argentine air attacks. The two ships were to co-ordinate the overall air defence of the amphibious Operating Area in Falkland Sound, using their radars and comprehensive plotting and communications facilities to vector the Sea Harriers onto the waves of attacking aircraft.

On 25 May the two ships were subjected to heavy air attacks. In the middle of the day two separate attacks were made, which *Coventry* handled with skill, shooting down three aircraft with Sea Darts. Operating to the north-west of Falkland Sound the two ships were in an exposed position, and the rest of the day must have seemed interminable. The end, when it came, was swift.

Four aircraft emerged from behind cover of land, where the ship's radar could not detect them, and raced the last ten miles hugging the surface of the sea. *Coventry* fired Sea Dart, the 4.5in gun, 20mm guns and even GPMGs and rifles, but although three aircraft were hit, the fourth got through and dropped four bombs. Three of them ripped into the port side, tearing open the plating and blasting the interior of the ship.

Immediately astern, *Broadsword* was a helpless spectator; she had been tracking the Skyhawks with her Seawolf Type 910 tracker, but a violent alteration of course by *Coventry* had blanked off the forward firing arcs. For a moment the ship's officers in *Broadsword* thought they might have inadvertently fired a Seawolf into *Coventry*, but they had other problems on their minds, as one of the Skyhawks' 1000lb bombs had bounced off the sea and gone through the helicopter flight deck without exploding, although it destroyed a helicopter.

Coventry's Operations Room took the full force of the bomb blast, and many of the 19 men killed were there, part of the 30-strong team directing the battle. The crowded compartment was immediately filled with thick black smoke—men's clothing was set alight, and all power and lighting failed. Later, Captain Hart-Dyke was to tell how he was so shocked and disorientated that he groped his way out to the port bridge wing and gave orders for the ship to steam at high speed to the east. *Coventry* was in fact listing to port at 50 degrees, flooding rapidly and on fire.

Nobody recalls hearing the order 'Abandon ship', but clearly the ship was doomed, and officers and ratings hurriedly put on life jackets and the brightly-coloured 'once-only' survival suits. Two Chief Petty Officers were still below, on their own initiative, checking compartments to make sure that anyone still alive had some chance of escaping. At least one rating owes his life to this last-minute search, for he was found unconscious, lying across a hatch above one of the engine rooms. All this had to be done by crawling along the deck, in the small space clear of toxic fumes, in darkness.

Fortunately the weather was calm, and the survivors could concentrate on helping badly burned men into life rafts. Help was on the way from other ships, and helicopters from the Royal Fleet Auxiliary *Fort Austin* picked up 55 survivors. The whole sinking took just over half an hour; the ship took roughly 15 minutes to capsize and then remained floating keel uppermost for another 15 minutes.

With the sinking of *Coventry*, four warships had been lost in three weeks. (The others were *Sheffield, Ardent* and *Antelope.*) In common with the other lost ships *Coventry* was also one of the fleet's most modern vessels.

Fortunately for Operation 'Corporate', however, the sinking of HMS *Coventry* did not mean the end of air defence, for on 23 May the Battle Group had been reinforced by the Sea Dart-armed destroyers *Bristol* and *Cardiff*, while the *Exeter*, with the much more effective Type 1022 radar, had joined a day or two earlier. In addition another Sea Wolf ship, the frigate *Andromeda*, four older frigates and three RFAs had arrived. The tide of battle had turned in the Task Force's favour at last.

Atlantic Conveyor, the 30-day wonder

On 25 May, with the beach-head firmly established at San Carlos, orders came to the massive container ship *Atlantic Conveyor*. She was to go into San Carlos Water to disembark the Wessex and Chinook helicopters.

What nobody knew was that two of the Argentine Navy's Super Etendard strike aircraft had picked up 'blips' on their radars, indicating sur-face ships at a distance of about 35 miles. Beneath their wings they carried two of the dwindling supply of AM.39 Exocet anti-ship missiles.

Subsequently, claims were made that the pilots had mistaken the bulk of *Atlantic Conveyor* for a carrier. But at that distance it seems likely that they fired 'blind'. The scene was set for one of the most spectacular tragedies of the war.

In peacetime, *Atlantic Conveyor* carried a formidable load when trade was good: 700 20ft containers, 990 vehicles on her car decks, and a further 72 40ft flatbeds on two trailer decks. When the Ministry of Defence's eyes fell on her, laid up in Liverpool, they saw an unusual 14,946 gross registered tons merchant ship, a combined deep hold and roll-off vessel, with stern ramp giving access to a pair of vehicle decks. She also had a flush upper deck for carrying containers or—in the nature of the circumstances—aircraft.

There was another special feature about *Atlantic Conveyor*, vividly recalled later by the man who surveyed her for conversion. The wooden planking which covered both the vast car decks was of lin marine plywood, which in the pitch and roll of ocean crossing had become soaked with oil from vehicles on board. It was a readily combustible mixture.

The decision to take up the merchant ships *Atlantic Conveyor* and *Atlantic Causeway* from trade, to reinforce the fleet of RFAs and STUFT merchantmen, was made comparatively late. Not until 13 April, a week and a half after the first mobilization orders, did Captain Michael Layard learn that he was to be appointed Senior Naval Officer aboard *Atlantic Conveyor*. His task was to supervise her conversion to an auxiliary transport and aircraft carrier—and be ready to go south by 25 April.

On 15 April Captain Layard met to discuss matters with *Atlantic Conveyor's* Master, Captain Ian North—universally known as Captain Birdseye. As the ship sailed for Devonport Naval Base, the design team was already on board, measuring and checking the thickness of pillaring. Despite her cavernous capacity, could *Atlantic Conveyor* take on the load that was to be taken south?

The types of aircraft she would be required to carry included the range of Army, Royal Navy and Royal Air Force helicopters, but in addition the requirement to carry Harriers and Chinooks imposed special problems. These big machines impose heavy landing loads, as well as their roll-up weight when parked on the deck, but in the event, tests proved the container deck strong enough for the burden.

Helicopter deck

By stacking the containers four-high on either side of the weather deck, it was possible to provide wind-breaks. The aircraft and helicopters were to be parked at the aft end of the deck, near the bridge-front, leaving the area of the hatch covers behind the breakwater clear for landing. Subsequently, this arrangement was reversed when the same designers converted her sister *Atlantic Causeway*. In that ship the Sea King helicopters were provided with a proper hangar by using light plating as a 'roof' over the containers. This simple hangar faced aft, and the landing area was just forward of the bridge.

The structural modifications proved relatively simple, but it was also necessary to provide accomodation for about 100 extra men of the Naval Party. They would maintain the aircraft on the way south, and man the satellite communications gear added at Devonport. At first the designers considered using Portakabins, but an exploration of the vast ship's bridge structure showed them that sufficient space existed. Not only were there spare cabins for conversion to mess-decks and offices, but sufficient space to fit the standard Navy three-tier bunks without encroaching on the existing crew-spaces.

The absolute urgency of the job and the need to use whatever materials were available stretched Devonport's ingenuity to the limit. A Naval HQ party of 35 (NP 1840) joined the Merchant Navy crew in the task of preparing the ship, manning a routine/regulating office, a sick bay, communications centre, stores organization, two flight decks, a battle damage repair team and even a Chinese laundry. The battle damage repair team of 13 men also had the task of replenishment at sea, damage control, aircraft refuelling and air engineering.

In addition to the aircraft arrangements the ship was also to function as an Army transport. Through the stern ramp were loaded thousands of tons of stores, food and equipment, including bombs for the Sea Harriers and sufficient tentage for a brigade. The ship was ready on 25 April, and as soon as she left Devonport and got into Plymouth Sound it was possible to carry out hurried Sea Harrier landing trials. After the six Wessexes of 848 Squadron FAA and five Chinooks of 18 Squadron had landed, Lieutenant Commander Tim Gedge, CO of 809 Squadron, landed his Sea Harrier on the forward flight deck. Then the ship had to carry out degaussing trials to check that her magnetic 'signature' was not excessive. One more exercise at an underway replenishment from a Navy oiler, and she was ready to go to war.

On the long voyage south to Ascension, *Atlantic Conveyor* was accompanied by another STUFT ship, *Europic Ferry*. They bunkered at Sierra Leone, but finally reached Ascension on 5 May. There she embarked eight Navy Sea Harriers and six RAF Harriers which had flown direct from the United Kingdom. The bulk of the NAAFI and naval victualling stores were transferred to the RFA *Stromness*, and the ship was ready to sail south with the Amphibious Group. In anticipation of the foul weather ahead, the aircraft parked on deck were swathed in plastic 'cocoons' to protect them from salt spray.

Battle Group rendezvous

In the light of earlier reports that an Argentine civilian airliner had tracked the Task Force, one Sea Harrier was kept in readiness, fully armed and ready to 'Hack the Shad' if it should put in an appearance. The ship's first task was to rendezvous with the Battle Group's carriers *Invincible* and *Hermes*, to transfer the Harriers and Sea Harriers. So far, *Atlantic Conveyor's* journey had been strenuous but smooth. And then on 25 May, at the moment of turning to gain the seemingly sheltered waters of San Carlos, disaster struck.

The missiles that sped from the two Argentine Super Etendards beyond the horizon were detected by the carrier *Hermes* and seduced off course by the firing of 'Corvus' chaff rockets. But apparently both Exocets re-acquired a target, which happened to be *Atlantic Conveyor* turning into Falkland Sound. The ship had received an air raid warning at 1930 hours (GMT) and only two minutes later the two missiles tore into her side low down on the port quarter.

As with HMS *Sheffield* the missiles generated intense heat and clouds of thick black smoke. The oil-soaked car decks burnt like torches. Within half an hour the fire was out of control. Large explosions were heard from the lower cargo decks, and the fire was spreading towards the aircraft bombs and kerosene fuel stowed forward. Although hoses were being played on the decks they were soon red-hot, and the order 'Abandon ship' was given by Captain North.

Twelve men died in the sinking of *Atlantic Conveyor*, including Captain Ian North. He went down the ladder just behind Captain Layard, but was not able to reach a life raft. Fortunately, the survivors did not have to wait too long for rescue. The carriers sent helicopters and the frigate *Alacrity* stood in dangerously close to haul the rafts clear of the blazing wreck. The abandoned hulk drifted for another 24 hours, wallowing in the swell as the fires and explosions wrecked her. The photographs of the wreck show a massive 'hog' of the hull amidships, indicating that she was about to break her back. She finally did break in half and sank in deep water.

The Ministry of Defence never divulged exactly what was lost in *Atlantic Conveyor*, but her loss has rightly been called a logistical disaster, which severely delayed the reconquest of the Falklands by the land forces. The helicopters lost included a Lynx, six Wessex HU5s and three Chinooks; it was the Chinooks, capable of lifting an underslung load of 12 tons, which were the most serious loss. The cargo lost included cluster bombs and Paveway laser-guided bombs, an emergency refuelling system for the RAF Harriers, a portable airstrip, as well as tents for 4000 men and other military stores. Although none of these losses prevented final victory, they increased the discomfort of the troops ashore, and narrowed an already finely calculated margin of success.

Atlantic Conveyor was called the '30-day wonder', but in her brief naval career she proved that big container ships can function as auxiliary aircraft carriers, and in the aftermath of the Falklands serious thought was given to a similar conversion. Another time, however, the opportunity would be taken to provide some elementary defence, in the form of chaff rockets or even containerized missiles.

21–28 MAY 1982

Waiting for the off

After the excitement of the successful landings, the first week ashore seemed like an anti-climax. The enemy wasn't so much Argentina as cold, wet feet, supply problems and frustration—at being spectators as ships were picked off in air attacks.

AFTER SPLASHING ASHORE in the early hours of 21 May, the land forces of the British Task Force made for their first objectives. As 40 Commando occupied San Carlos Settlement, 2 Para had to slog up Sussex Mountain and dig in on the hillside to protect the bridgehead from attack from the south. Opposite San Carlos Settlement, across San Carlos Water, 45 Commando took over the disused refrigeration plant at Ajax Bay. It soon became the main Dressing Station (MDS) or principal field hospital. Then 3 Para moved into Port San Carlos. At Ajax Bay was also located a key establishment: Brigade Maintenance Area—the 'base' clearing house of men, stores and ammunition.

These deployments, broadly speaking, are what made up the bridgehead. By the end of daylight on 21 May, around 3000 men—all five battalions—were ashore. They were digging in or had dug in, either high on tussocky hillsides which reminded them of Scotland or the Pembrokeshire coast of Wales, or close to the groups of islanders' red and white houses with their tin roofs and farm outbuildings, most looking as if they were three-quarters built.

It was cold but sunny on 21 May and everyone ashore was moderately cheerful. The most important unloading task, having got the men ashore, was now in train. Rapier batteries, which it was hoped would form a 'steel ring' of anti-aircraft defence around the bridgehead, and over the ships in San Carlos Water, were being transferred to the Sea King helicopters that would fly them ashore.

That day, and for the most of the following week, the average soldier's life was a question of waiting, mixed with all the countless chores connected with life under canvas or in a trench. A few lucky ones were housed in buildings at San Carlos Settlement, but for the others it was a battle against mud, cold and wet feet. In fact 2 Para had a particularly difficult time. Even on Sussex Mountain the water table was extraordinarily high and the bottoms of trenches and fox holes were awash at a depth of just two feet. Instead of trenches they had to make sangars by scooping shallow depressions and piling rocks round the perimeters.

Air attacks on the ground positions were expected hourly and digging in was quickly completed. But when the Argentine Air Force did arrive, it speedily became clear that their targets were the ships. The men ashore were left to watch in horror and fascination as Skyhawks and Mirages pressed home attacks unmolested by Rapier missiles, at this stage not operational.

One paratrooper, Lance Corporal Kevin Lukowiak, has particularly vivid memories of watching the ships being bombed in San Carlos Water. 'It was amazing. I can remember these three aircraft coming over us one morning and they went straight down the hill. And they see the ship, it was one of the nearest to us, and the three of these jets were nearly wing to wing and you could even see the little black things coming off them. It was pathetic, though; the pilots had got all that way, and then they missed. The bombs just splashed into the sea.'

When Argentine planes appeared, men blasted off thousands of rounds of small arms fire and mortar bombs, accompanied by shouts and catcalls. Logistics men, responsible for supplying them, squirmed with frustration at the waste.

They had good reason to be worried. On the first day ashore, the power of the Argentine air threat had been vividly demonstrated, leaving *Ardent* sinking and others damaged. As a result, Rear Admiral Woodward ordered all unloading of vital supplies to take place at night. As few supply ships as possible were to remain in San Carlos Water by daylight; instead they were to steam out to sea, re-stocking in the replenishment and logistics area, and then return in safety at night. Often enough, they could not manage the round trip in daylight hours, and so unloading schedules were seriously disrupted. As a result, everything was in short supply, from ammunition through petrol to helicopters. The sad fact was—as senior officers have ruefully admitted since the war—that peacetime armies forget how easily it is for supply systems to perform badly, or cease, when the action hots up.

Lt Colonel Hellberg, commanding the Logistic Regiment of 3 Commando Brigade, was one of those who bore the brunt of the supply problem. His first major setback was when the supply ships were ordered to sea on 21 May. There was not enough time to get all his supplies and back-up teams ashore and those left behind included a complete dressing station. It was not seen again until 1 June. Just as bad, MV *Elk*, one of Hellberg's supply ships, carrying tons of high explosive and ammunition, was ordered out of the landing area partly because it was a danger to neighbouring ships in air attacks, partly because her loss would be fatal to the ground forces.

Hellberg was entirely dependent on the timely arrival of air and sea supplies, none of which he directly controlled. Every request had to be submitted through Brigade Headquarters, and there placed on a priority list. Logistics requests always came lower on the list than battle supplies.

Typical of the mundane but crucial problems Hellberg had to deal with was that of jerrycans. The Task Force was woefully short of this humble item, probably because someone behind a desk at Whitehall had decided that refuelling from flexible tanks was the best method for modern fighting units. In reality, almost every unit needed refuelling as and where it happened to be situated—whether 1000ft up Sussex Mountain or miles down one of the Falklands' boggy tracks. There were few units operating out of or around San Carlos then, or after, that were not in some sense 'front line'; which could enjoy the luxury of turning back to refuel from a bulk tank.

The demand for petrol could never be satisfied; every unit had its generator, as did each Rapier battery. The Volvo BVs (snow vehicles) and raiding craft consumed the contents of vast numbers of jerrycans. The irony was that out on the ships in the logistics area, there was plenty of fuel. The problem was getting it ashore: this was mostly achieved by large rigid ranks carried on floats. Their contents had to be transferred laboriously into the inadequate number of jerrycans on hand.

If there was frustration at Hellberg's level after the landings, Brigadier Thompson, at this stage in charge of all land forces, had probably the worst week of his professional career.

Brigadier Julian Thompson, commander 3 Brigade, was at that time in charge of the landing forces because Maj Gen Jeremy Moore was still making his way south, incommunicado on *QE2*. Thompson started his day as usual, taking up his post in the Ops Room, in reality just a corner of the dense maze of dug-outs and camouflaged tents at San Carlos Settlement that passed for Brigade HQ. He stooped over his maps and carried on with the task that had obsessed him for days: he had secured the beach-head, from the land at least, and now he had to break out and advance on Stanley.

In essence, his plan was this: wait for the reinforcements of men, machines and supplies at that moment ploughing south through the Atlantic, and then mount a straightforward assault across East Falkland to Stanley. He saw no point in using precious resources to diversify the attack either to the south or the west. Stanley was the only target that made real military sense. He saw the assault in terms of a rapid series of hops as his men were lifted in helicopters—the big Chinooks—across the daunting terrain of the island. But all this was to change by the time the Brigadier came back into his sleeping bag long after dark on 25 May.

Attack again down Bomb Alley

The air raids began as usual: the hooting of the ships' sirens from the San Carlos Water and the cry of 'Air raid red' through the ships' Tannoys and over the radio sets spread through the hills. At first, it looked as if the air defences—on ship and land—were in for 'a good day'. The first wave of elderly Argentine Skyhawks was intercepted as they flew in over the sea from the north-west and were turned back after four had been shot down.

Then the pattern for the next two raids changed. The first pass came, as usual, screaming down Bomb Alley, a few seconds' worth of terror but, this time, little destruction. Then most of the Skyhawks and the Mirages flying with them changed direction to fly low across the radar clutter over the hills of West Falkland, dipping off the north of the Sound, heading, it seemed, for the northern picket set up by the Navy.

It was a ferocious assault on the two ships standing picket duty there, HMS *Coventry* and her Seawolf-carrying guard, HMS *Broadsword*. Most of the bombs were aimed at *Coventry*, and despite brave and effective retaliation, she was quickly sunk.

As Coventry sank, leaving the northern point of the Sound unguarded, two Super Etendards, armed with the dreaded Exocet missile, flew through the open corridor towards a large ship heading for the Sound and identified by Argentine intelligence as a high-priority target, the carrier *Invincible*.

This was the moment the Junta had dreamed of. To sink the aircraft carrier *Invincible* on their National Day would restore pride and severely hinder—if not cripple—the British effort. In fact, of course, it was *Atlantic Conveyor* that was crippled and then sunk by the lethal Exocets.

At about this time in the early afternoon, Brigadier Thompson was summoned to HMS *Fearless*, the flagship of the landing force, to talk over the satellite to headquarters in Northwood. Maj Gen Richard Trant came on the line—and within a couple of minutes, he had overturned everything that Thompson was working towards. He had orders; not suggestions, nor requests—orders. The demand from London was simply this: attack Goose Green and advance on Stanley.

Thompson's strategy in ruins

It remains unclear which came first: the orders to advance or the news that *Atlantic Conveyor* had been sunk. Either way, together they ruined Thompson's initial strategy, because *Atlantic Conveyor* was carrying the mighty Chinook helicopters, and about nine Wessex helicopters as well. All but one Chinook were lost, along with such comforts as tents for 4000 men. It was the biggest logistical blow of the war, and it cost Thompson the main plank of his strategy for getting his men across the Falklands. He was left with orders to advance for battle, with no apparent means of getting his men into assault position.

This dilemma was never seen in London. There, the political pressure was always intense to do something, to get a result. Britain had already lost five ships—the politicians wanted a success in return. There was increasing pressure for action before the UN ordered a ceasefire leaving Britain with nothing but the beach-head.

At least the unambiguous orders resolved the dilemma, even if they replaced it with a huge risk. Thompson called an 'O' Group—orders briefing—for his unit commanders. The COs' helicopters buzzed over to Port San Carlos, Sussex Mountains and Ajax Bay and then back to Brigade HQ. There, the para and marine colonels received the news with disbelief.

2 Para were to go to Goose Green—Brigade could just scrape up enough Sea King helicopters to take some guns and supplies there for them but the fighting men would have to walk. 3 Para and 45 Commando were to advance on Stanley, via the northern route. There would be no airlift. Further, since there were no vehicles capable of carrying men and equipment across that marshy, rocky, mountainous country, it would be a matter of walking—and of carrying enough gear to take on the enemy along the way if necessary, and rations to live on.

On the night of 26 May, 2 Para filed off the slopes of Sussex Mountains, south towards the battle for Goose Green. At dawn on 27 May, 3 Para and 45 Commando shouldered their kit to begin what was to become a famous foot-slog as they headed north and east towards Stanley.

In a way, that week after the landings was a battle of its own; after a few days, the cold and discomfort became a serious menace. Twice a day—at dawn and dusk—men were 'stood to'—routed out and obliged to man their positions, weapons ready in case of attack.

So the days went by—the men ashore feeling curiously remote from the drama going on below them. Certainly they cheered and shouted when they saw Argentine planes downed by missiles, gunfire or Harriers. But it was more like watching a war movie than actually being at war—until, that is, the evening of 27 May.

As dusk closed in, two Skyhawks screamed without warning over San Carlos Settlement and dropped parachute-retarded bombs. They drifted slowly towards 40 Commando's position and exploded, killing two men and wounding three others. Much of their force was absorbed by the soft peat.

Air raid surgery

Meanwhile, across Ajax Bay, three Skyhawks dropped 12 large retard bombs in Hellberg's own area. Mercifully, only four exploded, but they went off in the regimental galley and the echelon area of 45 Commando, killing six men and seriously wounding 26 others. Half an hour later, when the galley would be much busier, the number of casualties would have been unthinkable. Another of the bombs exploded among the 105mm and 81mm ammunition, and this, together with 45 Commando echelon's ammunition, carried on exploding all night.

Three bombs hit the Main Dressing Station, one passing straight through (and out the other side) and two lodging in the building itself. They failed to explode. Had they done so, half the regiment could have been killed. One of Hellberg's men was killed by Skyhawk cannon fire while blasting at an aircraft with his machine gun.

Throughout the raid, surgical operations were being performed inside the MDS. In the impact, some rusty meat hooks fell from the ceiling of the operating theatre, together with clouds of dust. But there was only one injury, and one Argentine prisoner whose wound was infected by rust.

It was a bad time for such a disruption, for the battle for Darwin and Goose Green was already under way. Casualties from 2 Para were soon to be flooding in. Two days before, in the Cabinet Room at 10 Downing Street, the question of a break-out had been debated. Rumour that it was indeed about to happen was rife in the British press, and in fact the advance on Goose Green was announced prematurely as 2 Para were on their way to spend their first night at Camilla Creek. Meanwhile, 3 Para and 45 Commando had also left the bridgehead and were making for Douglas Settlement, predictably enough on foot, for there were still not enough helicopters to take them to their objectives in swift, easy hops.

The paras win Goose Green

The radio message was terse: 'Sunray is down'. Colonel 'H' Jones died in the manner that he had lived, leading his beloved 2 Para from the front. It was a tragedy that showed the price of one of the war's major battles: the contest at Goose Green.

ON 15 APRIL 1982, 2 Para were warned to be ready to move to the Falkland Islands. These orders brought to an end the frustration of watching 3 Para sailing aboard *Canberra* and the feeling that they were missing a rare opportunity to test their training and organization.

Under Colonel 'H' Jones and his second-in-command, Major Chris Keeble, the battalion had been reorganized. A command and control structure was produced for 2 Para which enabled the colonel to concentrate on the battle and move freely with a small staff and signallers. His second-in-command had a skeleton staff which duplicated the colonel's tactical HQ. In addition, the main headquarters had two officers, the Operations Officer (a major) and his assistant (a captain), who were also assisted by an experienced warrant officer. These men could take the administrative load off the battalion second-in-command. The main HQ had the OC of Support Company (the mortars and anti-tank weapons) with the responsibility for artillery and air support.

The OC HQ Company was tasked with ammunition and casualty evacuation. They and the Main HQ were responsible for following the way the battle was developing and moving ammunitions forward where it was needed. The Adjutant handled the administration for the Colonel, and the Regimental Sergeant Major took care of ammunition re-supply and the evacuation of prisoners-of-war.

The Regimental Medical Officer, Captain Steve Hughs (RAMC), who had been with the battalion only 18 months, completely reorganized the medical training for the men. The aim was to give each man a firm grounding in the administration of a saline drip and morphine, the application of dressings, and resuscitation.

If a man was wounded, he was taught that the first priority was to take what steps he could to remedy the situation—then his battle partner 'buddy' would administer first aid. The section medic would assist if he was within reach. These skills, and the vital saline drip carried by each man in the top pocket of his smock, were life-savers in action. The battalion was to pay tribute to the helicopter pilots who flew at times in very poor visibility and evacuated men who might not have survived in the open without surgery.

A unique intelligence gathering organization was also developed by 2 Para in the form of their Patrol Company. Divided into a vehicle-mounted element and a four-man foot patrol and observation-post element, the Patrol Company is closely integrated with the Intelligence Cell and Intelligence Officer. In this way, they can be tasked to collect information and in turn this can be passed to the Colonel. The Company is commanded by a Major, while the Int cell retains its Captain as IO (Intelligence Officer). The advantage of the apparent dual command is that the Patrol Company OC can add the weight of his views when briefings on enemy plans and moves are given to the CO.

Finally the procedure for passing orders to the Company Commanders, and thence through the platoons to the soldiers, was reorganized. In 2 Para the Colonel would hold what is known in the SAS as 'a Chinese Parliament'. This means he would talk through, with the OCs of the rifle and support companies as well as the attached arms (gunners or armour), the options and ways in which the attack, or defence, could be conducted. Everyone has a chance to air their views and also to point out the problems or hazards of different course of action. By the end of the discussion everyone has a good idea of what lies ahead and then the Colonel prepares his orders. As a result, when the formal O Group was held, there were no surprises and company commanders had a clear idea of their tasks.

Any elite can thrive on its perception of itself as superior through its fitness, aggression and good training. However, these outward signs can hide the private fears of each man, and war can put pressure on men that can never be created even in the most demanding training. The Padre of 2 Para, David Cooper, was respected by the men, not only for the direct way he could talk to them, but also for the fact that he was a Bisley standard shot. Talking to the battalion as a group, and also to a few men at a time, he enabled them to think about fear and the loss of friends in action and gave them a few straightforward values that they could hang on to when they felt alone. Before the landing at San Carlos he addressed the battalion. Robert Fox of the BBC recalled in his book 'Eyewitness Falklands' the address:

'I don't think God is over-concerned with causes, as much as he is with people. Some of you will face fear and death. Some of you will die. I have to say this, because this is what I believe in. I want you to know that you will not be alone. God will be with you, and whatever happens this is not the end.' Fox commented that services in *Canberra* had generally been attended by officers, but here on *Norland* there was no distinction of rank between officers and men.

When the Falklands crisis blew up, 2 Para had been earmarked to go to Belize. One of the benefits of the planned tour of duty in Belize was that the battalion had drawn weapons for work in the jungle and had locked their own away in the armoury at Aldershot. In this way they had not only twice the number of General Purpose Machine Guns (GMPGs) but also such weapons as the Armalite rifle and the M79 grenade launcher. All were to be used in action, and the section with two GMPGs was to prove a far more effective sub-unit than the traditional fire group and assault group taught by the training manual.

The paras go in

On 21 April 1982 the battalion landed at Bonners Bay in Royal Marine-crewed LCUs. Though they had discussed and learned amphibious drills from an attached Royal Marine officer, this did not prevent the Paras from referring to landing craft as 'rubbish skips' and amphibious landings as 'rubbish skipping'. The first task for 2 Para was to move on foot to positions on Sussex Mountains. Here they dominated the southern approaches to the San Carlos beach-head and could observe any attempts by the Argentine forces to counter-attack from Darwin and Goose Green.

Patrols were sent out, but here the reconnaissance activities by Special Forces restricted the range of operations. It was frustrating for 2 Para, with their own excellent Patrol Company, to be restricted behind the screen of elements like the SAS, SBS and Mountain and Arctic Warfare Cadre.

On the night of the landings at San Carlos the SAS raided Goose Green. Approaching overland, they put in a heavy volume of automatic and anti-tank fire. It convinced the Argentine garrison that they were under attack from a large force and also deterred them from venturing northwards to investigate the operations at San Carlos.

Following the loss of HMS *Coventry* and *Atlantic Conveyor*, new orders were given for a raid on Goose Green. Earlier they had been cancelled because helicopters were not available to lift the battalion. Now 2 Para were not only going to Goose Green and Darwin—they were doing it on foot.

SAS patrols had reported that the area was held in approximately battalion strength. However, after these reports had been sent the Argentine forces were reinforced by men from 12 Regiment on Mount Kent. From a strength of about 500, with three AA guns and artillery, they had swollen to around 1400.

How this reinforcement came to be made was an area of controversy. Some sources said that ill-judged press and radio comment in the United Kingdom indicated that this would be the next British move after the landings; others pointed to the political leaks; and there was also the obvious fact that any good intelligence staff in Menendez' HQ would advise him that it was an obvious objective for the British.

Prior to the issue of orders, two patrols from 2 Para were able to confirm that enemy positions were at the northern end of the isthmus, and astride it just south of Darwin—notably on Darwin Hill, which dominates the community from the south. The patrols withdrew when they came under enemy fire.

Phased plan of attack

The plan of attack was a night and day operation in six phases It would have naval gunfire support from HMS *Arrow* and artillery fire from three guns of 8 Battery 29 Cdo Battery RA, augmented by two of 2 Para's 81mm mortars. The aim was to defeat the enemy in the hours of darkness, allowing the paras to identify and liberate the population of the two communities in daylight. After first light the battalion would also have Scout helicopters with SSII missiles as well as Harriers in a ground-attack role. Two Blowpipe detachments were attached for air defence from 4 Regt RA and the Royal Marines respectively.

The first contact with the enemy came when the paras entered the area of Camilla Creek House to the north of the isthmus. Harrassing fire from Argentine 105-Pack howitzers fell along the likely axes of advance.

It was at first light that the paras also captured an Argentine patrol. The enemy had driven up in a blue and white Land Rover they had comandeered from Goose Green. It was a standing patrol that covered the tracks from Darwin and Burntside House to Camilla Creek. Captain Rod Bell RM, a Spanish-speaking officer attached to 2 Para for the operation, questioned the two uninjured prisoners. The officer, Lt Morales, was a professional who would give little away, while Private Pedro Galva knew little, although he was more talkative. Two men had attempted to escape from the patrol and had been wounded; one of them was a sergeant who had a round through his leg. Captain Hughes, the RMO, attended to them, and afterwards remarked that it was something of a relief that the first battle casualties that he had treated were Argentines.

Though 3 Brigade's orders were to raid Goose Green and Darwin, 2 Para opted for a full battalion attack. The attack went in at 0230 hours on 28 May. HMS *Arrow* fired on the first line of enemy positions and Support Company moved to establish a fire base overlooking the enemy's left flank.

The main assault began at 0635 when A Company moved against Burntside House. The buildings were raked with fire and although the battalion had been told that there were no civilians outside Goose Green and Darwin, the paras were surprised to find that a family of four 'kelpers' (locals), including a grandmother of nearly 80, had survived the onslaught. The Argentine platoon withdrew and their artillery fire began to drop across the neck of the isthmus. Flares fired from their mortars hung in the air, creating shadows and highlights. Meanwhile, outhouses set alight in the attack on Burntside House reflected in the water of Burntside Pond.

Having secured their left flank, 2 Para cleared the neck of land to the north-west of the Pond. B Company crossed their start line at 0710 hours and cleared two positions on high ground to the west of Burntside Pond. In Colonel Jones's plan D Company would pass through B to continue south. In fact, they came under small-arms fire from enemy positions that had been bypassed by B Company and they put in an immediate attack and destroyed these positions.

While this fighting was in progress, A Company moved south past Coronation Point, a small promontory north of Darwin. Here they dropped off a platoon to give covering fire as the remaining two platoons hooked round the small bay to attack Darwin from the west. Some 1500 yards north of Darwin Hill, the Main HQ with the RAP, Defence Platoon and Robert Fox of the BBC and David Norris of the Daily Mail were digging in as they came under fire from mortars and artillery. The RSM, Malcolm Simpson, was taking charge of a trickle of prisoners—which was later to grow much larger. The RMO was busy with both 2 Para and Argentine casualties.

Colonel Jones with his Tac HQ had followed the track that led to the front of Darwin Hill, coming up behind A Company. A Company were about to assault Port Darwin when they came under heavy machine-gun fire from positions to the west. Now began a deadly process of reducing positions on Darwin Hill with GPMGs and 66mm LAWs. The tactic with the LAW was simple but risky: the para prepared the weapon for firing and then had to kneel and expose his head and chest as he fired at the Argentine bunkers. (The blast from this small anti-tank weapon killed some enemy without leaving any marks.)

The two GPMGs of each section hammered away at Argentine positions until they stopped shooting back. As dawn came up, the Battalion realized that they had probably just brushed against the screen during the darkness and now they were about to encounter the main positions. HMS *Arrow* had departed at dawn; her Mark 8 4.5in gun had malfunctioned during the bombardment and she had been unable to give the full weight of gunfire that had been planned. The weather at sea prevented Harrier support, and winds across the isthmus made spotting for accurate artillery fire very difficult. Argentine artillery fire was still falling between the forward troops and their re-supply of ammunition. Some paras were finding unused boxed

7.62mm rifle ammunition in captured trenches and had started using it themselves.

Death of 'H' Jones

A Company fought for two and a half hours against well-sited positions. The machine guns were sited to fire on interlocking arcs, so that as men moved forward to engage one, they came under fire from another. It was important that the impetus of the attack was maintained. The paras were now very exposed, and if they did not keep moving forward, they would suffer greater casualties. The OC of A Company, with a small party that included the Adjutant and Company second-in-command, made an assault up Darwin Hill but fell back in the face of intense machine gun fire which killed two of the officers. Colonel Jones had at the same time moved into a small gully to the right with part of his Tac HQ to take out a second position. In this assault he was hit by another gun dug in along the high ground.

The manner of his death has been the subject of much discussion since the end of the Falklands war. Was it foolish to risk his life and therefore the whole operation—or was it in the finest traditions of leadership to be at the front and share the risks with the men he commanded? He had gone forward to command the battle from the front, and after a quick consultation with A Company, he decided to call for mortar fire to provide smoke to cover the attack across open ground. The smoke ran out as the Tac HQ was exposed on the open ground, and under these circumstances the logical movement was forward against the machine guns that would otherwise kill the men where they were. Moreover, there is a time in many battles when even a small assault put in with vigour can carry the day. The surviving men of Tac HQ were extricated by fire from two 66mm LAWs which neutralized the enemy trenches.

Back at Main HQ Major Chris Keeble was organizing the PoWs and casualties and the re-supply of ammunition. The Main HQ was under mortar and artillery fire, the explosions making black scars in the peat soil. The news of Colonel Jones's death came in a terse radio message: 'Sunray is down'. When it was transmitted, no one knew the extent of the Colonel's injuries, but the battalion second-in-command knew that in the seniority list that had been prepared before the landings, he was the man to take command if the Colonel was injured or killed.

After receiving reports from the Battery Commander who controlled the fire of the attached 105mm guns, and the Commanders of A and B Companies, Keeble realized that the most vulnerable area was the right flank. He ordered the OC of B Company to assume local command until he could reach the forward edge of the battle. B Company was in an exposed position pinned down on the forward edge of a slope overlooking the ruin called Boca House. Here, besides small arms fire, they were subject to artillery and mortar bombardment.

As the day moved into the afternoon, A Company secured Darwin Hill. By 1510hrs, 18 enemy were dead and 74 prisoners had been taken, including 39 wounded.

The OC of Support Company moved the fire base of the heavy weapons, which included the Milan anti-tank missiles, to a position to the rear of A and B Companies. D Company, which had reorganized after the night attack, were also brought forward to be ready to move through B Company as had been originally planned. B Company had adopted positions on the reverse slope out of the line of direct enemy fire.

Incredibly, as B Company extricated itself from its vulnerable position at Boca House, the men under fire retained a crazy sense of humour. The radio operator of 6 Platoon, Pte 'Beast' Kirkwood, was heard over the air to say 'Hello 2 this is 23 over'; 2 replied 'Send over' and received the request, '23 for … sake beam me up!'

While the rifle companies were redeploying for their planned attacks, the men at Main HQ and the 105mm guns at Camilla Creek House came under attack by Pucará ground-attack aircraft. Both aircraft were shot down by Blowpipe teams but not before they had shot down a Scout helicopter piloted by Lieutenant Richard Nunn RM. The loss of this machine caused a delay in helicopter operations.

Major Keeble moved D Company to the extreme right of the positions by Boca House, and 11 and 12 Platoons worked their way along the beach to a forming-up point for an assault south-eastwards against Boca House. They were to remark afterwards that H Hour (the time for the attack) had been determined by the incoming tide. It was a remarkable piece of straightforward fieldcraft, where the men had to crawl forward below the slope of the shore line.

Assault on Boca House

The assault on Boca House was supported by Milan anti-tank missiles and sustained-fire GPMGs. Pulverized by this firepower, the Argentine position collapsed and between 40 and 50 prisoners were taken. With Boca House and Darwin Hill captured, the battle again became fluid and the paras were quick to capitalize on their successes. A Company was ordered to bypass Darwin itself and consolidate on Darwin Hill where they would detach one platoon to C (Patrol) Company as it passed through their position to seize the bridge north of Goose Green. As this attack was in progress D Company (who decided afterwards that they had earned the nickname 'the sloggers') swung east and using cover began to close on Goose Green. B Company, reorganizing on Boca House, were ordered to swing round in a wider hook to take them south of the airfield and allow them to seize the high ground which dominated the settlement from the south. Meanwhile, Support Company established a new fire base on the left shoulder of Darwin Hill.

As D and C Companies, and a platoon from A Company, closed in on Goose Green, the fighting became confused. A minefield deflected D Company from its axis. The sight of mine packing cases and associated refuse gave some indication of this obstacle. Afterwards senior Argentine officers admitted that they had no idea where the fields were laid—the job had been done by a corporal.

However, D Company had other problems besides mines—the 35mm and 20mm anti-aircraft guns emplaced around the airfield were switched to a ground role. These guns had earlier claimed two Harriers during attacks, though one pilot was subsequently rescued after he had evaded capture by the Argentines and awaited the outcome of the fighting at Goose Green and Darwin.

As C Company passed through A Company and moved down towards the bridge, they entered an exposed area of farmland that had been ruefully nicknamed by the paras 'the billiard table'. Here they came under heavy artillery, mortar and AA-gun fire. C (Patrol) Company HQ was almost wiped out on the forward slope of Darwin Hill. It was at this time that 'the white flag' incident took place. Attacking the trenches in front of the school house, Lieutenant Jim Barry of D Company saw a white flag over Argentine positions. He went forward to take the surrender of the position and then, according to Robert Fox, a British machine gun on the right opened fire. It was answered by an Argentine machine gun and Lieutenant Barry and two NCOs were killed. Fox wrote, 'Those at the scene do not think that this was deliberate treachery, with the white flag being used as a decoy'. Barry and the two NCOs were not the only men to die during the campaign attempting to save lives on both sides by persuading the enemy to surrender.

Combined assault

In a combined assault by C (Patrol) Company and D Company the school house was destroyed by a mix of M79 and WP grenades and LMG fire. It burned down and the Patrols Platoon of C Company remarked afterwards that this 'pleased the local kids no end'. The attack on the school house was put in by 14 men of Patrols Platoon with Captain John Greenhalgh of the Army Air Corps. About three Argentine platoons had defended the school house area and it is impossible to estimate how many men died in the explosion and subsequent fire in the building.

When the fighting at the school house was over, D Company came under attack first by two A4 Skyhawks and then by two Pucarás. The second attack included rockets and napalm, the only occasion this weapon was used by the Argentine Air Force. Three canisters were dropped, but fortunately they missed. Captain Rod Bell RM remembers a lone para, possibly a runner, hardly glancing back over his shoulder as the napalm burst in its orange and black explosion.

One Pucará came down when a Blowpipe missile, fired by a Royal Marine, took its wing off. The pilot was killed. The second aircraft fell to the small-arms fire of B and D Companies. The pilot baled out and was captured.

At 1925 a strike by three RAF Harrier GR3s hit the Argentine positions with BL755 cluster bombs and cannon fire. The attack arrived at an opportune time, giving Argentine morale a severe battering and silencing an Oerlikon 35mm AA gun on the seaward end of Goose Green.

At 2010, as darkness came on, an Argentine Chinook and six UH1B (Huey) helicopters were observed landing half a mile south of Goose Green, where troops were seen to disembark. Artillery fire was called up and B Company moved into a blocking position.

The paras settled down for a third night without sleep. A patrol by the paras cleared Darwin at night and discovered from Brooke Hardcastle, the manager at Darwin, that 114 civilians were held in the community hall at Goose Green. Earlier, Major Keeble had decided that he would, if necessary, call for an artillery bombardment of Goose Green rather than lose men in house-to-house fighting. The information that civilians were being held in the settlement changed his plans.

Keeble had requested 2000 rounds of 105mm ammunition, three more guns and six 81mm mortars. Brigadier Julian Thompson ordered forward Juliet Company from 42 Commando and told Major Keeble to halt and reorganize. In the night Captain Greenhalgh, with his crewman Sergeant Kalinsky, evacuated casualties and brought forward stores. He had been adopted by the battalion on the journey southwards, but detached after they landed at San Carlos. Hearing their requests for helicopter support, he had flown even though he was not equipped with night-flying aids. The helicopter pilots were widely respected for their conduct of hazardous operations which saved many lives by timely evacuation.

Negotiations for surrender

Realizing that he would have to negotiate the evacuation of the civilians, Major Keeble asked the Brigadier if contact could be made with the Argentine garrison in Goose Green to allow negotiations in the morning. This was done through a shortwave radio link between two farm managers, Allan Miller in Port San Carlos and Eric Goss, the manager at Goose Green. The Brigadier confirmed that the Argentines would receive a delegation in the morning.

Major Keeble proposed giving the enemy commander two options. The first was to surrender. The second was to accept the military consequences but to release the civilians. These were siege negotiations in an almost medieval tradition. Shrewdly, two Argentine Warrant Officers were chosen to go forward under a white flag. They did not seem too enthusiastic about their task and were told that, if they did not return, it would be assumed that the Argentine garrison had accepted the military consequences and would fight.

With the dawn, the two Argentine NCOs returned to announce that the enemy garrison would talk. A small party set off towards the airfield composed of Major Keeble, Major Rice (the Battery Commander) Major Hector Gullan (the liaison officer with 3 Bde HQ), Captain Rod Bell as interpreter and Corporal Shaw, the radio operator. The acting CO of the Battalion had requested that the two journalists join the party as civilian witnesses. They left their webbing and helmets behind in order to look as unwarlike as possible. At the airfield, in a corrugated iron shed, the talking began. On the Argentine side were representatives of the three arms. A naval officer introduced the senior officer, Air Vice Commodore Wilson Dosier Pedroza; the army representative was Lieutenant Colonel Italo Piaggi.

Finally the talking ended and the surrender was accepted. The Vice Commodore addressed his men, formed up in an open square, and then before they were dismissed they discarded their belts and helmets, as well as the rifles they had put down. There were about 250 air force men on parade. Assuming the same number of army and special forces, this would make up the battalion strength predicted by Intelligence. The parade was orderly and ended with a rendering of the Argentine national anthem.

It was then that the paras had a real surprise. More men began to emerge from the houses. Some of these men were from 12 Infantry Regiment, which had been flown in to reinforce the garrison. They were less disciplined, and after they had been formed up the British officers counted between 900 and 1000 men. On the order to ground arms, many of the men cheerfully threw their weapons down, happy that the fighting was over.

For the Paras the liberation of Goose Green had a curiously English ending. The 114 civilians who had been locked up in the community hall since 1 May—the day of the first Harrier attack—emerged to offer their liberators biscuits, sweets and tea in Falkland Islands Royal Wedding mugs.

2 Para suffered 18 fatalaties, including Lt Nunn RM, and 35 wounded. The Argentine casualties were reported as 250 killed and about 150 wounded. However, a Spanish-speaking eyewitness to the battle says that confusion arose when Major Frontera, second-in-command of 12 Rgt, and Vice Commodore Costa spoke of 250 men 'missing'. This was mis-translated. The burial service for the Argentine dead—a ceremony made grim by heavy rain which flooded the mass grave—would indicate fewer than

250. This in no way detracts from the bravery of 2 Para. They won a battle when the odds were stacked in favour of the Argentine defenders.

End of an ordeal

In the final stages of 2 Para's assault on Goose Green, Major Chris Keeble was preparing to flatten the tiny settlement's houses with artillery; the object, to soften up the Argentine garrison for recapture and avoid heavy casualties to his own men.

But at the last moment, as extra guns were being flown to Camilla Creek to mount the barrage, a message came through from Brooke Hardcastle, the Falklands Islands Company manager at Darwin. It informed Keeble that well over 100 islanders were imprisoned in the community hall at Goose Green. Their chances of surviving an artillery barrage were minimal. Keeble had to think again.

Back in early April, soon after the Argentine invasion, Goose Green had been placed under the command of Air Vice Commodore Wilson Dosier Pedroza and a hard-line army officer named Piaggi. Both were deeply suspicious of the islanders. On 1 May, after the first strike by Harriers on the Goose Green airstrip, the officers decided to imprison the entire community in one place to minimize the risk of clandestine signals being sent to the Task Force. The deserted houses could then be used by officers.

The community hall was the obvious choice of prison: 80ft long by 40ft wide, it was the largest inhabitable building in the settlement.

Using a security meeting to discuss air raid precautions as a pretext, the Argentines brusquely herded the 114 islanders out of their homes at 0900. Some were half-dressed, some still wore their slippers, and one old lady hadn't had time to put her dentures in. That first day they remained locked up without food—or explanations. In the evening they eventually received some tinned provisions. That night they had to sleep on the floor without bedding, in their clothes. An armed guard was posted outside at all times. If the islanders asked why they were being imprisoned, they were fobbed off with comments such as 'for your own safety'.

On the second day, the islanders were allowed to fetch bedding from their own homes. They began to organize themselves: blankets were hung up to partition the space into family areas, and mattresses were laid out on the floor.

A catering corps was established, and each day, two of its members, always women, were escorted to the store to collect the daily rations. Towards the end of the month's captivity, food ran critically short.

In a last-minute orgy of vandalism before 2 Para arrived, the Argentine officers who occupied islanders' houses smashed up furniture, ornaments and radios. The inhabitants of Goose Green returned to homes in which floors, baths, even chests of drawers had been used as lavatories. In some cases, excrement was plastered around the walls. In the store, cameras, jewellery and watches had been looted. The manager's house had been occupied by 34 Argentines, who had slept in the beds with their boots on, plundered the garden, put a 40-gallon oil drum in the bath and relieved themselves on the bedroom floor.

One good thing may have come out of the islanders' ordeal. Their presence in the wooden jail could just have helped persuade the Argentine officers that they could discuss surrender with honour once 2 Para had surrounded the settlement, so averting further bloodshed.

Five Brigade at South Georgia

The journey south on *QE2* was a voyage into the unknown for 5 Brigade, not least because they were aboard Britain's premier merchant ship. Her vulnerability dictated that she steer a course for South Georgia rather than the Total Exclusion Zone.

ON 27 MAY, after a two-week voyage, *QE2* arrived at Grytviken in South Georgia, her great bulk dwarfing the long-stay vessels in the harbour.

Five Brigade had set sail from Southampton in *QE2* on 12 May but, unlike 3 Brigade, did not stop at Ascension, which was merely seen as a blur on the horizon. Then, on 22 May, with the *QE2* now south of Ascension, the Brigade was placed on Active Service. This meant not only introducing the necessary drills of darkening ship and manning the ship's anti-aircraft defences, but was also important from the legal point of view.

Indeed, this procedure was laid down by the Army Act 1955, since some offences such as desertion in the face of the enemy only applied to Active Service. This is a standard drill carried out at all times when British troops are likely to be involved in armed conflict.

The long journey south gave officers and men ample opportunity to think about and discuss the task that lay ahead. Inevitably there were nerves, heightened perhaps by the unreality of the setting. Browning machine guns looked out of place among the perfumery boutiques of the shopping arcade. Every day the Gurkhas, wearing life jackets and full battle dress, plunged into the icy waters of the swimming pools to accustom themselves to the freezing weather that lay ahead.

Concern at Northwood

Throughout *QE2*'s passage south, Task Force Headquarters at Northwood had been very conscious of her status as the premier British merchant ship. Should she be lost, especially to enemy action, the blow to prestige and morale would be incalculable. Hence, great efforts had been made to keep her exact whereabouts secret during the voyage, and it was for this reason that she did not put into Ascension.

Allowing *QE2* to enter the Total Exclusion Zone (TEZ) would put her at even greater risk and was, therefore, unacceptable. Admiral Sir John Fieldhouse ordered *QE2* to make for South Georgia, now back in British hands, and once there, the intention was to transfer 5 Brigade to other ships.

Meanwhile, the landings at San Carlos had taken place and a firm beach-head established in the teeth of fierce attacks by the Argentine Air Force. *Canberra* and *Norland* had been in the thick of the action, and both had experienced near misses from Argentine bombs. During the day of the landings, 21 May, both ships had taken aboard casualties, and *Canberra* had also received the survivors of HMS *Ardent*. The original plan was for *Canberra* to remain at San Carlos to de-store and then convert to a rest and recreation ship, but in view of the air threat, it was decided that both she and *Norland* were too vulnerable. Both were therefore ordered to dis-embark their remaining troops and slip anchor by midnight.

This done, they retired to a position 170 nautical miles NE by E of Port Stanley and transshipped the balance of their stores to RFA *Resource* on the 23rd. They remained here until the 25th, when they received orders to rendezvous with *QE2* off South Georgia. In fact, the signal giving these orders was not actually received on *Canberra* until she arrived off South Georgia, but Captain Burne, Senior Naval Officer on board *Canberra*, anticipated the move from his reading of the situation.

At lunchtime on Thursday 27 May, the two ships anchored at Grytviken, having previously identified themselves to the Royal Marine Garrison on shore.

Almost immediately after the two ships dropped anchor, the converted trawlers of 11 Mine Countermeasure Squadron (MCM), which had been detailed to carry out the transfer of 5 Brigade from *QE2*, came alongside. *QE2* had been expected that morning, but had sent a signal to say that she was held up by thick fog and ice and would not arrive until that evening, which she did at 2000 hours.

The plan was for the Scots and Welsh Guards, with Brigade supporting arms and services, to cross-deck to *Canberra* while the Gurkhas went on board *Norland*. At the same time, the casualties and survivors on these two ships would be transferred to *QE2* which would take them back to Ascension. For those on *Canberra* there was some speculation as to why she and not the *QE2* was to return to 'Bomb Alley' and, without knowledge of the real reason, the general consensus was that *Canberra* was not experienced as an assault ship and, being a little smaller, was more manoeuvrable in the narrow waters of Falkland Sound.

However, everyone recognized the urgency, and transshipping began that very night. While the ships of II MCM ferried the troops across, the heavy stores and equipment were transferred by helicopter. It was a hectic time, and no one got much sleep for the next 24 hours.

Transfer of survivors

The final task was a poignant one, the transfer of the survivors of *Ardent* from *Canberra* to *Leeds Castle*, which was to take them across to *QE2*. Dressed mainly in white boiler suits supplied by *Canberra*, 177 of them climbed down onto the *Leeds Castle* flight deck, watched by the crew of *Canberra*.

The Royal Marines Band played all the tunes that those on *Canberra* had come to know so well during the long voyage south, and in reply the *Ardent* survivors sang that well-known rugby song beloved of every Devonport sailor, the 'Oggie Song'.

Now came the moment for *Canberra* and *Norland* to weigh anchor and proceed towards the 'sound of battle'. For the crews of both ships, it was 'more of the same', but for 5 Brigade it was the start of a voyage into the unknown.

The long tab, the long yomp

The good news was that the men of 45 Commando and 3 Para were to break out of the bridgehead. The bad news was that they were to do it by forced march, across punishing terrain. Charles Lawrence of the *Sunday Telegraph* accompanied them; this is his account.

LIEUTENANT COLONEL Andrew Whitehead, commanding officer of 45 Commando, Royal Marines, came striding up the steep slope overlooking Ajax Bay, picking his way between slit trenches. He had come from an 'O' Group with his company commanders and HQ staff, a tight circle of well-camouflaged men blending into the scrub further down the hill. His face bore its familiar determined set.

Colonel Whitehead settled for a moment in the bracken and said, 'Well, we're breaking out. We'll be leaving first thing tomorrow. That's the good news. The bad news is that we're yomping.'

Yomping. As a Falklands correspondent, I had been with the Marines long enough to know what the word meant. It meant marching: a forced march, carrying everything a 650-man Commando needs to live and fight. I had yet to experience the full flavour of the effort that word now conjures.

'How far are we going?'

'About 21 miles, to start with.'

That didn't sound too bad, calculated against a limited memory of country walks. 'That's fine, we'll come along. We can hack it.'

This last boast in the military's own language caused the colonel's clipped moustache to rise in one of his ironic smiles. He seemed to know something I didn't.

Hostile terrain

Yomping—'tabbing' to the paras—turned out to be punishingly hard. It was partly the terrain. The Falklands consist almost entirely of hilly, marshy moorland. You can climb all the way to the top of a mountain, and at the top you will find more ankle-sapping sludge between the rocks. And then there is the grass itself. Called 'tussock', it grows in clumps on the soft, peaty earth, trying to twist the ankle at every step. Every yard of a march requires a concentrated effort.

On top of this, there is the weight. Men of 45 Commando set out carrying their full packs as well as weapons and 'fighting order', the complex of webbing and pouches carrying ammunition, water bottles, trenching tools and enough gear to survive at least 24 hours. This kit could weigh up to 140lbs, and the 'bootnecks' had to hump it all through the mud, marsh, rocks and darkness.

The march began on 27 May, six days after we had run up the beaches on to East Falkland for the D-Day landings. The battle of Bomb Alley had raged continuously over the landing beaches, but now the intensity of the Argentine air attacks was easing. About 100 of our men died, mostly on the ships, but we estimated that as many as 70 Argentine jets had already been shot down.

The helicopters that, in the original plans, would have been ferrying troops of 3 Commando Brigade across the island had been lost in *Atlantic Conveyor* on 25 May. But the pressure on the brigade's leader, Brigadier Julian Thompson, to advance from the bridgehead, to start getting results, had been relentlessly building up from London. On 26 May he was ordered to move with whatever means were available.

The means of transport available was, in Thompson's own favourite phrase, the LPC. The Leather Personnel Carrier—the boot.

In the early hours of 27 May, well before dawn at 1100 hours London time, some 2500 men of the élite Royal Marines and the Parachute Regiment began to lace up their boots with that little bit of extra care. Then they shouldered their kit and formed restlessly into company marching order.

Two Para filed off Sussex Mountains and headed south towards Darwin and Goose Green. Three Para, who had taken Port San Carlos Settlement on D-Day, headed straight out east and slightly north from their trenches by the settlement. They were to follow the direct route to Teal Inlet on the east of the island, which lay half-way to Port Stanley. Meanwhile, 45 Commando were to take the most northerly route, the long way round, clearing Douglas Settlement before yomping on to Teal behind the paras.

These last two units set the style for the epic march. They always remained ahead of any available helicopter lift, and in the end they yomped all the way to Stanley. They fought battles, too, but at the end of the campaign it was the march which gave them a special distinction.

Lt Col Hew Pike, CO of 3 Para, a lithe and energetic man who runs marathons for fun, had scrounged some transport while his unit was dug in at Port San Carlos. He persuaded the local farmers to hitch trailers to their tractors and follow them over to Teal carrying some of the heavier equipment, including the back-packs.

He kept his men in basic fighting order and took advantage of the light weight they were carrying to set a blistering pace along the trail through the hills. It seemed as if the paras were on a fast patrol rather than a route march of over 20 miles. Their approach was typical of the paras: they charged in, suffered badly, but, apart from a few twisted ankles and exposure cases, nearly all of them finished the march ready to fight.

On Ajax Hill there was just time to brew a 'wet', as the marines called any kind of drink, and stuff away sleeping bags, poncho ground sheets and hexamine stoves before 45 Commando left for the jetty down by the refrigeration plant in the Bay that had become the field hospital and logistics base for the Brigade

We had to cross San Carlos Water and round Hospital Head to the paras' base at Port San Carlos using landing craft, before we could move along the route over Cushy's Hill. Inevitably, the operation conformed to the military maxim, 'hurry up and wait'. The LCUs, always busy in the struggle to get the shipping unloaded in the midst of the air raids, were late. Half that day's meagre eight hours of light had passed by the time 45 were on their way across the Falklands.

As if in a farewell gesture from Bomb Alley, the air raid sirens sounded as we were splashing across the water. The marines, never keen to go down without a fight, promptly lined the stately tub with machine guns and clambered on to the wheelhouse roof with Blowpipe missiles. In the middle of it all, a sergeant handed out mail and for a few moments we could shut out the war as we crouched below our water-proof hoods, lost in a letter from home.

Boggy peat and wet boots

Routes across the Falklands are marked clearly on the maps, but they are not marked on the landscape. An occasional scar in the marsh from the wheels of tractors points the way, but otherwise the tracks are no more than the easiest route over the ground. You find your way from reference points: jagged rocks, peaks or a line of fencing marking settlement boundaries.

It was such a track that 45 Commando followed that first day. After no more than a mile, up the hill from Port San Carlos, legs and shoulders began to feel the strain, and the laden bootnecks were breathing hard through open mouths.

The day was clear enough, but the peat was horribly boggy. Leather army boots, fitted with canvas spats, could hold out the surface water, but as they sank into the mud the damp soon crept through. There were no dry feet after the first few miles.

Distance is deceptive on the open moorland. A peak could look a mile away, but in fact was four or five. We slogged on, the Volvo-tracked snow vehicles carrying radio gear and ammunition grinding slowly up the hills with HQ company. After an hour, we could still see San Carlos Water as an air raid struck home, sending belches of black smoke into the sky. Later we learnt that bombs had hit the refrigeration plant and men from 45 Commando had died, their first dead of the campaign.

By now the Commando was spread out over three or more miles in a heaving, struggling column. The rifle companies were in front, spread on each side of the route, each man keeping at least ten yards from his neighbour. This was a precaution against air attack—with no cover, the column was critically vulnerable to strikes by Argentine Pucará ground-attack aircraft.

The first casualties came surprisingly soon—caused not by enemy attack but by the ground. Twisted ankles, pulled muscles, and even a sudden asthma attack. They were left by the trail to be picked up and squeezed on to the heavily laden Volvos. Soon men were clinging to the sides of the vehicles, hitching a lift for a few yards or nursing minor injuries. Once, we had to pause to call in a helicopter to evacuate a suffering bootneck.

Most of the men looked utterly miserable at being left behind, as if they had failed the course for their Green Beret. The senior NCOs and officers would bark at them but always with a veiled sympathy for the injured.

'Bottle', said the RSM, Pat Chapman. 'That's what it is, lack of bottle.'

The pace was agonizingly slow. Every delay took its toll—a man hurt or a Volvo stuck, a stream to be waded or an air raid warning to be waited out lying on the turf.

Colour Sergeant Bill Eades, a man never lost for a colourful phrase to be bellowed out at drill-sergeant volume, remarked: 'Don't know about the assault on Stanley, looks to me more bloody like the retreat from Moscow.'

It seemed to take an eternity to cover the first ten miles and darkness was falling when Lt Col Whitehead—yomping at the front—called a halt for 'scran' (a meal).

Hungrily, we broke open ration packs and struggled to light the primitive hexamine stoves. I was desperate for a hot drink, but just as I put the mess tin on to the flame, an air raid warning sent out the order to kill all lights.

So it was without hot food that the column moved off again into the dusk. We waded another stream, miserable at the thought that at night the chances of drying out were low. We stumbled along for another six hours.

Last hurdle to Stanley

We got as far as Newhouse, a shepherd's summer base, now deserted. There was time for a few hours' sleep, and most of us fell to the ground in our sleeping bags, not bothering with the intricate business of rigging up a shelter on an open moor.

Then it rained. Everybody was soaked. Even the marines, who so far had scarcely seemed to notice the hardship, looked miserable. Col Whitehead appeared as we rolled up our sodden bags. 'Sense of humour still intact?' he asked.

Bill Eades, as usual, had the answer. 'Humour? You've got to laugh, or you would bloody well cry.'

The forward units of 3 Para had reached Teal that first night and as 45 Commando strode into Douglas, finding that an enemy patrol just left, Hew Pike was leading his men towards Estancia House, huddled at the base of the mountains, and the last hurdle to Stanley.

Two nights and a day were spent resting at Douglas by 45 Commando. The locals, recovering from being locked in the little Community Hall and clearing up their looted homes, helped to fire up peat stoves to dry us out. Senior NCOs inspected dozens of feet—some were white and puffy in the first stage of trench foot—and had us digging trenches, just in case. It finally stopped raining.

That first yomp proved to be the hardest. The terrain was at its worst, and from now on Lt Col Whitehead made sure we would march without the burdensome back-packs, even if it meant nights without the luxuries packed inside.

The path to Teal was much easier. The temperature stayed at zero all day, freezing the mud to a hard surface, while the marines, trained in Norway, had no fear of the blizzards.

Most of the paras had moved through Teal—a settlement boasting some of the few trees to survive on the Falklands—by the time we filed in that evening. To the west, Goose Green had fallen in the first major land battle of the war, and the assault down the northern route seemed unstoppable.

But we were way ahead of our supply lines and getting dangerously close to the Argentines' main defences in the hills around Stanley. Brigadier Thompson decided to call a halt. It is testimony to the determination of the advance that he had to fly across the island in person to stop 3 Para at Estancia.

A helicopter lift was promised 45 Commando from Teal to our next stop, the assault base for Stanley on Mount Kent and just within sight of Stanley. The mountain had been cleared by the SAS and 42 Commando and a 105mm battery had been flown into position there.

The prospect of an airlift brought sighs of relief from the weary bootnecks. This was more like modern war. But the weather closed in and after a day's delay the Commando was back on its feet.

The sun was shining as we left Teal Inlet, the view over the water towards the foot of Mount Longdon in the distance breathtaking in the clear light. It was a steady yomp and we had passed the paras at Estancia by the time we made camp for the night.

The last day of the yomp started badly. We were shaken from our sleeping bags well before dawn and sent off down the track before we could brew tea or light a cigarette, neither of these luxuries being allowed in darkness. We had to walk for two hours before a half-hour breakfast stop was called. Little things like that make all the difference.

But Bill Eades found the words to encourage his boys: 'The only way out of this bastard is through Stanley, so let's get on with it!'

When we reached the camp on Mount Kent on the afternoon of 6 June, greeted by a howling blizzard, 45 Commando had covered some 60 miles from Port San Carlos. It had been a gruelling march, and from now on there was not so much as a hut or a peat stove to provide comfort in the deepening winter.

It is fitting that, in the end, when the Argentines ran up the white flags, 45 Commando and 3 Para yomped the final few miles into Stanley.

Taking Mount Kent

When the Brigade Commander said 'Go!', they went—2 Para to Goose Green and glory, 3 Para and 45 Commando on their epic yomp across East Falkland. But it was 42 Commando who saw Port Stanley first—from the summit of Mount Kent.

ON 1 JUNE the first British artillery shells landed on the outskirts of Port Stanley: they were fired from the back of Mount Kent by a gun battery attached to 42 Commando. It was an exhilarating moment. Less than a week after the landings at San Carlos a major British unit was literally within striking distance of the ultimate objective. How they got there, and how they dominated the area, is a story as important as any in the campaign—even if Goose Green, the long march, and the sinking of the big ships were the features that seized the world's headlines at the time.

Back on 25 May, Brigadier Julian Thompson had been ordered to break out of the San Carlos beach-head. Reluctantly, unhappily, he had issued his orders: 2 Para were to go for Goose Green; 3 Para and 45 Commando were to march west to Douglas and Teal Inlet; 40 Commando were to remain at the beach-head in case of an enemy counter-attack. And 42 Commando? There was only one way left for them to go—south-east, towards Stanley.

It was fortunate, in this respect, that the SAS had set up a forward patrol base on Mount Kent, from which they had been operating for some time.

In the chain of high ground that runs eastwards from San Carlos, there are a number of peaks that give a good view of the surrounding country. Whoever holds these peaks can dominate the area. Mount Kent, at the extreme eastern end, is 1400ft high. It overlooks Mount Challenger to the south and is substantially higher than Two Sisters and Longdon to the east. In effect it is the key to the whole chain, and indeed to the eastern approaches to Stanley.

By 27 May the mountain was more or less under their control. Even more fortunate was the fact that the Argentine 12 Regiment had been helicoptered to Goose Green—although 2 Para were less than happy to find them there. It was a rare chance to move forward and seize the initiative over the Argentines—possibly to dominate high ground to the west of Stanley. The problem was, how to get 500 men that far forward in one fell swoop?

The answer was to fly them in. But how? Helicopters were more highly prized than almost anything else in the Falklands. There were not many of them, and they were all being used to ferry stores and casualities around. For two days Brigade HQ struggled with the arithmetic; some 500 men; Sea Kings with a capacity of 27—at a pinch; 20 helicopter lifts in all. And there were the guns and mortars and food, and extra ammunition and Milan anti-tank weapons and extra Milan ammunition to be considered.

There are some risks that simply must be taken. It was finally decided that K Company of 42 would fly in and seize the mountain top on the night of 30 May. This plan was foiled by a total whiteout created by the severe driving snow. Then next night they tried again—and succeeded. Two colonels—Nick Vaux of 42 and Mike Rose of the SAS—crammed into two helicopters with the rest of K Company and flew in. Two hours later the sole RAF Chinook brought up a 105mm gun battery and 300 rounds. The summit was in British hands and all that could be done was to wait for either reinforcements, an enemy artillery strike or a counter-attack.

Hedge-hopping across no man's land

It was the reinforcements which arrived. On the night of 1 June, Lt Commander Simon Thornewill led the Sea Kings back to Mount Kent with the rest of the Commando. Wearing Passive Night Goggles (PNGs) the pilots literally hedge-hopped across the no man's land in the centre of the island. Sticking to below 20ft, they made it in successive lifts, and deposited the men, company by company, on the LZ partly sheltered from Port Stanley and the Argentines' big guns by the mountain.

One company was missing—'Juliet', the composite force made up of odds and sods, and the men of Naval Party 8901 who had last seen Port Stanley on 3 April. Juliet, under the command of Major Mike Norman, were now veterans, after the fierce fire-fight at Port Stanley. It was possibly for this reason that they were tasked to assist 2 Para at Goose Green. On 28 May they were flown forward in response to a request from 2 Para's acting CO, Major Chris Keeble, for extra firepower during the planned dawn attack on 29 May. The attack didn't go in, as the Argentines surrendered.

For the rest of 42 Commando, the war became a period of great boredom, punctuated with the odd artillery 'stonk' from the Argentine guns in Stanley. The main enemy was not, in fact, the Argentines but the weather. The men of 42 are trained in Arctic warfare and the techniques of survival in a hostile environment; they were to need every scrap of knowledge and experience as they shivered and huddled on the top of the mountain. Strangely enough, the lower the temperature—when there is snow on the ground—the more comfortable it is possible to become. When the temperature hovers around freezing point, ice melts and men get wet. And the wet is the real killer. Dry men, so long as they are sheltered from the wind and can huddle in their sleeping bags to keep warm, can remain in the open almost indefinitely. Wet men cannot. They begin to suffer from exposure, hypothermia, trench foot—all the classic horror stories from mountain rescue operations.

Under these circumstances every bit of equipment came into play: Wellington boots or plastic bin liners kept feet dry—and so did the rubberized overboots issued with NBC defence suits. Waterproofs were worn at all times, elaborate bivouacs were fashioned from ponchos and ground sheets—and patrols were sent out all the time.

The patrols were a vital part of the intelligence-gathering programme. Many were simply reconnaissance patrols—a small party of men who would creep into the countryside to watch for enemy positions and identify obstacles. Not a few were fighting patrols, sent out with the express purpose of looking for trouble. Such forays were always nerve-racking. The patrol might set an ambush for unwary Argentines, or they would attack an Argentine position that was lightly defended. Their purpose was to wear the enemy down and, if possible, bring back information about their strengths, weaknesses, numbers, locations, firepower and morale. There were inevitable casualties. Someone had to find out where the minefields were, and the incredibly brave sappers and assault engineers who probed their way through these minefields are perhaps the least appreciated heroes of the entire campaign. The information they brought back was invaluable, their rewards few beyond the satisfaction of knowing that not many others could do this sort of job.

Securing the range

While Mount Kent was the main base for 42 Commando, the unit spread far and wide over the surrounding hills. They secured Mount Challenger to the south-west, Mount Wall, and—most important—Bluff Cove Peak, a feature to the west of Mount Kent which overlooks the low ground near Estancia House. It was here, on 1 June, after their epic march, that 3 Para set up their headquarters and patrol base. Three days later, on 4 June, 42 were joined by an even more footsore 45 Commando. With these three units dug in around Mount Kent, the eastern approaches to Menendez' defences around Port Stanley were secure. Julian Thompson's 3 Commando Brigade now firmly controlled the north and north-west side of the island.

This move of 42's was a daring stroke, and one that made the long march possible. If the Argentine 12th Regiment had still been on Mount Kent, if 3 Para and 45 Commando had been forced to fight their way on to the high ground, if 2 Para hadn't drawn the Argentines to the west and Goose Green, the story might have been entirely different. Certainly the war would have gone on much longer. The taking of Mount Kent was one of the most important actions of the war, though it has received little appreciation as such. Perhaps it was the success of Julian Thompson's initiative that tempted his fellow Brigade Commander Tony Wilson to try the same thing again at Fitzroy.

On reflection, the only reason why the helicopter lift to Mount Kent was unique was because there were so few helicopters. Had *Atlantic Conveyor* survived with her Chinooks and Wessexes, the entire brigade could have been moved by helicopter. The fact that they were able to tab—or yomp—when they had to merely emphasized the men's adaptability. If 42 thought they were lucky in not yomping, they were wrong. They had the mountain to contend with.

Five Brigade ashore

The arrival of 5 Brigade in the Falklands added greatly to the punch of British land forces; it added to their organizational problems, too. As ever in war, getting the right people in the right place, on time, proved unexpectedly difficult.

ON 1 JUNE the land forces on East Falkland received the major reinforcement they had been waiting for. The Fifth Infantry Brigade, which had sailed from the United Kingdom in *QE2*, landed without mishap at San Carlos. Admiral Fieldhouse, Commander of the Task Force operations in the South Atlantic, could not risk a prize target like *QE2* in San Carlos Water, or for that matter inside the Total Exclusion Zone. So, on arrival at South Georgia on 27 May, the Brigade had been cross-decked to *Canberra* and *Norland* with the help of the ships of 11 Mine Countermeasures Squadron. The operation took two days, and the Brigade sailed into San Carlos Water on 31 May. First off the next day were 1/7th Gurkhas from *Norland*; after came 2nd Bn Scots Guards and 1st Bn Welsh Guards from *Canberra*.

Ashore, the tactical situation was still fairly simple. In the north, 45 Commando and 3 Para had completed their epic 50-mile 'yomp', securing Douglas Settlement and Teal Inlet on 30 May. In the south, 2 Para had fought their famous action at Goose Green, thereby removing the Argentine threat to the south, while 42 Commando, making maximum use of available helicopters, had seized Mount Kent and Mount Challenger on the western approaches to Stanley. Major General Jeremy Moore had also formally taken over command of the land forces from Brigadier Julian Thompson, and was now planning the thrust on Port Stanley.

General Moore informed Brigadier Wilson, Commander of 5 Brigade, that his task would be to take the southern route to Port Stanley, and that for this purpose he was to take under his command 2 Para, now in the process of sorting themselves and their prisoners out at Goose Green. Brigadier Thompson's 3 Commando Brigade would cover the centre and northern approaches, thereby producing three simultaneous thrusts on Stanley.

2 JUNE 1982

Paras move on Fitzroy

It was one of the most remarkable advances of the whole campaign – and it all hung on one phone call. In the Falklands you don't find a phone box on every corner. The nearest to 2 Para was 20 miles away, and there was no guarantee that it was working.

FLEET STREET made much of Wilson's 50p telephone call. Brigadier Tony Wilson of 5 Brigade, it was said, had made a 50p call from a telephone box to find out whether Fitzroy was still occupied by Argentine forces before advancing. But in reality, there were no telephone boxes in the Falklands, and the 50p coin is not part of the islands' currency. A telephone call was made but not by Brigadier Wilson. So much for the myth...

After their victory at Goose Green, 2 Para were allowed to rest for four days, and they were given the chance to spend one night each in a shack which soon became known as the R and R—Rest and Recreation—Centre.

Bluff Cove and Fitzory were the paras' next objective. They lie southwest of Port Stanley on a deeply indented coastline. Fitzroy straddles a small headland that juts out eastward into the South Atlantic. Bluff Cove is on a small natural harbour, and the two communities are linked by a narrow bridge that crosses the inlet of the eight- to ten-mile-long bay of Port Fitzroy. The track from Darwin crosses that bridge. To bypass it would take vehicles up into the rocky foothills of the mountain chain that runs across the northern part of East Falkland.

The paras had special interest in the enemy strength in this area. In an analysis prepared in Buenos Aires, the Argentine intelligence staff had listed Fitzroy as a possible landing site for British forces. It was close to Port Stanley and would offer the British the opportunity to make a fast attack over little more than 30 miles into the capital of the islands. General

Menendez would have had good reason to deploy troops to cover this prospective landing site. So before moving ahead again, 2 Para needed further intelligence on the enemy's movements and disposition.

It was Brooke Hardcastle, the Falkland Islands Company manager at Goose Green, who suggested that a phone call might prove fruitful. The lines from Goose Green were down but the telephone at Swan Inlet might still be connected, he said.

Swan Inlet is a 20-mile march along the coast, half-way from Goose Green to Fitzroy. But it is a fairly hard slog over soft ground. So a heliborne reconnaissance with armed escorts of Scouts with SSII missiles was proposed to 5 Brigade, who now commanded 2 Para. Brig Wilson gave the go-ahead and B Company was assigned the operation. One troop-carrying Scout would be used, along with two missile-armed escorts. When they arrived at Swan Inlet, Major John Crosland of B Company ordered the escort to fire their missiles close to the house there. If there were any enemy in the area, this would dissuade them from retaliating, he reasoned. Four SSII exploded around the house and the paras landed and raced towards the building. There was no enemy, in fact there was no one about at all, so Colour Sergeant Morris broke a window and climbed in. He found the phone and wound its handle twice—that was the code for Swan Inlet.

The famous phone call

His call was answered by a teenage girl who fetched her father, islander Ron Binney. The conversation between the para and the manager was guarded until they established that there were no Argentine forces in the area. Binney said that they had left after demolishing the bridge.

While this famous telephone conversation was in progress, 2 Para were completing the handover of Goose Green to the men of the 1/7th Gurkha Rifles. They would garrison the area and clear the peninsula of Lafonia to the south.

When Major Crosland returned to Goose Green with the news that Fitzroy was clear, Brig Wilson saw a unique opportunity. If he could get troops forward to seize Fitzroy he would not only get 5 Brigade into a position where it could secure the right flank around Port Stanley, but save his men the long advance on foot around the south shore of East Falkland.

The next move was to send two patrols forward to establish that Bluff Cove and Fitzroy were indeed free of enemy. This was done by the Patrols Platoon of C Company. They were able to put in the visitors' book at Bluff Cove the entry 'First in—heli-borne—callsigns 31 and 31E', along with a list of eight names.

Scout helicopters were used in the initial sortie. Four men sat on the floor of the cargo area of each helicopter with their feet braced against the skids. Their bergens and other kit could then be stowed in the centre between the back of the two rows of men. The pilot took the little machine low over the ground to the landing zone. But the low-level flight often proved hair-raising for the troops.

With the men of Patrols Platoon in position in Fitzroy, it was vital to put in as many men as possible before dark. Brig Wilson decided he needed the use of the only Chinook heavy lift helicopter available on the Falklands to move the maximum number of troops forward. The other Chinooks had been lost aboard *Atlantic Conveyor* and this single remaining machine was invaluable. There was a strict bidding procedure for its use and officers were supposed to get clearance through headquarters at San Carlos before they could use it. To short-circuit this laborious process, Brig Wilson simply 'hijacked' the Chinook.

The San Carlos staff had assigned the Chinook to bring 5 Bde HQ forward to Goose Green after it had flown the prisoners to the cage at Ajax Bay. The helicopter had suffered a minor flying accident a few days earlier and the pilot said that he was not sure the instruments were 100 per cent reliable. It was only supposed to carry 40 men and some kit. In the event that number was doubled, though some of the men of A Company had been sent off without their bergens. They had to brave the harsh winter conditions of Fitzroy for two days without bergens and sleeping bags.

On the high ground around Mount Challenger and Smoko Mountain, two OPs put out by the Mountain and Arctic Warfare Cadre of the Royal Marines had observed helicopter activity in the fading light. Among the machines they recognized a Chinook—the Argentine forces had used one to reinforce the garrison at Goose Green—and the smaller Scouts that could easily be mistaken for Bells in the gathering dusk.

A contact report was sent back through 3 Brigade HQ to Ajax Bay. No British helicopters were reported to be that far forward. As far as Brigade Headquarters knew the Chinook was still moving PoWs back to Ajax Bay. The grid references were reported back and two batteries of 29 Commando Regiment RA were tasked with a fire mission. They were to shoot a mix of air-bursts and white phosphorus on the given grid reference.

'Cancel, cancel, cancel...'

As the information was being passed over the air, a Royal Marine Corporal saw to his horror that the Chinook had RAF markings. With his finger on the transmission button of the radio he jammed the air with a desperate message: 'Cancel, cancel, cancel, cancel ... it's got "Royal Air Force" along the side, it's got RAF markings, the door is missing ...' and rattled off all the recognition features of an RAF helicopter. Just in time the gunners had heard the message and cancelled the order to fire.

Even 5 Brigade HQ had little idea that the Chinook had been hijacked, and they were surprised by the reports that it was not shuttling north and south. The staff then contacted the pilot and his position tallied exactly with that given by the Mountain and Arctic Warfare Cadre observation posts that had seen the helicopters. The mystery was unravelled. This incident prompted a staff officer at Ajax Bay to confide to his diary that the operation was 'grossly irresponsible'.

There was also some disquiet about the fact that 2 Para had been placed out on a dangerous limb where they would be very hard to support if the Argentine forces had put in a heavy and concerted counter-attack. As it was, 2 Para's rapid advance had been spotted by an Argentine observation post as well and the troops were to come under the first 155mm fire of the campaign. But after the experience of mortar and artillery fire at Goose Green they were prepared and had already dug the turf sangars that were known as 'grouse butts'.

It was about this time that Colonel David Chaundler arrived to take command of the battalion, following the death in action of Colonel H Jones. Colonel Chaundler had made a parachute jump into the sea from a Hercules as it flew near a Royal Navy warship.

When D Company were visited by their new Colonel they were told that 2 Para were 'ten feet tall and had electrified Britain'. The paras put this description down to 'jet lag'.

Once Bluff Cove and Fitzroy had been secured, the battalion had been able to establish better positions along the coast. By the use of landing craft, they also had a chance to zero their weapons on an improvised range there.

The Assault Engineer Platoon of 2 Para were assigned the task of repairing the bridge at Bluff Cove which links the settlement with Fitzroy. This was not as cushy a task as they imagined. They were to recall later that Sergeant Bell and Private Horrocks were almost flattened by Colour Sergeant Hirst who had made a hasty withdrawal when he saw that some of the charges that had been attached to the bridge by the Argentine forces had failed to explode.

Brig Wilson was interviewed on television. While admitting that the helicopter lift was not entirely according to the rules, he was resolute.

'I've grabbed my land in this great jump forward. Now I want to consolidate it!' he said.

3 Para on Mount Estancia

The long tab was over for the time being, and Port Stanley was in sight. For 3 Para Estancia House represented a chance to relax and build up for the final assault on Port Stanley. It was also a chance to apply pressure on the Argentine positions.

IT IS A MILITARY AXIOM that space can be traded for time. Faced by German attacks in World War 2, the Russians were able to withdraw over vast areas, but now the Argentine forces on the Falklands were running low on both space and time. In the press in Buenos Aires there was brave talk of a defensive 'horseshoe' around Stanley, but the grim reality was that the garrison was becoming constricted as they withdrew from outlying positions, under pressure from 45 Commando and 3 Para. The men of 42 Commando were already on the vital high ground of Mount Kent where they had survived bitterly cold days and nights.

While they were holding the high ground 3 Para had closed in on the small community of Estancia House. The population of this sheep farming ranch had been increased by kelpers who had left Stanley and Green Patch Settlement to escape the dangers of military action. In a house with only four bedrooms 14 men, women and children were enduring the South Atlantic winter.

On the night of 31 May, they were awakened by the crack of a flare as it exploded above the farm and in the flickering light they heard a man shout, 'Open up! It's the British Army!' For the owner Tony Heathman there was a moment of doubt and then he opened the door to see a face smeared with camouflage paint and topped off with a camouflaged helmet.

Mind if we come in?

In contrast to the Argentine soldiers who had demanded the use of the farm Land Rover, this soldier asked, 'Mind if we come in? It's awfully cold outside.' As he talked, the rest of 3 Para began to deploy around the buildings and dig in. Digging was a drill that came naturally—'bombing and shell fire make trench diggers out of everyone', an officer remarked after the campaign.

Estancia House is north-west of Mount Kent and at the most southern end of the long stretch of enclosed water called Port Salvador. The track to Stanley here crosses a saddle of high ground that links Mount Kent with features to the north including Mount Estancia and Green Hill and Long Island Mount. These features make up part of the 'Horseshoe' around Stanley.

As 3 Para settled in around Estancia their positions became more substantial. Lt Col Hew Pike of 3 Para was photographed outside a bunker which bore the name 'Rumour Control' with a sketch of a parachute, and which also sported a Union Jack and a letter from No 10 Downing Street. The bunker was dug under the guidance of Sergeant Graham Colbeck, of whom Pike was to say, 'Give him 24 hours and you would think Sergeant Colbeck had been on the Somme for three years.'

The Quartermaster, Captain Norman Menzies, established his stores in one of the barns. He had learned to live with his nickname 'Norman the Storeman', and Robert Fox of the BBC was to comment that 3 Para ran 'probably the best supply operation in the entire British Land Force on the Falklands'.

3 Para were quick to push out a screen of patrols to dominate the ground to their front. Though a strong Argentine company had been in the area, these forces had withdrawn before 3 Para arrived. The Intelligence Officer, Captain Giles Orpen-Smellie, said that positions had been found with abandoned equipment and even rations including fruit juice. The positions had been bombarded by the battalion's 81mm mortars and indications of casualties included field dressings and blood trails. Later, Argentine soldiers began to surrender in small groups, unarmed and without their personal equipment.

The initial deployment of the battalion was Tac HQ with A Company on Mount Estancia, C Company on Mount Vernet and B Company on the southern shoulders of Mount Vernet covering across the valley to Mount Kent.

From these positions the paras were able to see the approaches to Stanley, including the craggy slopes of Mount Longdon, which was to be their next objective. Poor flying conditions prevented the movement of artillery and so it was not until 3 June that the guns of 79 Battery RA were lifted into the area to support 3 Para.

Argentine artillery fire included the French-built 155mm guns as well as 105mm Pack howitzers. In addition, high-level night bombing runs by Argentine Canberras were reported to be 'fairly accurate and very noisy'.

Assistance from 'Rubber Duck'

On 3 June, A and B Companies moved eastwards to set up patrol bases to reconnoitre Mount Longdon. Each rifle company sent out fighting patrols and Patrol Company put its four-man teams within a few yards of enemy positions on Mount Longdon. The fighting patrols had the desired effect of reducing enemy confidence and dominating 'no man's land'.

The Mortar Fire Controllers (MFC) of Support Company moved forward to observe and engage targets and the Argentine forces struck back with increasingly accurate artillery fire. The farmers of Estancia House braved this fire to assist the paras with transporting stores, casualties and ammunition using their tractors and trailers.

Patrolling and mortar and artillery fire missions were conducted between 3 and 10 June, and a detailed intelligence picture was built up for the battalion.

During these operations the paras were assisted by a man who was given the signals code name of 'Rubber Duck'. He was Terry Peck, a bearded 44-year-old ex-Stanley policeman and a member of the Islands Legislative Council. He was given the more flattering nickname by the paras of 'the man with the built-in compass'.

Part of the purpose of the patrol operations was to learn as much as possible about the Argentine positions on Longdon. The minefields had to be located, and enemy bunkers and trenches. The snipers, who had intrigued journalists on the journey south on *Canberra*, were also out picking their targets—though in at least one instance this was a brace of Upland geese, which were a welcome dietary supplement.

An attack on 3 Para by Argentine Pucarás was witnessed by the Surveillance Troop of 45 Commando. Second Lieutenant Andy Smith recalls: 'As the two white aircraft banked towards the paras the sky was suddenly filled with tracer and evidently a "surface-to-air" 84mm round was fired ...' The moral of this story is that it is perhaps not a good idea to attack the British soldier when he is 'stood to'.

Reagan rides in

As far as the Falklands War was concerned, the Versailles summit was a farce for the Americans, but a final hurdle for the British. With the support of her European allies, Britain was ready to finish the job. The talking was over. All that remained was the war.

AMONG TREATIES SIGNED at one time or another in Louis XIV's Palace of Versailles was that in 1783 ending the American war of independence. Almost 200 years later, at the opening of 1982's economic summit, held amid the mockingly lavish splendour of the palace, Mrs Thatcher may have reflected that times had changed. The Americans were on the side of the colonialists these days. Only hours before, she had strolled amid the rich summer scents and colours of the American Embassy rose garden in Paris with President Reagan, in a reassuring mood, beside her. It was 4 June, the British forces were closing in on Port Stanley, and there was no wavering in American support; or so it seemed.

'We had very deep things to talk about', she said at the end of the talks. The Americans remained staunch allies. 'They are firmly on our side.'

Those countries which were participating in the economic summit were, in addition to Britain and the US, Canada, France, Italy, Japan and West Germany. All, to varying degrees and with reservations here and there, backed Britain. Mrs Thatcher was to thank them all, particularly their host, President Mitterand, for their support.

Despite the calming nature of her talks with the President, the Prime Minister was a little less confident about the Americans than she appeared. There was still a smell of uncertainty about them. The divided loyalties caused by America's desire to show the Latin Americans that the US was also a devoted member of *their* club were still in evidence. The US Ambassador, Mrs Kirkpatrick, was badgering Haig from the UN once more. The debate on a Spanish-Panamanian Security Council resolution calling for a ceasefire and withdrawal by both sides was due to be voted on in New York later that same night, a Friday.

Still, as she sat listening to the opening remarks at the summit, the Prime Minister believed the Americans would stick to their agreement to join Britain in vetoing the resolution. Mrs Thatcher wanted nothing to go wrong in the countdown to victory and she wanted the additional strength that would come from shoulder-to-shoulder support from the Americans in the Security Council. Other members of the summit, such as France and Japan, did not matter so much.

New York is six hours behind Paris which meant that the Security Council was moving towards a vote around midnight or later, so far as the relevant delegations at the summit were concerned. In New York, Mrs Kirkpatrick kept a line open to Paris in the hope up to the last minute that Haig would change his mind and tell her to abstain. The history of relations between the two over the Falklands was well known as being abrasive. Mrs Kirkpatrick in one exchange had accused the Secretary of State and his aides of being 'amateurs—Brits in American clothes'. He, for his part, had told her that she was incapable of understanding the issues.

The vote came without the hoped-for response from Haig and a reluctant Mrs Kirkpatrick joined Sir Anthony Parsons in vetoing the resolution. Then followed a moment of near farce. Haig changed his mind. Reagan, who had gone to bed, was not consulted, despite the fact that he had assured Mrs Thatcher earlier in the day there would be an American veto. But Haig's message reached Mrs Kirkpatrick too late. Nevertheless, she informed the surprised Security Council—including a shaken Parsons—that the vote was a mistake. The intention had been to abstain.

Morally, this was a victory of sorts for Argentina. But did it matter? In retrospect, whether America vetoed or abstained can be seen to have been of small importance. The British attack on Port Stanley was not delayed; the outcome of the war was unaffected. It was only amid the tension and the heightened apprehension that surrounded the British government's determination to keep its major ally 'on side' that it seemed important. Mr Pym, woken from his sleep in the early hours of Saturday morning by a phone call from Haig, found the news dismaying. The later suggestions that the American Secretary of State had actually been engaged in a clever display of having his cake and eating it were never received with much credulity in the British camp.

Reagan rides out

At a press conference Haig brazened out a storm of questions. No, he had not woken up the President. The decision was his alone. 'Frankly, I felt it [the resolution] was firm because it was explicit in supporting UN Resolution 502, which calls for a ceasefire and withdrawal as well as a political solution.' The decision to abstain was no more than a nuance in the American position and totally within 'my category of responsibility'. Frankly, he added, if he woke up the President every time there was a nuanced vote in the Security Council, the man would be up 24 hours a day.

At a lunch for the seven heads of government later that day, Mrs Thatcher was besieged by reporters. 'I don't give interviews at lunchtime', she snapped.

But at least there had been some soothing music at the end of the summit when Mitterand responded to her account of the war's progress by stating on behalf of the participants that they expressed complete solidarity with Britain, whose international pride and national interests had been injured.

A few days later Reagan was in London, riding in Windsor Park with the Queen and speaking of the enduring solidarity of the Anglo-American alliance. The incident still rankled in British minds, but much was forgotten, and forgiven, in the warmth generated by the visit.

What was now clear was the impossibility of a negotiated settlement. The politicians in London, who had been demanding a quick victory, were now prepared to defer to the expertise of the military—the more so once the difficulties of taking Port Stanley without causing a bloodbath had been explained to them. At the beginning of the week, Al Haig had urged restraint on the British—or at the very least 'magnanimity in victory'. There was little doubt now that the victory would indeed be Britain's. Nor was there any doubt that, however much certain figures in British politics might dislike the idea, the Islands would remain British. A much-quoted British NCO summed up the rapidly hardening mood when he stated in front of a reporter, 'If they're worth fighting for, they must be worth keeping.'

In Buenos Aires, now that the last chance of an honourable peace had evaporated—and with it the political career of the Argentine foreign minister, Nicanor Costa Mendes—Galtieri sealed the decision with one simple order to the troops on the island: the garrison, he ordered, 'must fight to the last man'.

Disaster at Fitzroy

The advance was leapfrogging ahead. The important features west and south-west of Port Stanley were now in the hands of 2 Para. Once 5 Brigade was brought up, the final assault could start. It was then that the biggest disaster of the whole campaign struck.

BY NIGHTFALL on 3 June, Brigadier Tony Wilson was congratulating himself on the speed with which his 5 Brigade had gobbled up the miles between Goose Green and Port Stanley. With the last helicopter lift of the day 2 Para had established themselves around Fitzroy, just 20 miles from Stanley, and the British right flank was well on the way to being secure. It was a bold stroke—if unpopular with certain members of General Moore's staff—and Wilson was jubilant. Less than a week later, his plan seemed to be in ruins. In the single worst disaster suffered by the Task Force, some 150 men were killed or wounded and two vital ships were out of action, bombed as they sat at anchor near a little hamlet called Fitzroy.

Like 42 Commando a week before, 2 Para had 'leapfrogged' forward to capture the important features west and south-west of Port Stanley. With the area secure, 5 Brigade could build up quickly for the final push. It was now a question of getting the rest of the brigade across to join 2 Para. Due once again to the shortage of heavy-lift helicopters and the appalling weather conditions which had now set in, an air lift was impossible. The 1st Battalion Welsh Guards (1WG) set out from San Carlos in an attempt to march, but the going proved very difficult and the Snocats with them kept breaking down. After 12 hours they were called back. A sea passage was the only answer. The assault ships *Fearless* and *Intrepid* were pressed into service. While this was going on, the Scots Guards' Operations Officer and the Commanding Officer of the Welsh Guards, Lt Col Johnny Ricketts, flew up to the two settlements on 4 June to liaise with 2 Para.

The plan drawn up was for the Scots Guards to embark with *Intrepid* on the night of 5 June, while the Welsh Guards with supporting elements of the Brigade would follow in *Fearless* the next night. The Gurkhas would then follow them, using whatever helicopter support and shipping was available. It was decided that the two assault ships would proceed no further than Lively Island at the entrance to Choiseul Sound because of the threat from land-based Exocet missiles. There the troops would cross-deck into Landing Craft Utilities (LCUs)—four of which were carried in each ship, manned by Royal Marine crews—for the final stage of the journey. As a preliminary, a joint Royal Engineer/Special Boat Service recce party went in and checked the beaches and exits at both settlements for mines, obstacles and the enemy.

One redeployment on 5 June gave 5 Brigade and especially 2 Para some comfort and extra security. This was the flying in of J Company 42 Commando, which contained many members of the original Falklands garrison, to a position south-east of Mount Challenger. From there, they could give early warning of, and delay, any Argentine attack on Bluff Cove. Meanwhile, 2nd Battalion Scots Guards (2SG) were boarding *Intrepid*. Their Commanding Officer, Lt Col Mike Scott, had received his final orders from Brig Wilson at Darwin. That evening they set sail from San Carlos and reached Lively Island. Here the transfer to the LCUs went without problem, but the rough seas and poor weather conditions, added to the fact that the LCUs were only designed for inshore work, meant a very cold and cramped seven-hour voyage. There was a tense moment when star shells burst overhead. At the time these were thought to be from an Argentine 105mm gun, and everyone expected them to be followed by high explosive. But the warship HMS *Arrow* appeared through the spray. She had thought the LCUs were Argentine. Having picked them up on her radar, she had fired the star shells to help investigate at close quarters. Frantic Aldis lamp messages were flashed and *Arrow* then turned away, satisfied that they were friendly.

Exposed to the weather

Eventually, a soaked, frozen battalion arrived at Bluff Cove just before dawn and was met by guides from 2 Para. The original plan had been for 2SG to move out immediately and dig in further up the coast but, in view of the appalling weather, this was cancelled. Instead they were to relieve 2 Para at Bluff Cove while the latter concentrated at Fitzroy to guard the Brigade Headquarters to be set up there. One company, Left Flank, took over the 2 Para positions forward of Bluff Cove. Right Flank took up positions to the west, while G Company occupied Bluff Cove itself. Left Flank's position was badly exposed to the weather, but had a good view of

Mounts Harriet, Tumbledown and William and Sapper Hill—names which would become well known before the next week was out.

At this time, however, Lt Col Scott was more concerned about the danger of his men succumbing to exposure than anything else and he arranged for G Company to relieve Left Flank after a short time. Like 2 Para, he made maximum use of the sheep-shearing sheds for his soaked men to dry out. The locals were more than helpful, as they had been to 2 Para, and used their tractors to help ferry stores and heavy equipment from the beach—as well as providing a non-stop service of 'tea and wads' for those coming back from the forward positions to dry out.

While the Scots Guards were establishing themselves, it was the turn of the 1WG to make the trip. The weather had worsened considerably during 6 June and that night. This and the shortage of LCUs meant that it was possible only to send half the battalion on from Lively Island. The balance returned to Goose Green in *Fearless*.

The Task Force Headquarters then said that it was too risky to use the assault ships any more and offered *Sir Tristram* and *Sir Galahad*, and two RFA Landing Ships Logistic (LSLs) instead. *Sir Tristram* was committed to moving stores and ammunition and arrived at Fitzroy on 7 June. *Sir Galahad* was earmarked for the Welsh Guards and other units. Brig Wilson also wanted to get his own tactical headquarters up there early. Most of its equipment, especially the communications apparatus, was mounted on Land Rovers and an attempt to get it to Fitzroy overland had, like the Welsh Guards', failed because the tracks were impassable. So he commandeered a local coaster, MV *Monsunen*. This and an LCU were to move the headquarters round to Fitzroy on the evening of 7 June, but because of a breakdown of communications the LCU failed to show up to lift the balance of equipment until midday on 8 June. *Monsunen* would remain at 5 Brigade's service for the next three days, transporting the Gurkhas.

Meanwhile, 2SG had launched their first operation. They had been tasked by Brig Wilson with destroying two 105mm guns and a radar site believed to be in the area of Port Harriet—actually at Seal Point, almost due south of Stanley and well within the Argentine lines. The task was given to the Recce Platoon, who established a patrol base seven miles forward of Bluff Cove. Shortly after last light on 7 June, they set off for their objective, accompanied by a Forward Observation Officer from the battalion's supporting battery and an Engineer recce party. First, they went to Port Harriet House which, after a silent approach, was found to be unoccupied. Leaving a patrol there to act as an anchor, the remainder set out to try and locate the two guns, without success. But they did find the radar site, which was using the Israeli Rasset system. While the bulk of the platoon returned to Bluff Cove, the Port Harriet House patrol was tasked with dealing with this on the night of 8 June. But on the morning of the 8th, an SAS patrol, not under the battalion's command, arrived to operate in the area.

Since it had no immediate task on hand, and its members were willing, it was decided to leave it at Port Harriet House to help deal with the radar site. An attempt was made to get more food up to 2SG's patrol. Two civilian Land Rovers were used to do this, but the leading one ran over an anti-personnel mine just short of the house. A wheel was damaged and both vehicles had to be extricated. The wheel was changed and it was decided that the group should return to Bluff Cove. But, as they were struggling to get out of the minefield, disaster struck the LSLs, now anchored at Fitzroy.

The Welshmen's dilemma

It was a clear day. This meant that the danger of an Argentine air attack was very much increased, and a dilemma fell upon the Welshmen. They were now on board *Sir Galahad*. But should they weigh anchor and get out to sea and safety? Or get on with their move to Bluff Cove and hope for the best?

Ewen Southby-Tailyour, the Royal Marine major who had mapped the coastline in 1978, was horrified to see the two ships in Port Pleasant outside Fitzroy. He went aboard *Sir Galahad* to find out what was going on. She had been intended to go to Bluff Cove, but the LSL couldn't get up the narrow channel to the planned disembarcation beach. She went instead to Fitzroy. There she unloaded the Rapiers that would give local air defence to the troops now in position. But the guards had no intention of going ashore anywhere but Bluff Cove, and then only in LCUs.

Bluff Cove and Fitzroy are some five miles apart as the crow flies, linked by a a short track and a bridge over a long, narrow inlet. But Argentines had blown the bridge so 1WG would face a walk of some 20 miles—right round the inlet. Not on, said the senior Guards officer, not after all the messing around of the previous few days. Southby-Tailyour pleaded with the Guards to get ashore and let the ships get out to sea. Finally they agreed. But 5 Brigade's medics, 16 Field Ambulance, who were also aboard, were to disembark first. They had the more urgent job of setting up a field hospital. Besides, they were *supposed* to be at Fitzroy, while the Guards were not.

Air warning red

At 1300 hours that day 2SG got an air warning red—and saw what they mistook to be Harriers. They were, in fact, two Skyhawks and two Mirages, They screamed low over Fitzroy, taking everyone by surprise, and went for the ships. For the first time the Argentine Air Force got it right—they had attacked troop-carrying ships. Their bombs ripped into the undefended LSLs, exploding deep in the bowels of the two ships. Some men were killed immediately. Others were burnt in fierce fires started by the bombs.

1WG's mortar platoon was aboard *Sir Galahad* with all their mortars and ammunition. They suffered the most. Almost everyone below decks was burned—their uniforms and hair caught on fire. Petrol from the Rapier missile generators flew in all directions, feeding the flames. Men vividly recall being hurled into the air by the force of the explosions, and then watching as the skin on their hands melted and feeling their hair and berets burst into flames.

Somehow, order prevailed. Blinded by the smoke and their own wounds, men staggered to the sides of the ships, some helping two and three other men at a time. The lifeboats and rubber liferafts were launched. These were in the water within seconds. On board *Sir Galahad* medical orderlies from 16 Field Ambulance—many of them badly wounded themselves—gave life-saving first aid to wounded men, remaining in danger on the burning ships as they worked. Finally, they too were evacuated. All the time, ammunition was exploding.

Controversy rages over the incident to this day. A scapegoat is still sought, but too many factors contributed to the disaster; too many people were involved for the blame to be laid at any one door. Some have said that the Welsh Guards sealed their own fate because they were too lazy to walk round the coast. This is unfair. They could have done the march—they are among the best troops in the British army—but they had been messed around too much to be bothered. On top of that, they hadn't seen the battle of Bomb Alley and didn't know just how devastating the Argentine air attacks could be.

Brigadier Tony Wilson has attracted a great deal of opprobrium for trying to go too far too fast—but he was engaged in a desperate race against the weather which was taking a heavy toll on the commandos and paras up on the mountains. He couldn't afford to hang around. The Harriers are blamed for not shooting down the enemy aircraft—but they were engaged elsewhere taking on another five Mirages who were attacking HMS *Plymouth* off West Falkland.

And finally, it is said that the unloading went too slowly. Normally, the technique was to drive an LCU up to the ramp on the LSL, but *Sir Galahad's* ramp jammed. All loading had to be done laboriously over the side. There weren't enough LCUs around, anyway. And so it goes on. Different observers have different viewpoints, but it is hard to apportion blame. War is a matter of risks.

On to Wireless Ridge

Two Para saw more action in the Falklands than any other unit. As they sorted themselves out at Fitzroy, they were ordered to move again, to the scene of their last battle, Wireless Ridge. It was fitting that they should win the race to Port Stanley.

FOR THE PRIVATE soldiers of 2 Para—the Toms—things were getting pretty bad by 10 June. For one thing, 5 Brigade were running out of food. For another, the food they did get was too much for stomachs used to army compo rations. By now, many ungrateful Toms felt they had been poisoned. The next day, however, they brightened up—they were on the move again and, more importantly, back on compo rations. They were also under the command of 3 Commando Brigade and on the final stretch of their long haul to Port Stanley. One final push and they'd be home and dry.

Their new commanding officer, Lt Col David Chaundler, had joined them just four days after the battle of Goose Green. As a personal friend of Colonel 'H', the news of the latter's death at Goose Green had come as a great blow. At the time, Chaundler had been working at the Ministry of Defence in London and heard the first news of 2 Para's victory on the night of Friday 28 May, just before he went to bed. The following morning he discovered what the victory had cost: 18 killed and 35 wounded. He was horrified. That morning he was told he might have to fly out there himself to take over, but dismissed the idea. That same night he was at RAF Brize Norton.

What happened next has become something of a legend. He jumped, they tell us, from 25,000 feet over the Falkland Islands, using a black parachute to avoid detection. A Hercules had been laid on specially for him, reports say, and he arrived bearing news vital to the course of the war.

The truth is rather simpler. He flew to Ascension Island on a VC10, arriving there on Sunday 30 May. He flew from Ascension at 0200 hours on Monday 31 May ('everything happened at 2 o'clock in the morning', he was to reflect wryly). The Hercules he flew in wasn't his own, but one of many doing a routine drop of supplies and mail to the Task Force out at sea. With his parachute strapped on, he helped push out the containers full of mail and vital military spares, and followed the heavy loads out of the open tail gate. He was plucked out of the sea by a helicopter, flown to one of the ships, and given a chance to dry off before being flown to HMS *Hermes* for a brief talk with Admiral Woodward.

His next port of call was Major General Jeremy Moore's headquarters where he was brought up to date on the course of the war, and only then, weary and slightly deaf from his long Hercules flight, did he join 2 Para.

His next task on arrival was to meet his fellow officers and debrief them on what had happend at Goose Green. On hearing the full story, he vowed that never again would 2 Para go into action without the fire support they had lacked at Goose Green.

When 2 Para moved out of Fitzroy, they knew that another battle was in the wind. Their first move was—unusual for the paras—by helicopter. Following the issue of final orders some days before, the units making up the Task Force (which amounted now to about divisional strength) knew exactly what they were to do. As far as 2 Para were concerned, this meant waiting for 3 Para and 45 Commando to put in their attacks on Mount Longdon and Two Sisters.

The divisional plan was for 3 Commando Brigade to mount three simultaneous attacks: while 3 Para and 45 Commando were taking their objectives 42 Commando would take Mount Harriet. 2 Para were to be the brigade reserve, lying on Bluff Cove Peak to back up any unit that needed help.

The second phase of the divisional plan was for 5 Brigade's major units to take the high ground to the south-west of Port Stanley. Mount Tumbledown was the objective of the Scots Guards, Mt William the objective of the Gurkhas, and Wireless Ridge the objective of 2 Para—their second pitched battle of the campaign.

The third phase of the attack was the one that nobody was really looking forward to: a street fight in Stanley involving almost the whole of 3 Commando Brigade. In the event it wasn't necessary.

'Prepare for action'

On the morning of 12 May it became clear that 3 Commando Brigade's attack had gone without a hitch. Although 45 Commando and 3 Para had taken heavy casualties, their objectives were secure and 2 Para could march round the back of Mount Longdon to take up their positions for the attack on Wireless Ridge. Expecting to go in that night, they carried no bergens, only their fighting order and as much ammunition as possible. Their sense of humour had survived intact. L/Cpl Kevin Lukowiak remembers one practical joker in particular: 'At one halt on the march we stopped for a breather and I flopped on to my back. The guy next to me gave me a nudge and whispered, "Message from the front—you can have a fag." I thought, great, and passed it on to the next guy, then started hunting through my 30,000 pockets for fags and lighter. Then the guy nudged me again: "One between two", he said. Fair enough, I thought, and passed that on as well. I had just got the fag into my mouth when the bastard nudged me again and said, "But you're not to light them!" '

Back on Bluff Cove Peak the battalion's mortars and heavy machine guns received a nasty jolt: Skyhawks, on the lookout for Brigade HQ, strafed their positions and delayed their planned move forward. As a result there was no chance of them getting up to Wireless Ridge in time to be dug in and zeroed before the assault. Despite this apparent setback, however, 2 Para had one ace up their sleeves: massive fire support from 2 Scorpions and 2 Scimitars of the Blues and Royals. Lt Col Chaundler wanted fire power, and he got it.

The ring of steel

Less than two weeks had passed since the landing at San Carlos and already the British forces had achieved a dominant position on the islands. The main Argentine force, which had remained in Port Stanley, was now surrounded. The end was in sight.

BY 10 JUNE 1982 the Argentine garrison at Port Stanley was surrounded. Land to its west was being gripped by the two British brigades; the sea to the south, east and north was dominated by the Royal Navy. Overhead, Harriers and helicopters were able to fly unmolested (except for anti-aircraft artillery fire) to deliver their loads of rockets and bombs. General Menendez had permitted the initiative to pass to the British amphibious Task Force.

Frigates and destroyers of the Royal Navy delivered gunfire support to the troops on the ground and bombarded shore targets within the Argentine pocket. The ships used for these tasks were mainly the County Class destroyers *Glamorgan* and *Antrim*, the type 21 and the Modified Type 12 frigates. The type 42 destroyers, *Cardiff, Glasgow* and *Exeter*, helped too, when they could be spared from air defence duties.

The number of shells fired by the ships was phenomenal. *Glamorgan* fired 1245, *Avenger* 1075, *Yarmouth* 1441, *Arrow* 902 and *Active* 633 of their 4.5in main armament in naval gunfire support (NGS) to the troops. The presence of the ships was a vital factor as the weight of fire of a naval gun on a RN warship is far greater than the weight of fire of a Royal Artillery battery (six barrels) of 105mm Light Guns. NGS was frighteningly effective.

There were five Naval Gunfire Support Forward Observer (NGSFO) teams with 148 Forward Observation Battery of 29 Commando Regiment Royal Artillery, and these were divided among the land forces on the basis of one team each for 3 Commando Brigade and 5 Infantry Brigade—the remaining three teams being deployed with the special force patrols. The

NGSFO parties were able to call an awesome weight of fire on to Argentine positions and key points with considerable accuracy and devastating effect. As the British land forces put in their attacks on the various hill lines, creeping closer to Port Stanley, each battalion-sized major unit had one of the RN ships dedicated to it to give NGS on a particular objective. The ships were able to come and go at will, and were largely unmolested by the Argentines. Only one hit was scored by Argentine fire from the land when an MM.38 Exocet missile, which had been dismounted from a ship and fitted to a towed flat-bed trailer, struck the rear of HMS *Glamorgan*. This caused loss of life but did not put the ship out of action. One reason for this was that the warhead failed to explode—typical of the Argentine lack of thoroughness.

Controlling the heights

With the seizure of the hills, the British were able to observe the Argentine positions and their gunlines. This gave the troops of the Royal Artillery about a week before the fall of Port Stanley during which to register all the observable targets.

As the enemy's perimeter shrank, it became easier to determine where their locations were. Harrier GR3s were used for air strikes against Argentine positions, being called in and directed on to the targets by the Tactical Air Control Parties (TACPs) with the RM Commandos and by Forward Air Controllers (FACs) marching with the troops. Helicopters were also used in a gunship role to attack the enemy, often using GPMG-SFs, manned by the crewman firing through the right-hand door port, and 68mm SNEB rockets mounted in pods fitted to the outboard pylons.

General Menendez also had to contend with the possibility that Task Force warships would try to force a passage into Port Stanley harbour or land troops in Argentine-held territory. The British had enough troops available to put ashore parties of up to battalion strength. To guard against the threat—especially the possibility of Port Stanley being taken out—Menendez had to deploy troops to guard the vulnerable coasts and various key points to the east and south of Port Stanley. This limited the number of Argentine soldiers and marines available to face the main British advance.

Defence of the Vital Ground

It was clear that Vital Ground, without control of which General Menendez's position would become untenable, was the series of hills close in to Port Stanley. Menendez had to hold Sapper Hill, Mount William, Mount Tumbledown, Mount Longdon and Wireless Ridge at all costs. Farther out from these, and constituting 'ground of tactical importance' (without the control of which his position would become difficult to defend), were Mount Harriet and Two Sisters Hill. Farther out still to the west were the key features of the Murrel Heights, Mount Challenger and Mount Kent. These hills would allow a potentially successful attack to be launched on Two Sisters and Mount Harriet and later on the hills of the Vital Ground. Possession of Mount Challenger by the British would allow the settlements of Fitzroy and Bluff Cove to be used as resupply bases— either forward brigade maintenance areas (FBMAs) or distribution points (DPs)—which would greatly simplify an attack.

The British approached Port Stanley with a two-pronged advance, or pincer movement. The northern route was taken by 3 Commando Brigade and the southern one was the line of march of 5 Infantry Brigade. Patrols from G Squadron 22 SAS Regiment were able to report that Mount Kent was only lightly defended during the last days of May 1982, and D Squadron was helicoptered forward to take the hill, which they held until relieved by K Company 42 Commando some five days later. The Royal Marines were rapidly reinforced by two 81mm mortars and three 105mm Light Guns. The rest of 42 Cdo were soon moved up to reinforce K Company, and consolidated themselves in possession of Mounts Kent and Challenger to it south.

On 30 May, 45 Cdo had reached Douglas Settlement and 3 Para were in Teal Inlet Settlement. The paras then moved on to Estancia House, where they had a stiff battle with the Argentine defenders, and then they consolidated on the high ground. The CVRTs of the Blues and Royals moved southwards from Teal to Kent and Challenger to give armoured and direct fire support. It became a priority to move forward the three field batteries (7, 8 and 79 Batteries) of 29 Cdo Regt RA with 1000 rounds per gun. This was a task which strained and reduced heli-lift capability of the Task Force after the loss of *Atlantic Conveyor's* Chinook and Wessex helicopters. Most of the movement of the gunners was by air, while 5 Inf Bde moved by sea.

A telephone call by Maj John Crosland of 2 Para to Reg Binney, the farm manager at Fitzroy, on 3 June had established that the Argentines had pulled out the day before. Using the sole remaining Chinook, 2 Para were quickly flown forward to secure the settlement, thus saving 5 Bde a time-consuming advance to contact. On 4 June, the Scots Guards were shipped round the southern coast on board LSL *Sir Tristram* and the LPD *Intrepid* to Bluff Cove. A similar move on 8 June resulted tragically in the casualties to the Welsh Guards at Bluff Cove. But the gamble meant that both the brigades were holding basically the same north—south line.

Advance on Port Stanley

The plan was for a three-phase divisional advance towards Port Stanley. In phase one, 3 Cdo Bde were to take Mount Longdon, Mount Harriet and

Two Sisters in the early hours of the morning of 12 June. The tasking was for 3 Para (with HMS *Avenger* in direct support) to assault and capture Mount Longdon. To their south, 45 Cdo (with HMS *Glamorgan* in direct support) was to take Two Sisters, and farther south again the Welsh Guards (one company with two companies of 40 Cdo under command) were to secure a Start Line from which 42 Cdo (with HMS *Yarmouth* in direct support) would assault and capture Mount Harriet. The Welsh Guards—40 Cdo composite battalion would remain in reserve. D and G Squadrons 22SAS Regiment, with HMS *Arrow* in direct support, were to launch an attack on the Murrel Heights in the area of Murrel Bridge. Phase two was to take place on the night of 12–13 June, and was to be carried out by 5 Inf Bde. The tasks were for 2 Para (with a troop of the Blues and Royals attached) to take Wireless Ridge after passing through 3 Para; 2SG (with HMS *Yarmouth* and *Phoebe* in on-call direct support, and 4 Fd Regt RA and 7 Battery of 29 Cdo Regt RA at priority call) to capture Mount Tumbledown; 1/7 DEOGR (with the same gunfire support) to assault Mount William; and the IWG-40 Cdo composite battalion to take Sapper Hill. When these objectives were secured, 3 Cdo Bde in phase three would assault the Argentine positions in and around Port Stanley itself by immediately passing through the 5 Inf Bde objectives. In the event, phase two was delayed for 24 hours—to the night of 13–14 June—and phase three was rendered unnecessary by the Argentines' surrender.

Phase one of the divisional plan was carried out as planned. There was stiff resistance. On Mount Longdon, 3 Para fought a fierce battle with the Argentine 7 Inf Regt, who had dug themselves in among the crags and used their snipers (equipped with second-generation image-intensifying sights) very effectively. The capture of the feature cost 3 Para 23 dead and 47 wounded. On Two Sisters 45 Cdo attacked a reinforced company of 4 Inf Regt, who had .50in calibre machine guns in strong positions; the Commando lost four killed and eight wounded. The rest of 4 Inf Regt were on Mount Harriet. The Welsh Guards Recce Platoon, under Lt Willy Sims, put in a diversionary attack on the west side of the feature using Milan ATGWs, while 42 Cdo came round the south and assaulted it from the rear. This classic infantry tactic took the Argentines by surprise and 42 Cdo were able to take the feature with one killed and 13 wounded.

Thus in the morning of 12 June, the British were in possession of General Menendez's Vital Ground, and poised to take the next step. He was truly surrounded by a ring of steel, from which he could not escape, and his military defeat was only a matter of time.

The night of battle: Mount Longdon

The looming mass of Mount Longdon lay like a fortress between 3 Para and the western end of Port Stanley. Between a minefield to the south and enemy to the east on Wireless Ridge the paras had little room to manoeuvre.

THE CAPTURE OF Mount Longdon was a key objective in 3 Commando Bde's plan of advance for the night of 11–12 June, which was phase one of the overall divisional plan for the capture of Port Stanley. The weather was closing in and resupply of food and ammunition was becoming a problem: the high ground had to fall quickly if the British were to succeed. It was with some relief that 3 Para took the orders to assault the mountain for, as one Para officer remarked afterwards, 'steady shelling by 155s eventually makes you rather shaky'. He recalled how many non-smokers had taken to tobacco, becoming at once veteran 40-a-day men. The feature that they had to take was no easy nut to crack. It was clear afterwards from captured maps and the interrogation of prisoners of war that the mountain had been defended by the complete 7 Infantry Regiment, reinforced by specialist elements and snipers from 601 Company of the Argentine special forces and from the marines. These snipers used their second-generation image-intensifying night sights very effectively. The feature was also protected by numerous minefields. The enemy had had two months in which to prepare his bunkers and sangars on this long, narrow, craggy mountain. His position was supported by 120mm heavy mortars, numerous Browning '30 cal' and '50 cal' heavy machine guns, 105mm recoilless guns and anti-tank missiles. Each of the positions turned out to have been pre-registered as mortar and artillery DFs (defensive fire targets). It was clear that Mount Longdon was the lynch-pin of the Argentine defences of Port Stanley, and the enemy was prepared to fight long and hard to keep it.

The feature had to be taken piecemeal from the west, and the lie of the summit dictated that only one company could fight along it at a time. Outflanking was not an option because of a large minefield to the south and known enemy company positions on Wireless Ridge to the east. The summit of Mount Longdon dominated the very open ground around it for several thousand yards, adding to the hazards of even night movement. Reconnaissance patrols had been surveying the 600ft high hill for almost two weeks, and were fairly certain that all the likely areas where anti-personnel mines could have been laid had been identified. It had also become clear that there were two principal defended positions on the mountain. One, which was given the codename *Full Back*, was on the eastern side of the summit and the other, *Fly Half*, was a nearby ridge towards the western edge of the summit. This latter was a known enemy command post and was well defended. *Full Back* was known to be heavily defended by machine guns and snipers. The northern side of the summit was codenamed *Wing Forward* and, continuing the rugby football analogy, the attack start line which also served as a report line was called *Free Kick*. This was located on the eastern edge of the FUP (forming up point), on the far bank of a stream which runs south—north to the Murrel River.

The plan of attack was simple and flexible. Moving by independent routes, under Patrol (D) Company guides, Tac HQ and A, B and C Companies were to close at night with the objective. A and B Companies were to move north and south in a pincer-like movement. A Company's task was *Full Back*, B's was *Fly Half*, and C was in reserve.

Fire support

Heavy supporting fire was to be provided by HMS *Avenger*, 79 Battery RA (from 29 Cdo Regt RA), and the battalion's own machine guns and mortars of Support Company, who were to establish two firebases—one at the 300ft contour west of the mountain and the other at *Free Kick*. Engineer support was to be given by 2 Troop, 9 Parachute Squadron Royal Engineers. The Sappers also provided defence for the 300ft contour firebase by manning a .30in Browning heavy machine gun, to neutralize a similar one known to be operated by the Argentines on Two Sisters to the south-west (the objective of 45 Commando for the same night). There were two FOO (Forward Observation Officer) parties: Capt McCracken with B Company and Lt Lee with A Company. B Company had one MFC (mortar fire controller) and A Company had two. Once Longdon had been secured, it was intended to pass C Company through and onto Wireless Ridge. In the event this proved impossible to do, as Tumbledown was not captured the same night and this heavily defended hill dominated the ground and the Ridge.

The start line was crossed at about 2100 hours local time. The approach required a four-hour-long night infiltration march across diverse routes. As the start line was crossed, a good moon rose to the east of Mount Longdon revealing the jagged nature of the feature and the extent to which it dominated the surrounding countryside. The move to the start line from the assembly area went well. There was one incident which could have affected the mission and which caused the B Company commander, Maj Mike Argue, to alter his approach route to the mountain. One of the battalion fire support groups (the sustained-fire GPMG and Milan teams), when moving to their positions, cut the B Company column with the result that part of Five Platoon and all of Six Platoon lost contact with the rest for about 30 minutes. As a consequence of this lost time, Maj Argue decided to approach the objective directly from the west, thus travelling well south of the original route and well to the right of A Company.

The bright moonlight prompted a further adjustment to the B Company plan. The platoons were ordered to move in closer to the rocks so that best cover for the Fight Through could be used—the excellent night vision provided by the moon made this possible. The attacking formation chosen was somewhat unconventional. The three rifle platoons were formed, with Company HQ slightly to the left and rear. Six Platoon was on the right and attacking from the south-west of the feature. Four and Five Platoons were to the west and north-west with Four Platoon on the left. Once the rocky ground was reached, Five Platoon fanned out and upwards into better cover but Four Platoon were still on low ground about 700 yards away from the first Argentine trenches. At this moment, the forward left section commander of Four Platoon, Cpl Milne, stepped on an anti-personnel mine receiving serious leg injuries, and the element of surprise had been lost. The Argentines responded with mortar, artillery and machine gun fire, but fortunately this time it was somewhat inaccurate. Five Platoon were in good cover given by the rocks, and Four Platoon raced forward through the minefield to close with the enemy. Six Platoon made contact at the same time. They had occupied *Fly Half* without any fighting, although they had grenaded a number of enemy bunkers on the way through. In the dark they bypassed a bunker with at least seven enemy hiding in it. These Argentines opened fire on Six Platoon's rear causing some killed and injured before they were dealt with.

Under heavy fire

After advancing through *Fly Half* towards the east of the feature, the platoon came under accurate rifle and automatic fire, suffering eight casualties—four of them fatal. The Platoon Commander asked to be allowed to pause so that he could reorganize and treat the wounded. This was granted, but he was informed of the situation facing Four and Five Platoons and warned that he might have to move forward to give them fire support. On the northern side of *Fly Half*, Four Platoon had moved up on the left side of Five Platoon and one of its sections had become intermingled with the other platoon for a time. In their advance up the feature, Five Platoon had come under heavy fire from an Argentine GPMG and a .50in Browning HMG (heavy machine gun). A GPMG team was pushed further up the rock face to fire into the enemy position, and the Argentine GPMG was taken out with 66mm LAWs and 84mm MAW fire. As soon as this had been done, more enemy automatic fire came from further east along the ridge from the '50 cal'. This was taken out by another section attack, with the gun group giving covering fire while Ptes Gough and Gray charged forward and grenaded the position. At this time Four Platoon was still on the left and slightly to the rear. It was largely out of contact, but was engaging targets to the east and above Five Platoon's forward elements.

As the two platoons arrived at an area forward of the summit of *Fly Half*, where the rock ridges started to break up and the ground began to slope away to the east, the *Full Back* feature could be seen in the distance. Both platoons immediately came under fire from the western end of a company defensive position. Their immediate problem was to deal with a well-sighted platoon position which was beefed up with at least two FN MAG 7.62mm GPMGs, a 105mm RCL (recoilless gun), and a .50in HMG. The position also had a number of snipers equipped with passive night sights. In the initial burst of fire, the Platoon Commander of Four Platoon was hit in the thigh and his signaller in the mouth. They continued to fire from their position, and the signaller carried on transmitting until he was relieved some time later. It was while attempting to take out the HMG that Sgt Ian McKay VC was killed, for the platoon position seemed to be organized around its defence. The weapon was sited in a substantial sangar and protected by several riflemen. The heroic efforts of Sgt McKay and his team substantially reduced the enemy resistance, but unfortunately failed to neutralize the gun.

Heavy casualties

With the Platoon Commander injured and the Platoon Sergeant killed, Sgt Fuller was despatched from Company Headquarters to take over Four Platoon. It was decided to withdraw the two platoons to evacuate casualties and to reorganize for a Company attack on the HMG position. Six Platoon at this time had met up with the stretcher bearers who were evacuating their casualties. The Battalion Commander had also by this time arrived on the feature with a fire support group, under Major Peter Dennison, which had occupied a position on the summit of Mount

Longdon and were bringing machine gun fire down on the enemy further east along the ridge. B Company HQ was in an OP overlooking the enemy position and was putting down heavy automatic fire on them. Covering fire for the withdrawal from contact of the two platoons was provided by everyone available plus artillery and mortar rounds.

From the start of the advance, the artillery guns had been laid on recorded targets on *Full Back*. When Cpl Milne had stepped on the AP mine the order had been given to fire on the targets, and from that time onwards throughout the action the guns and mortars had been firing on the enemy, sometimes with rounds landing only some 50 yards away from 'own troops'.

The withdrawal was supervised by the company sergeant-major, who was particularly concerned at the large number of casualties lying forward of the position. These were, however, recovered. Further casualties (one fatal and several minor) were sustained during the withdrawal itself.

'Regroup'

The assault on the '50 cal' position was to be a straightforward 'left flanking' attack supported by machine gun fire from the summit of the mountain and by mortars and artillery. Four and Five Platoons were merged into a composite force and, accompanied by a small group from Company HQ, they were to approach along the route just used for the withdrawal as this was known to be clear. They moved up the ridge to the north, and waited while the final 'fire for effect' came down on the enemy positions. When the FOO moved along the fire further east, they moved forward and immediately came under fire from point blank range after having gone only some 30 yards. The muzzle flashes could be seen from Company HQ but not by the platoon. The OC ordered the FOO to fire a 66mm round at the position to identify the target, which was done 'with enthusiasm'. Even so, the platoon commander was not sure where the enemy were but ordered the section to his rear to throw grenades so that he could extricate himself and his radio operator. No more fire came from the position, so the platoon commander and a rifleman both fired 66s at it and ran forward firing their rifles. Three enemy dead were found immediately and more after first light. Nothing had been heard from the '50 cal' for some time and it was hoped that it had been neutralized, and there seemed to be less activity in the area of its position since the bombardment. As B Company left cover to move forward they came under automatic fire from two flanks: one from a position further east of the HMG and another from the north-east where it was known that there were a number of enemy trenches. It was decided to move back and up onto the ridge to try and come at the enemy from behind. As this move was being carried out more fire came down, causing three more injuries. B Company's numbers were now critical, and so it was decided to pass A Company through them to continue the action eastwards.

As A Company had approached their objective from the north, they had come under increasingly accurate fire from the Argentine positions at the east of the feature. Due to lack of cover, they moved forward to a series of peat banks with One Platoon on the left and Two Platoon on the right. Tac HQ was behind One Platoon and Company HQ was left and to the rear. Three Platoon was right rear. In seeking the cover of the peat banks, the company sustained their first casualties. The initial Argentine fire had been onto planned DFs, but they soon began to adjust this indirect fire back onto the A Company and the reserve C Company positions. It became obvious that the company could not move forward as originally planned across the very open ground without sustaining more casualties from the accurate machine gun and sniper fire from the high ground to their front, so they were ordered to pull back and move round to the western end of the mountain, and pass through B Company to assault their objective (*Full Back*) from the west.

B Company's fight had established that outflanking the Argentines from the north of the feature would be too costly. A Company then decided to attack along the ridge and Coy HQ Support Group under the second-in-command, Capt Freer, moved forwards to position two GPMGs to cover the advance. The FOO attached to the company also moved forward and began to call down artillery fire. Once covering fire was coming in, the platoons began to cross the ridge by crawling on their stomachs towards the Argentine positions. The advance was slow and the enemy fire accurate. In spite of the weight of covering fire, the lead section had to use all its own grenades and its 66s, together with the following sections's 66s to clear the enemy positions as they moved forward. As the third section of the leading platoon crossed the crest, some of the enemy could be seen starting to withdraw. As One Platoon followed Two Platoon over the crest, the supporting fire had to be stopped as it was becoming hazardous to own troops. The two platoons then fixed bayonets and proceeded to clear through the Argentines with bullet, grenade and cold steel, a brutal but efficient business. As the platoons advanced more enemy could be seen withdrawing to the east, and these were engaged by the support groups. Eventually, after an action lasting ten hours, the mountain was in British hands.

Ferocious attack

As daybreak came the companies were reorganizing on the feature. Mercifully, a heavy mist shrouded the mountain, hiding them from the Argentine guns on the hill to the south and east around Stanley.

But the price of victory had been high. The paras had lost 23 killed and some 47 wounded. The Argentine casualties had been much higher (over 50 died), and many of them could never be identified. The killing went on afterwards, however. When the mist cleared the Argentine guns claimed six more lives, and many others wounded.

Mount Harriet: steep and lonely

There is a military proverb that says: 'Sweat saves blood and brains save sweat.' It is amply borne out by the attack and capture of Mount Harriet where meticulous planning and the use of surprise achieved victory at very low cost.

THE ATTACK TOOK PLACE on the night of 11 June and Lt Col Nick Vaux took a route that was least expected by the Argentine troops on Harriet. He attacked from the east, after taking the Commando through a minefield to the south and making a 180° turn to approach the feature from the least expected axis.

Harriet is a rugged outcrop of limestone due south of Two Sisters. Between them the features of Harriet and Two Sisters offer a natural screen for Mounts Longdon, Tumbledown and William further to the east. Harriet and Two Sisters, as well as Mount Challenger to the west, are linked by saddles of high ground that are not only exposed by day, but are so featureless that they make navigation very difficult by night. Between Challenger and Harriet is Goat Ridge.

Lt Col Nick Vaux, who as a young troop commander had landed at Suez, had been in the area since elements of 42 Commando had landed at Mount Kent. The good visibility had allowed him to assess the positions on Harriet and prepare his plan. However, before he could proceed with detailed planning a more complete picture of enemy positions, and particularly minefields, had to be built up.

K and L Companies sent out patrols and tragically two marines in L lost legs when they triggered anti-personnel mines. K Company, tasked with the route for the attack, also put out fighting patrols to inhibit the enemy. While men were prodding in minefields, the fighting patrols ensured that the Argentine garrison remained in their bunkers. And Sergeant 'Jumper'

Collins led two patrols to find paths through the minefields and a covered approach south of Mount Harriet.

A fighting patrol by 1 Troop worked its way to within 20 yards of enemy positions on Harriet, when they came under fire. But their reply—66mm and 84mm anti-tank weapons and gunfire directed by Captain Chris Romberg—enabled them to withdraw without loss, after killing six Argentines.

Shell fire from Argentine 105mm and 155mm guns, and bitterly cold weather, made life more unpleasant for the men of 42 as they readied themselves for the next phase of operations. Diarrhoea and trench foot already affected a number of men. Rations were generally the dehydrated Arctic type. Everyone had been warned about the liver fluke in the Falklands water and it took time to collect and boil or sterilize water—a chore performed grudgingly by men who might have been out for 16 hours in the night probing enemy positions.

At the Orders Group

Vaux quietly told his men: 'Surprise and absolute silence are vital. If necessary, you must go through the old business of making every man jump up and down before he starts, to check that nothing rattles. Persistent coughers must be left behind. If you find yourself in a minefield remember that you *must* go on. Men must not stop for their oppos, however great the temptation. They *must* go through and finish the attack, or it will cost more lives in the end … The enemy are well dug-in in very strong positions. But I believe that, once we get in among them, they will crack pretty quickly.'

The plan for 42 Cdo was to secure Harriet with a night attack in which K Company would outflank the enemy with an assault from the rear, before L exploited this advantage to overrun forward positions. J Company would secure the start line before moving forward to consolidate on the captured feature.

The approach march along the south of the feature was going to be a nerve-racking phase—the ground was completely open and an alert sentry on Harriet could bring down fire on the Royal Marines.

The Reconnaissance Platoon of the Welsh Guards were tasked with securing the start line with J Company, and there was a maddening delay of one hour as the guardsmen failed to link up in the dark. Once they were in position K Company moved off. During the move Lt Col Vaux kept the men well spaced out as they weaved through the minefield. They had reached a point 100 yards from enemy positions before they were detected. Then the fight began. The tactics used were similar to those employed in house-clearing with grenades, 66mm and 84mm gunfire all coming into play. And naval gunfire from HMS *Yarmouth*, 105mm Light Guns and 81mm mortars hit positions in front of the men as they advanced.

During the night the Commando had four batteries on call to give a 'full regimental shoot'—one of the heaviest artillery concentrations since World War 2. The CO of 29 Commando Rgt RA co-ordinating fire support for the night actions had 'on call' a list of 47 targets. During the night his guns fired 3000 rounds, some shells falling only 50 yards from friendly forces.

When the Commando used their 66mm or 84mm anti-tank weaons they would shout 'Sixty six' or 'Eighty four' as a warning to men who might be caught in the back blast. Captain Ian MacNeill recalled the effect of these weapons: 'The demoralizing effect of even near misses must have been considerable—most of the members of K and L Companies closest to the explosions testified that they, too, speedily got their heads down, such was the impact of the missiles exploding.'

The men of K Company were later to recall Corporal Newland who appeared to be relaxing against a rock pulling on a cigarette—he had, in fact, been shot through both legs, but continued to man the radio and command his section.

L/Cpl Koleszar had the surprising experience of finding that two 'dead' Argentine soldiers, whose boots he was trying to remove, were very much alive and jumped up to surrender.

As the men reached the summit, an enemy hut caught fire and gave the Argentine gunners a good aiming point. Shell fire wounded members of the Company HQ including the second-in-command. It also interrupted the fire fights as each side dived for cover. But with first light, the Sergeant Major of K Company collected nearly 70 prisoners.

L Company had to assault uphill through the rocks. Though artillery fire forced them to take cover, they realized that the real threat was from the .50in machine guns and groups of snipers with excellent German bolt-action weapons. Many of the bunkers around Goat Ridge had been pinpointed by patrols of the Royal Marines Mountain and Arctic Warfare Cadre and so Lt Col Vaux was able to use Milan anti-tank missiles against them. He admitted it was expensive—they cost about £10,000 each—'but it was our job to get rid of them'. By first light the men had overrun their objectives with two officers and five marines wounded.

J Company were ready to move off on the very cold morning of 12 June. All went well until they reached the slopes of Harriet where enemy defensive fire from artillery was still falling. But it ceased before the marines were on the upper slopes.

The marines' revenge

With dawn J Company began to sweep through the positions to clear the remaining enemy who seemed happy to surrender. Within three hours, 58 prisoners had been processed and despatched for Company HQ. For the men of J Company, the victory at Harriet was a more personal triumph since they were made up of men who had been in Naval Party 8901—The Royal Marines who had defended Government House back in April when the Argentine forces landed—and Major Mike Norman, their erstwhile OC.

Harriet yielded over 300 prisoners as well as documents that were of great value to the intelligence staff at 3 Brigade. Elsewhere on the feature among the well-built bunkers there was a litter of .50in machine guns, rockets and ammunition amongst which were some hollow point 9mm rounds—or 'dum dum' bullets. In the simple shelters the marines found foam rubber mattresses and ration packs that compared well with their GS or Arctic packs. Argentine soldiers received a pack which included powdered fruit juice, beef pâté and soap and razors. There was even a small bottle of whisky with the doubtful name of 'Breeders Choice.' Finally, in an unopened crate a battlefield radar set was discovered near the summit.

A dozen Argentine prisoners collected at the foot of Harriet were told by sign language that they should walk, not run, otherwise they would be shot. They misunderstood and thought that they were being ordered to run not walk so that they could be shot. The message was got across to them eventually: their war was finally over.

The taking of Two Sisters

Most of the young marines expected some sort of visual impact: flashes of explosive, men running, or falling. In fact, the 45 Commando attack on Two Sisters was all noises and, to everyone's relief, only a few casualties.

IT WAS DAYLIGHT and Lieutenant Chris Fox, together with his recce patrol, was lying up on the enemy slopes of Two Sisters. They were efficiently concealed, as well they might be: it was several miles back to their assault base across a wide open valley and over the ridge of Mount Kent.

They had moved forward to this dangerous position just 24 hours after completing, with the rest of 45 Commando, their epic yomp from San Carlos. Their mission was to locate Argentine bunkers, and now they were waiting for darkness to fall before returning to base. Darkness is the only truly effective cover on those bare Falkland hillsides.

An Argentine patrol literally stumbled on them. Rifle fire poured down without warning from above, most of it frighteningly accurate. Fox received a bullet through the hand. He had no orders to fight back under these circumstances; on the other hand he had no choice. He and his men returned a devastating hail of SLR and sub-machine gun fire. Twelve Argentines were killed, and a further three suspected hit. When darkness arrived, the marines slipped away without casualties. It was an interesting start to 45 Commando's battle for Two Sisters: almost as many Argentines died in the clash as in the main assault which followed later.

Lt Fox was flown back to the medical centre at Ajax Bay, but soon rejoined his unit with a stitched hand and scarred finger. His work was to earn him an MC.

No one knew at that stage when the real attack on Two Sisters would take place; most of the men had been expecting to go into the assault within

24 hours. As Colour Sergeant Bill Eades had said on the march, 'There's only one way out of this bastard, and that's through Stanley', and now Stanley was tantalisingly close beyond the twin rocky peaks of Two Sisters. You could see the airport and the harbour from the ridge above the commando base on Mount Kent.

Maximum artillery

But in the end they had to wait eight days for 5 Infantry Brigade to arrive as reinforcement, and for Brigadier Thompson to decide to give the order to go. Learning the lesson of the under-supported attack at Goose Green, he had decreed a maximum level of artillery support for the battles in the hills around Stanley. Whenever the mist and blizzard let up, the helicopters would come droning up the valleys with huge pallets of ammunition slung in nets under their bellies. Eventually five batteries were dug in around Mount Kent, each with six 105mm guns, every gun with 1200 rounds.

Two nights before the attack was finally called, 45 was hit by their worst disaster of the war—a 'blue on blue' or 'friendly-friendly' clash between their own mortar troop and a patrol. In the dark, the patrol was taken for Argentine; the mortars opened up, to be met with a withering return of fire. In the confusion, five died, including the mortar troop sergeant, and two were wounded. It was one of those tragedies that are inevitable in war, but while 45 took it philosophically enough, everyone felt it a blemish on their exemplary record in the Falklands.

If anything, the tragedy increased the determination of the CO, Lt Col Whitehead, to take Two Sisters with the minimum casualties. He had been critical of the level of casualties at Goose Green and said before his own assault: 'Let's finish what promises to be the last lap in style. I want no futile and useless casualties.'

The battle plan for the night of Friday 11 June was described by one officer as a 'straightforward, Warminster-style assault'. By this he meant the orthodox infantry attack plan taught since World War 2. Although the approach to the enemy lines would be 'silent', the battle itself would be 'noisy' with the maximum weight of artillery hurled at the Argentines as the riflemen stormed their positions. While 45 would take Two Sisters, 3 Para would assault Mount Longdon to the north and 42 Commando Mount Harriet to the South. HMS *Glamorgan* was to provide naval gunfire support.

Late start to the battle

The Start Line was at Murrell Bridge, a rickety structure over the Murrell River at the foot of Mount Kent. The lead rifle company for the assault,

'X' or 'X-ray', led by the able and articulate Captain Ian Gardiner, should have been there at midnight.

But the commandos were two hours late at the start line, bogged down by peat and slowed by fearsome rock-runs over which they had had to hump the heavy weapons. Whitehead was on the radio net threatening to 'come down and kick' the rifle company into action as they finally began to cross the dead ground towards the southern ridge of the hill. Capt Gardiner's company made the lower ridge of the southern peak of the Two Sisters without problems but were then promptly pinned down by ferocious machine gun and mortar fire.

A night battle on this scale is an extraordinary experience. Most of the young marines expected some sort of visual impact, with men running, guns firing, targets falling and so on. In fact it is nothing like that. Sound is the predominant impact: the whoosh and thunder of incoming artillery, the enormous bang from the British guns behind, the steady pok-pok of the Argentines' 0.5in heavy machine guns sending down a stream of red tracer from the bunkers above.

As X-Ray scratched what cover they could from the rocks and peat ridges, trying to pin-point the enemy bunkers and working out routes to their trenches, Whitehead coolly decided to change the whole battle plan. It was clear that there was no way X-Ray could storm the twin peaks without massive casualties, so he decided to bring in the other two companies to advance up the northern peak. In a series of quiet commands typical of the colonel's style, he repositioned his men for a steady, stealthy assault up the hillsides each side of the main saddle between the peaks.

As the rifle companies found what shelter they could on the peaks, enemy artillery still pounded in, sending up sprays of peat from the saddle between them. The marines were carrying no sleeping bags or shelters. Exhausted, they began to slump down in the snow drifting between the rocks. Whitehead, anxious for their welfare, ordered them to find what kit they could among the Argentines' positions, and as the morning drew on, his men could be seen setting up an instant camp from salvaged ponchos and sleeping bags.

The aftermath

As the helicopters crept along the contours of the hill to pick up dead and wounded, seemingly oblivious as usual to fog or enemy fire, Whitehead gave his characteristically curt verdict on the fortifications he had just stormed: 'Give me 120 men and I could die of old age defending this hill.'

For the men of 45, the battle of Two Sisters had been no pushover, however. Whitehead's inspired planning had kept the level of casualties to a minimum, but the paras on Mount Longdon hadn't seen it that way: the sheer weight of fire coming down on the marines had excited the sympathy even of the paras. By the same token, the marines watched with awe the firefight on Mount Longdon, one man saying 'Not even the paras'll be able to walk on water after this one.' A young marine, asked to write a minimum of ten words about the battle, had only this to say: 'It was a cold and dark night the time we took Two Sisters. I am still trying to forget that night, so I will write no more about it.'

Others dug in and waited for the next battle, numbed by what they had experienced. They had all been professionals before, but now they were truly battle-hardened veterans.

The cost of battle

After the battle for Mount Longdon was over, Colonel Hew Pike summed up the feelings of much of 3 Para when he echoed the words of the Duke of Wellington: 'There is nothing half so melanchony as a battle won ... unless it be a battle lost.'

WITHIN A GROUP as small and homogeneous as a ship, battalion or Commando it is possible for the commanding officer to know something about each man. In 650 or 800 men there are the characters, the problems and the men who can be relied on to keep going in conditions of great physical and personal pressure.

Since the British forces are volunteers there is a stronger sense of cohesion than in a conscript army. Against this background the loss of men killed in action is profoundly felt. The lieutenant, captain or colonel would know a great deal about the soldier or sailor under his command.

But the hardest experience during the campaign fell to the mothers, wives and friends who were at home watching the news and listening to the at times ambiguous statements from the MoD.

Robert Fox wrote in *Eyewitness Falklands* of a conversation with the wife of an officer in the Parachute Regiment after he had returned from the Falklands: 'You bloody journalists out there don't understand what hell we went through back here, we wives. Can you honestly know what it was like looking after all the wives? To tell one with two babies crawling round her, and her stomach out two feet expecting another, that her man isn't coming back?'

Telling the next of kin of the death of their son or husband fell to the men who remained at home. The Married Families Liaison Officer with the Royal Marines, or the Families Officer with an infantry battalion would take some of the weight of grief and worry. The families in the married quarters too were a source of strength—all of them sharing the fears and concerns with one another.

But for the young unmarried servicemen with parents living away from the depot, home port or barracks, the responsibility for breaking the news of a son's death would fall to the local police force.

At the South Concourse of the Ministry of Defence the first public news of casualties came in typewritten and photocopied lists. They carried the full rank, Christian name, surname, age and home town of each man if he came from a ship, or arm of service if he was a soldier or Royal Marine.

All these experiences were in strong contrast to those of the Argentine conscripted servicemen who were flown to the Malvinas. When British-supervised burial parties started to collect the dead they discovered that some of the Argentine soldiers' identity tags only bore their blood group. The British forces carry two—each with the blood group, name, service number and religion. In the event of death, one tag is left with the body and the other collected as a record. When subsequent re-burial takes place the body can be identified. For many Argentine next of kin the fate of their relatives is still unknown, simply because the British undertakers who re-buried them at Darwin have no idea who they were.

The Exocet's last victim

The Exocet had an awesome reputation. It had already knocked out *Sheffield* and *Atlantic Conveyor*. Now one crashed into the helicopter hangar of *Glamorgan*, killing 13 men. But prompt action saved her. *Glamorgan* took an Exocet and survived.

GLAMORGAN'S OUTDATED RADARS never even saw the fast-moving, low-flying missile. It was the Officer of the Watch on the bridge who first spotted the incoming Exocet. It was 0235 hours on the morning of 12 June. With lightning reactions, he executed the classic evasive manoeuvre. He turned hard to starboard.

Ten seconds later, the turn not quite completed, the missile struck. It skidded along the main deck and crashed into the helicopter hangar, then through the galley below. Thirteen men were killed and a further 22 injured. But it could have been a lot worse. *Glamorgan* survived to sail back to Portsmouth. The month before, *Sheffield* had been hit and later sunk beneath the waves of the South Atlantic.

The first *Glamorgan*

The Royal Navy maintains a fierce tradition in the naming of its warships. The crew of *Invincible*, for example, would have been well aware that an earlier ship of that name had defeated Vice-Admiral Graf Spee's squadron near the Falklands in World War 1. The crew of *Exeter*—the fifth Royal Navy ship to bear that name since 1680—would have known that another *Exeter* had fought the pocket battleship *Graf Spee* in the same area in World War 2. And they would have known that an even earlier *Exeter* had been part of a squadron which captured the first *Ardent* from the French in

1746. But the *Glamorgan* that had gone south with the Task Force was the first ship to bear that name.

Before that fateful 12 June, though, *Glamorgan* had already done enough to earn a place in the history books. She had led the Task Force south, flying Admiral Woodward's flag as commander of Task Force 317 until he transferred to HMS *Hermes*. She had proved a tower of strength to the rest of the Task Force all the way. She had repeatedly landed and assisted Special Forces on the Falkland Islands and laid down a devastating bombardment on the airstrip at Pebble Island with her twin 4.5in guns.

She had supported the diversionary raids on 21 May, then had joined in with the forces defending San Carlos on the next day. Though her anti-aircraft and anti-submarine weapons systems were a generation older than the latest systems being used by the Royal Navy, her guns were tireless in providing firepower support for the forces ashore. And it was in her Naval Gunfire Support role that *Glamorgan* became popular with the marines and soldiers. Had it not been for the events of 12 June, *Glamorgan* would have fired more NGS rounds than any other vessel. As it was, only the undamaged *Yarmouth*, another ship popular with the troops, fired more.

In the time between San Carlos and the final assault on Port Stanley, there was only limited NGS work to be done. And since the Task Force had been strengthened by the arrival of seven destroyers and frigates on 23 May, Rear-Admiral Sandy Woodward felt that he could spare *Glamorgan* from operations in the combat zone to look after the Towing Repair and Logistics Area. TRALA was a box of sea, some 200 nautical miles east of Port Stanley, outside the combat radius of most of the Argentine air force. In the TRALA were a varying number of tugs and repair ships, logistic ships and vessels which were not immediately needed but had to be kept close by and out of harm's way.

A very rich target

In effect the TRALA was a stationary convoy which presented a very rich target to any Argentine air, surface or submarine attack. *Glamorgan's* job was to defend these vessels—though as the sole escort it could probably only have countered an Argentine attack—and to co-ordinate the activities of the TRALA. These could become very complex with several ships leaving and entering the area at any one time to replenish their ammunition or provisions, or to repair damage.

Her peaceful sojourn as TRALA manager came to an end on the evening of 11 June. On the islands the British forces were, of course, outnumbered, so these attacks needed all the support they could get. As much NGS as possible was needed. *Glamorgan* was recalled to the gunline.

It was now well known that the gunline was a risky place to inhabit.

Already *Ardent* had been sunk and *Plymouth* had been badly damaged there. The regular course followed by ships bombarding the coast made them vulnerable to attacks from submarines, fast-attack craft, coastal artillery and missiles; and there was the ever-present fear of air attack, though this was reduced as most of the NGS now occurred at night.

The threat from submarines and fast-attack craft was contained by the Royal Navy's anti-submarine and helicopter forces. The Argentines did use their battery of 155mm Model 77 howitzers against the bombarding ships; but without proper fire control they found it impossible to hit what were, in effect, relatively small moving targets at long range.

The Argentines did have some effective weapons, though—two Exocet MM.38 surface-to-surface missiles mounted in launch boxes on trailers. The missiles had been removed from the light frigate ARA *Guerrico* which had been immobilized, ironically enough, when the ship strayed too close to South Georgia on 3 April. The Royal Marines who were defending the island kept up a sustained fire on the ship with machine guns, small arms and a Carl Gustav anti-tank weapon. *Guerrico* was returned to Argentina so badly damaged that she never left port again, but her weapon systems were stripped from her and flown out to the island.

Ten seconds to turn

Glamorgan was on the gunline 18 miles from shore, and at the alert, when she was hit. But neither the Type 992Q Target Indicator or the Type 965M surveillance radars detected the incoming Exocet. These old radars were unable to see such a low-flying, fast-moving, small target against the background clutter. The first warning of the approach of the missile came when the Officer of the Watch on the bridge of *Glamorgan* made a visual sighting. With great presence of mind he performed the classic naval manoeuvre. He turned the ship away from the missile so that it would be presented with the smallest possible target area, the ship's stern.

Turning the ship so that the stern is facing the incoming threat was a tactic first developed to combat the torpedo. It was used as long ago as 1916 in the Battle of Jutland. The ploy has two effects. It reduces the size of target that the ship makes for the missile by a factor of about ten— *Glamorgan* is some 520½ft long but its beam is only 54ft wide. This makes the task of decoying the missile a great deal easier, but in *Glamorgan*'s case there was no time to deploy the chaff decoys. There were only ten seconds between detection and impact.

Though no part of a ship can ever be described as a good place for a missile to hit, the stern of the ship is probably the least worst. This is because a ship is more likely to remain afloat with her stern blown off than her bow, and a missile hitting a ship broadside is likely to hit vital machinery or a control centre. In either case the ship would be paralysed and left a sitting duck for further attacks. Worse still, it might hit one of the magazines which would destroy the ship outright with great loss of life.

But it wasn't just the good handling of *Glamorgan* which saved her. She also had a piece of good luck. Just like the air-launched AM.39 Exocet that hit *Sheffield*, the surface-launched MM.38 failed to detonate on impact. Had the warhead detonated, it would have caused massive damage to the stern of *Glamorgan* and would probably have meant the loss of the ship. As it was, *Glamorgan* limped back into Portsmouth on 10 July. Her shattered hangar was shielded from the elements by a large tarpaulin, but in all other respects her superstructure remained intact, adding weight to the theory that the Exocet, on its last legs at the end of its run, had failed to explode.

The lone raider

One of the most audacious attacks of the whole war could have wiped out Menendez and his staff in one blow. For Lt Manley and Petty Officer Ball, it was nearly a moment of glory; for the Task Force, it might have ended the war early. It failed—just—but it was worth a try.

ON THE MORNING of 12 June, while 3 Para were enduring bitter weather and enemy shellfire on Mount Longdon, one of the most unusual operations of the entire campaign took place. A lone Wessex helicopter attacked a building in Port Stanley and all but succeeded in destroying the Argentine command structure on the Falkland Islands.

It began, predictably enough, with the Special Forces. An SBS patrol in the Port Stanley area noticed that, every morning, some sort of conference would take place in the town hall. The road outside would be thick with parked vehicles. It seemed likely that Menendez, Joffre and their staff were, if not the reason for the meetings, at least regular attenders. The SBS, not unnaturally, felt that this daily conference represented an ideal opportunity to 'take out' the entire Argentine command structure. The temptation was irresistible.

While knowing very little about what the SBS and SAS were doing in the Port Stanley area, it is possible to draw some tentative conclusions. The town hall stands on the waterfront, facing away from the harbour towards the main road. An OP on Sapper Hill might have seen the vehicles congregated outside, but any OP across the harbour near Wireless Ridge would have noticed the vehicles coming and going as well. Observation must have lasted several days so that any sort of pattern could be detected and some plan of attack worked out.

It isn't clear whose idea it was to attack the town hall, but it certainly wasn't an original idea: since the middle of World War 2 audacious commandos have made several attempts to destroy the enemy's high command. In 1942 Lt Col Geoffrey Keyes won a posthumous VC after leading an unsuccessful commando raid on Rommel's headquarters in North Africa. In 1944 Major Otto Skorzeny of the German Friedenthal Organization put the fear of God into the Allied high command during the Battle of the Bulge: it was rumoured that he planned to assassinate General Eisenhower in Versailles. He had no intention of doing so, but the threat frightened the Allies so much that they tied themselves in knots looking for Skorzeny and his commandos.

The precedents were clear, and so, at this stage, was the need. General Moore's divisional plan called for a three-phase attack on Port Stanley: the first two phases would be brigade-strength attacks on the high ground to the west; the third phase was to be an all-out battle in the streets of Port Stanley. If Menendez and his senior staff were 'taken out', ran the thinking, the Argentine forces would collapse without any sort of leadership. The sooner it happened, the better. With a bit of luck, they might crack before the final assault went in. At worst, they wouldn't be able to offer any kind of organized defence.

Quite possibly the thought of revenge had entered a few minds: just two days before, a flight of Skyhawks had bombed 3 Commando Brigade's headquarters at Bluff Cove Peak. There had been no casualties, but both Brig Thompson and Maj Gen Moore were there at the time, and the possibility of losing them didn't bear thinking about. Or did it? Tit for tat? We may never know, but the upshot was a decision to attack the town hall.

Exactly who tasked the helicopter is not clear. It would have been logical to use a Harrier for the job and drop a laser-guided bomb; cannon fire or a salvo of 68mm rockets might have done equally well. But a Harrier goes very fast—too fast, some might say, for accuracy, especially when 1000lb bombs are concerned. And there were the civilians in Port Stanley to be considered. By the same token a sneak, terrorist-style attack by the Special Forces was out of the question—there might be reprisals against the civilians. So it had to be a helicopter. But what kind?

Raising the roof

A missile-armed helicopter would have to be used, but not the Gazelle as it was too vulnerable. A Scout, or Wasp? They both carry AS12 missiles and they're both light, agile machines. Wessex 5 helicopters carry AS12s as well, however. It seems that the choice of a Wessex 5 was made for a variety of devious reasons: The SBS reputedly put the idea to an officer in 845 Naval Air Squadron; he heartily approved the idea. 845 and the SBS worked out a reasonable plan and took it to higher authority.

The idea was approved, and so, on the morning of 12 June, the weary British troops up in the mountain had a grandstand view of a single Wessex 5, flown by Lt Peter Manley and with Petty Officer Arthur Ball as gunner, swooping low over Port Stanley after a low-level flight through the mountains, and letting fly at the town hall. The first AS12 hit the roof of Port Stanley police station and blew it off; the second missed, hitting some telegraph poles and landing in the harbour.

There was no time to do more. As every gun in Port Stanley opened fire, the helicopter 'bugged out', back to the safety of the mountains. In the six weeks since the first air raids on Port Stanley the Argentine gunners still hadn't learned from their mistakes—this time they shot down one of their own helicopters in the confusion.

It was a brave attempt that could have only been tried once. A single pass over a heavily defended target didn't allow the pilot and his air-crewman who aimed the weapon to get the range and bearing. But it was a worth a try, and is said to have shaken up the senior Argentine officers considerably.

12 JUNE 1982

The Queen is back!

It was a mixture designed to bring out the patriotism in all but the most half-hearted: famous ocean liner, precious cargo of survivors, victorious home-coming. For those there to meet them, Southampton Water would never be so memorable again.

ON SATURDAY 12 JUNE *QE2*, flagship of the Cunard Line, and most famous of the civilian ships commandeered for duty in the South Atlantic, glided up the Solent for her home port of Southampton to the sort of jubilant reception not seen since the end of World World 2.

In a month-long epic voyage, the mighty Queen had covered 14,000 miles, her great engines propelling her 67,000 tons through some of the most dangerous waters in the world.

As the liner began to pick up her welcoming escort of small boats on her slow run into Southampton Water, her decks were packed with nearly all of the 629 survivors of HMS *Coventry*, *Ardent* and *Antelope*.

It had taken the liner just 13 days to make the homeward trip. The route back had taken her well to the east in order to be certain that there was no danger from land-based Argentine aircraft, though as one of her crew officers pointed out, there was always the danger of a one-way kamikaze-style attack. She refuelled once from a Royal Fleet Auxiliary tanker, the first time that she had ever been refuelled at sea.

Among the survivors on board were 21 wounded, and seven of these spent the return trip in the ship's hospital under the expert care of Sister Jane Yelland and her staff. Some of the casualties she had treated for superficial burns, but others had shrapnel wounds that were far more serious. It was a tribute to *QE2*'s hospital team that on disembarkation only one man still needed hospitalization.

Perhaps the most important service carried out by the Cunard crew of 700 on the homeward leg was the boosting of their passengers' morale. These men had suffered the shock of being bombed and sunk, had lost friends and comrades in the most horrific circumstances, and were returning as survivors rather than as victors. The Cunard crew must have done their job, for the men lining the decks were in a genuinely festive mood. The 22 women of the Cunard crew were given a boisterous return journey, and had dates booked for weeks ahead. There had even been exchange of suspender belts and panties for the rather less glamourous khaki underpants of their charges.

Five hours before *QE2* docked, a group of journalists was flown out to the liner in RAF helicopters to conduct interviews with anyone who would listen. While still in the Solent, one of the first to greet the liner was the Royal Yacht *Britannia*. While an RM band crashed away behind her, the Queen Mother waved from the foredeck, and received wild cheers from the men on *QE2*. Now the flotilla of little boats began to swell in number and the excitement mounted. There were tugs and pleasure craft, coasters and yachts. Time and time again they gave the liner a three-blast salute, and each time the sonorous hooter of the liner responded. In the sky overhead, helicopters clattered and light aircraft circled. With a great roar, a military jet thundered past, dipping its wings in salute.

On the dockside, a riot of flags and bunting fluttered in the sea breezes, while two military bands competed to hammer out patriotic airs and the crowds roared. Over 6000 people crammed the quay, cheering, singing, holding up children, laughing and crying. As the great ship edged into its berth, the men at the rails could read their own names on specially printed 'Welcome Home' T-shirts.

They disembarked in order. First came the 255 men from *Coventry*, then the 177 men from *Ardent*, then the 197 men from *Antelope*. They carried their kitbags, and many still wore the rubber flip-flops they had worn on deck. They seemed very young. The bands played, and the laughter and tears mixed, and wives and children and parents tried not to look too startled at the newly healed scars. For most, this was their first and last voyage on an ocean liner. *QE2* herself would go for cleaning up, refitting, refurbishing. The next passenger list would look very different when she sailed to New York in August. But the crew would not forget this extraordinary human cargo in a hurry.

Paras take Wireless Ridge

For the men of 2 Para, Wireless ridge was just another battle; after this one, they thought, the last would be a street fight in Port Stanley. But it never came to that. Under their firepower, the Argentines broke. 2 Para chased them into Port Stanley.

THE ASSAULT and capture of Wireless Ridge is unique in the Falklands campaign on two counts. It was the only action fought by a battalion that had already fought a major battle, and it brought into play a broader array of weapons than any other engagement to make it a truly 'all arms' battle.

The men of 2 Para had fought at Darwin and Goose Green on 28 May, and at Wireless Ridge on 13–14 June they used the lessons they had learned there. Not only did they bring in naval gunfire support and land-based artillery, they also deployed CVR(T) Scorpions and Scimitars, armed Scout helicopters and their own Milan and 81mm mortars.

From Fitzroy 2 Para had moved by helicopter to Mount Kent. Back under the command of 3 Brigade, they were initially tasked with support-ing the attacks by 3 Para and 45 Commando on the night of 1 June. They weren't needed and, after the attacks on Mount Longdon and Two Sisters, moved by foot to a position to the north of Mount Longdon, where they dug in at an assembly area under a scarp slope that gave some protection from the Argentines' 105mm and 155mm artillery.

Battalion HQ were rather startled when they got the order 'It's Wireless Ridge tonight' from Lt Col Chaundler when he returned with orders from 3 Brigade on 12 June. But the attack planned for that night was postponed for 24 hours and gave them more time to prepare detailed orders. This was as well as the positions on Wireless Ridge were reported to be held by men from the Argentine 7 Regiment from La Plata and the 1st Argentine Parachute Regiment.

An attack by seven Argentine A4 Skyhawks narrowly missed 3 Bde HQ and caused a delay in the movement of the mortar and machine gun platoons. The Royal Artillery forward observation officer was also delayed and he had to register targets after the previous night using illumination rounds.

As 2 Para's attack was being planned they discovered that a feature called Hill X to the north-east of Mount Longdon was still in enemy possession. A small headland on the mouth of the Murrell River to the north-east of Wireless Ridge was also held by the enemy and positions between these, the approaches to Wireless Ridge, were held in greater strength than had earlier been reported. So a new plan was drafted. This called for a four-phase noisy attack. The decision to go noisy rather than use the silent tactics employed by other battalions was significant. Silent attacks had the advantage of surprise, but once battle was joined it was sometimes difficult to use NGS or artillery fire effectively because the two sides were mixed together.

The new plan called for D Company to attack the position to the east of 3 Para, A and B to go for the centre and provide fire support for D as it swung left and attacked Wireless Ridge from the west. C Company which had carried out the reconnaissance of the route forward and secured the start line would then hook round to the left to take the position on the banks of the Murrell River mouth.

Firepower!

After their problems with fire support at Darwin and Goose Green, 2 Para were to have two batteries on priority call, the mortars of both 2 and 3 Para and two Scimitar CVR(T)s with 30mm Rarden Cannon and two Scorpions with 76mm guns. NGS would also be given and the Milan platoon was tasked to manpack their firing posts forward to give direct support.

The battalion moved out at last light, 2030 hours. But as they were on the move Lt Col Chaundler received information that a captured enemy map showed a minefield in front of A and B Companies' objective. By now there was no time to call a halt, so the attack went on.

At 0045 hours on 14 June after 30 minutes of artillery fire, D Company moved up to the start line. 'Once again finding the start line proved an interesting exercise', as they commented later. But right on time they crossed it and seized their objective, nicknamed 'Rough Diamond'. As they took the Argentine position 155mm air-burst shells sent them diving for cover. Much to the amusement of the 'toms' the company second-in-command and a para found that they had dived into the enemy's latrines. The position itself had been vacated by the enemy some time before.

A and B Companies watched as supporting fire fell on the enemy positions. 'It was a great comfort—better than a Warminster Fire Power Demo,' said one para. Over 6000 rounds fell on Argentine positions that night. The CVR(T)s with their second-generation night-viewing equipment were able to engage targets, even when flares giving white light were being used. (First-generation night sights become temporarily ineffective when flares are used.) The tactic was for the CVR(T)s to hit a bunker with their main gun, and then, as the enemy attempted to escape, engage them with their co-axial GPMGs. The effect was dramatic, and the paras loved every minute of it.

A and B Companies began their advance, but as they approached their objective, they saw the enemy running away. The presence of radios and telephone cable there indicated that the position had probably been part of the 7 Regiment HQ. Fire from other positions was quickly silenced. Then, like D Company, they came under accurate 155mm fire. The Argentine gunners had moved one of their French-built 155mm guns into Stanley where it was difficult to locate and neutralize. The shelling went on for some nine hours as the companies dug in in the soggy peat.

C Company now moved round to the small hill to the west. Here they found abandoned tents and even 'warm boots', indicating that the enemy had departed somewhat hastily. And before they returned to the battalion, the company commander, Major Roger Jenny, had the satisfaction of sitting in an abandoned Argentine officers' mess.

As A and B companies reorganized, it was time for D company to be moved to a new start line at the western end of Wireless Ridge. The CVR(T)s of the Blues and Royals, commanded by Lieutenant Robin Innes-Ker, moved up to A and B Companies to give covering fire. It was here that the machine gun platoon set up a firebase. By the end of the operation they had fired over 40,000 rounds of ammunition and almost burned out three GPMGs.

Watching the CVR(T)s as they moved into position, one para commented, 'Bloody fools, they stuck themselves above the skyline and just kept blazing away.' But for the Blues and Royals it was a chance to prove their worth—throughout the campaign so far they had enjoyed no real opportunities to demonstrate how effective their tanks could be in action.

D Company moved through 'the start line' quickly and were now poised to clear along Wireless Ridge. But there was a pause as the fire support was co-ordinated. The company had the unnerving experience of being shelled by their own guns at one point. After 90 minutes the mix of illumination and high explosive rounds was deemed to be right and the attack went ahead.

An Argentine survivor from 7 Regiment called Guillermo recalled the attack in *Los Chicos de la Guerra:* 'Seven or eight of their machine guns fanned out and began firing at one of ours. They fired tracer bullets—they were luminous so you can see their trajectory in the air. And we saw a hail of bullets, like red rain in the shape of a fan, home in on the position.'

The paras pressed their attack home and came under heavy machine-gun and artillery fire. The reorganization was also very hazardous since they started to come under fire from Tumbledown and Mount William which had not yet been cleared by the Scots Guards and Gurkhas.

A counter-attack launched by Argentine troops was broken up by small arms and artillery fire. But Lt Page, the new commander of 12 platoon, had a nasty experience. A sniper's shot 'split the difference between two grenades and penetrated a magazine en route'. The Company Sergeant Major and Company Quartermaster Sergeant kept up the vital work of moving ammunition forward and casualties back as Argentine artillery fire burst above and around their stretcher parties and ammunition carriers.

The 2 Para mortar platoon fired illuminant rounds during the night and switched to high explosive rounds with the dawn. A universal problem in the Falklands was that the ground was either too soft or too hard for mortar base plates. On Wireless Ridge, as the 81mm mortars fired on supercharge, four of the platoon held down the base plates with their feet, knowing the enormous shock that would be transmitted through to their ankles. To keep the fire going down, the paras took this hazardous duty in turn and in turn four men suffered broken ankles.

The battalion had been supported by the men of their B Echelon. These are the men who normally work as cooks, clerks and storemen, but on Wireless Ridge they were in the thick of the action as additional stretcher bearers and ammunition carriers. In the light of their experience at Goose Green, 2 Para knew that ammunition was a vital priority as was the speedy evacuation of wounded. And the 'stretcher race' remembered from their P Company days at Aldershot took on a grim new meaning.

With first light, 2 Para found that they were looking down across a snow-covered slope towards the old RM barracks at Moody Brook. They had a chance to get a brew going and look around the enemy positions. These had been well dug. One platoon commander remarked that once down in the bunkers you couldn't hear the shelling. They may not have heard it, but some of the Argentines certainly felt the effect of the shelling. The bunkers were littered with clothing, weapons and corpses.

Lt Col Chaundler also heard at first light that 2 SG had taken Tumbledown so his men would not be exposed to fire across Moody Brook. At about the same time, 2 Para were subjected to an unexpected enemy counter-attack of about platoon strength. It was thought that this attack was mounted by men of the Argentine 1st Parachute Regiment.

The men of 2 Para watched as a combination of small arms fire with mortar and artillery fire broke up the attack. The failure of the attack seemed to break all resistance and the enemy began to stream back. Artillery fire directed on them sent men tumbling in the snow.

The Argentine artillery however, kept up a steady and heavy fire. Lt Col Chaundler asked for an airstrike to knock them out. At that stage weather conditions were unsuitable. But two Scout helicopters made two attacks with SS11 missiles at guns across the valley from Moody Brook.

By now there was every indication that the enemy were broken. A and B Companies were ordered forward with the CVR(T)s of the Blues and Royals. As they breasted the skyline of Wireless Ridge, 'it was like a scene out of *Zulu*', remembered Lt Col Chaundler.

3 Commando Brigade HQ was asked for permission to advance into Moody Brook and along Port Stanley Road. But it was initially denied until the Brigadier came forward to see the situation. At that time he still thought that Argentine forces would put up a stand. A final phase with formal attacks on Moody Brook camp and Sapper Hill were now being planned. During the battle for Wireless Ridge, 2 Para lost three men killed with a further 11 injured. Of the estimated 500 Argentines occupying the ridge some 100 were killed and 17 prisoners were taken. The rest fled.

Tumbledown: the final battle

The noose had tightened and the Argentines were now cornered in a small peninsula with Mount Tumbledown at its head. Its taking would seal their fate. Nobody knew how ferociously they would defend this, the last major objective before Stanley.

DESPITE THE DISASTER which had befallen *Sir Galahad* and *Sir Tristram*, on 9 June most of 5 Infantry Brigade were firmly entrenched in the Bluff Cove—Fitzroy area. The Gurkhas and the final support elements were on their way from Darwin in the MV *Monsunen*. And preparations for the final advance on Port Stanley could now get under way.

Brigadier Tony Wilson assembled the battalion commanders at Fitzroy in order to plan the brigade's part in this operation. He had been told that 3 Commando Brigade would seize Two Sisters and Mount Harriet on the night of 11 June, with 3 Para putting in a feint on Mount Longdon. It was then to be 5 Brigade's task to take out Mount Tumbledown, Mount William, Wireless Ridge and Sapper Hill—the last feature before Stanley itself. Brig Wilson's first idea was for the brigade to make its attack the following night, with 2 Para taking on Wireless Ridge and the Gurkhas mounting active patrols against Tumbledown and William on the same night as 3 Commando Brigade attacked in the hope that these would fall too. The Scots Guards, with a company of Gurkhas under their command, would move in step with 3 Commando Brigade, covering their south flank. If Tumbledown and William did not fall to the Gurkhas, the Scots Guards were to attack both of them at first light on 12 or 13 June. The Welsh Guards were down to only two effective companies, and Brig Wilson intended to keep them as his reserve.

Lt Col Mike Scott, commanding 2nd Battalion Scots Guards (2SG), had as his first concern, on returning from the Brigadier's conference, the recall of his Recce Platoon which was still forward of Bluff Cove at a covert patrol base. It would be needed for other tasks during the main advance. He sent a helicopter forward to bring the platoon commander back for briefing. But in the late afternoon, before the platoon itself could be withdrawn, it came under mortar and small fire arms fire, and it seemed as if the Argentines were about to attack.

A retreat under fire

Platoon Sergeant Allum gave the order to pull out. This manouevre was performed under intense mortar fire which wounded three men, including Sgt Allum. The casualties were taken to an emergency rendezvous and were lifted by helicopter direct to the main dressing station in Ajax Bay. The remainder of the platoon picked their way through a minefield which barred their retreat, then hitched a ride to Bluff Cove on the Scorpions and Scimitars of the Blues and Royals troop now with 5 Brigade. The important thing about this action was that it showed that the Argentines were well prepared to meet any threat from the south, along the track from Bluff Cove to Stanley.

This information made Lt Col Scott unhappy about having to attack Tumbledown from the south. Having held a planning meeting with his company commanders, supporting battery commander, adjutant, operations and intelligence officers, the concensus was that the long uphill assault at daylight across the harsh ground of Tumbledown's southern slopes would be suicidal. So he went back to Brig Wilson and said he would prefer to take Tumbledown from the flank by night, using positions the commandos had already secured to the west. Wilson agreed and incorporated it in his formal orders on 10 June.

The new plan was that once Tumbledown was captured, the Gurkhas would take Mount William, then the Welsh Guards would pass through and seize Sapper Hill.

Scott gave his orders later that afternoon. His plan was for a silent attack in three phases, each based on a company attack, with companies passing through one another until Tumbledown was secured. For supporting fire, he had been promised Harriers in a fighter ground attack role, five batteries of 105mm light guns, the mortars of 42 Commando RM and the Welsh Guards, and naval gunfire support from HMS *Active* and *Yarmouth*. And just prior to the main attack, he planned a diversionary attack from the south, the direction from which he believed the Argentines were expecting him to come.

The attacks by 2 Para and the Scots Guards were now scheduled on the night of 12 June, and the guards were to be lifted to their assembly area west of Goat Ridge at 0800 hours that day. But no helicopters arrived and

Lt Col Scott went to Brigade Headquarters to find out what was happening. There he learnt of 3 Commando Brigade's successes of the previous night. In view of the delay caused by the shortage of helicopters, his attack would be postponed until the following night. But he was able to take his company commanders forward by helicopter, and give them a good look at Tumbledown from Goat Ridge.

The following morning, the helicopters did arrive. The men were airlifted to the assembly area and sangars were dug—which was as well as the Argentines shelled the position for most of the day. Only one man was wounded, though. The platoon and section commanders had a chance to get forward and look at the objective during daylight which would be of immense benefit in taking it in the dark. At 1400 hours, Scott gave his final orders.

The initial estimate was that the Argentines probably had a company occupying Tumbledown, and that they were likely to be well dug in. The battalion would advance down Goat Ridge in a line-ahead formation by companies, with G Company leading, followed by Left Flank, then Right Flank. (The Scots Guards name their companies after the positions they take at the full dress ceremonial parades: G Company is in the centre with the companies Left Flank and Right Flank on either side.) G Company would take the most western part of Tumbledown, which was thought to have one Argentine platoon on it. Left Flank would then pass through them to deal with the next part, and finally Right Flank would seize the remainder.

H-hour was fixed for 2100 hours. Each man was in light order, leaving his rucksack in the assembly area; but six sleeping bags per company were carried to help with the treatment of casualities. The actual assault would be made wearing berets, as steel helmets were awkward and uncomfortable when scrambling over difficult terrain. Helmets would be carried, however, and worn when close to the objective as protection against mortar and artillery fire.

The diversionary attack went in first at 2030 hours. It was commanded by Major Richard Bethell, who had done a tour with the SAS, and consisted of three four-man assault sections from the Recce Platoon and a fire support group from Battalion Headquarters and A1 Echelon, the battalion's immediate logistics element. In support were the Blues and Royals and two sappers, a forward observation officer and mortar fire controller.

Earlier, during the day, signs of the enemy had been seen, but now there appeared to be nothing in front of Bethell's men. So he sent the Scorpions and Scimitars off towards the Stanley road in order to draw fire. The lead one ran over an anti-personnnel mine, luckily without injury to the crew and without attracting attention. The advance continued on foot.

Then a sangar was spotted. With the fire support group taking up position, the assault group closed in. They spotted further sangars and snoring could be heard. The group split up to deal with these dug-outs and came under heavy fire. Two men were killed immediately and four more wounded. But after two hours' hard fighting, the position was eventually secured. Then came the withdrawal.

Maj Bethell and the piper with him, who were providing covering fire for the withdrawal, were wounded by grenade shrapnel and later four more men were badly wounded in a minefield. Then Argentine artillery fire opened up. Luckily, it had little effect with the shells burying deep in the peaty ground. But at this stage, the dead had to be abandoned and the party got back to their starting positions just after 0000 hours, in time to see Tumbledown lit up by artillery fire and 0.5in tracers from Mount Harriet.

G Company advanced in two parallel columns for the 1.8 miles from the start line to their objective. Amid sporadic snow flurries and artillery and mortar fire, as well as star shells, all from the Stanley direction, they managed to get onto their objective, only to find that the Argentines had abandoned it. But they heard Spanish being spoken further up the hill and they remained undetected. The Left Flank passed through them at 2230 hours. G Company gave supporting fire. This drew mortar and artillery fire onto them and they suffered some casualties. Meanwhile, two platoons of Left Flank closed with the enemy.

The right-hand platoon came under accurate artillery and machine gun fire and began to take casualties, while the left, under Second Lieutenant James Stuart, who had only been with the battalion for four months, had problems negotiating the rocks. His platoon sergeant and one other man were killed and two more were wounded, including the company sergeant major.

Both platoons tried to dislodge the enemy with 84mm and 66mm rounds and M79 grenades, but the Argentines, who turned out to be regulars of the 5th Marine Battalion, were not to be budged. It was a question of fighting through crag by crag. The FOO and MFC called down fire, but they had problems getting it to fall in the right place and there was a serious danger that the attack would grind to a halt.

Company Commander Major John Kiszely spoke to Battalion Headquarters on the radio just before 0230 hours. He said he was going to attack with fixed bayonets, and he led his men forward in a charge. The sangars were overrun and enemy killed, but it was tough fighting. Major Kiszely himself had a lucky escape. An enemy round lodged in the compass on his belt and he killed one Argentine with his bayonet.

During the move forward, guarding the prisoners and clearing out the sangars had swallowed up most of his men. Maj Kiszely found himself on the top of the mountain with only six men, three of whom were immediately wounded. He then went through some very anxious moments: what should he do if the Argentines counter-attacked? Luckily they did not, and Right Flank soon came up. But the attack had taken seven hours' hard fighting and had cost Left Flank seven men killed and 18 wounded.

The enemy were still holding on to the last part of Tumbledown, and at 0600 hours Right Flank moved forward to deal with them. Maj Simon Price planned to do a right flanking action with two platoons, using his third to give covering fire. He had to move quickly as it would be daylight in half an hour. He had no artillery support and very little mortar fire.

He attacked with the leading sections firing their anti-tank weapons as they went. Ricochets off the rocks flew in all directions and the enemy returned heavy fire. The Guards did manage to secure a forward position. But then, as with the Left Flank, it became a question of individuals using their initiative to move forward. Many acts of bravery were recorded. By 0800 hours, the objective was finally secured, with several Argentines killed and 14 captured. Right Flank had achieved this at the cost of five wounded, including Lt Robert Lawrence, who was later awarded the MC.

Tumbledown had proved to be a remarkably tough nut to crack because of the nature of the ground and the determination of its defenders. For a battalion which, only two and a half months before, had been on ceremonial duties in London, the taking of Tumbledown was a remarkable achievement.

Mount William: brink of victory

With the Scots Guards fighting on Tumbledown and 2 Para firm on Wireless Ridge, the next phase of the 5 Brigade plan could begin. It was now the turn of the Gurkhas to get stuck in—and of the Welsh Guards to avenge their losses at Fitzroy.

THE TASK OF THE GURKHAS was to take Mount William, which lies south-east of Mount Tumbledown, and then allow the Welsh Guards through to seize Sapper Hill, the final obstacle before Port Stanley. Intelligence estimates gave Argentine resistance as being two companies on Mount William, with one more in reserve.

The Gurkhas' battle began late. The 'Jocks' had been taking a hammering on Tumbledown, where they found themselves up against the Argentine marines—the best troops Menendez had on the island—who were dug in in battalion strength. For Lt Col David Morgan, commanding the Gurkhas, the delay was frustrating. His battalion were waiting, frozen, in their forming-up point to the north of Goat Ridge, listening to the battle going on to their east. Morgan went forward to the Guards' command post to offer Lt Col Scott some help, but he was told they weren't needed.

Morgan was worried, however. The longer the battle for Tumbledown continued, the less chance there was of his men putting in their attack under the cover of darknes. At length, Brigadier Tony Wilson told him to move out. By the time they reached the objective, the Scots Guards should be firm on theirs. Now another problem presented itself—mines. To the north of Tumbledown there was a minefield nearly a third of a mile square. The Gurkhas could either skirt round it to the north, or feel their way through it at its southern end. Morgan wasted no time in arguing the pros and cons: he ordered his men to go through it at the southern end.

Immediately, the entire battalion moved out in one long line. As they crossed the saddle separating them from their objective, they came under artillery fire, but they never faltered. The little men from Nepal plodded gamely onwards, determined to get to grips with the enemy. Morgan had absorbed the lessons of Goose Green, and intended to put them to good use—all the battalion's machine guns and Milans went with them, while the mortars had set up a fire base near Goat Ridge to give them and the 'Jocks' covering fire. Among the Gurkhas' weapons was a selection of 0.5in Brownings. At 84lb each without ammunition, they were a fearsome load for the diminutive mountain men. But as Lt Col Morgan said later: 'They appreciated the firepower even if they didn't much like the weight.'

His plan was to skirt along the northern edge of Mount Tumbledown under the covering fire of the Scots Guards, then hook round to the south to pass round the easternmost 'Jock' position and to attack Mount William from the north.

The reality was slightly different, but at least they missed the minefield. However, the Argentine shelling had already claimed eight men by the time they came abreast of Tumbledown. As the battalion climbed a small re-entrant to approach the summit, B Company swung off to the left to take the eastern end of the feature. There they took some prisoners, part of the reserve company who had been planning a counter-attack. The mere presence of the Gurkhas had changed their minds. The Scots Guards company nearest them were very relieved; in the course of their bloody hand-to-hand battle for the summit, they had all but run out of ammunition.

The next phase of the plan was for A Company and all the support weapons to form a fire base on the summit to support D Company's attack on Mount William, which was now only a mile away.

It was at this stage that the Argentines' own propaganda backfired on them. Stories had been bandied around portraying the Gurkhas as semi-human cannibals who never took prisoners and went into battle crazed with drugs. The Argentines on Mount William were already feeling insecure after the fall of Mount Tumbledown and Wireless Ridge. When they realized they were about to be attacked by the Gurkhas, it all became too much for them.

One Argentine, awe-struck, recalls the sight of the little men from D Company advancing towards them, screaming and yelling. He fled. So too did his comrades, almost an entire battalion of them. Lt Col Morgan's plan had again misfired—Mount William was taken unopposed, and his men were bitterly disappointed.

Meanwhile, back on Tumbledown, the Scots Guards were concerned with trying to get their casualties, some of them in poor shape, evacuated from the mountain. They brought the wounded down to the west end of the feature, where a rocky outcrop provided some shelter from the elements. Now the six sleeping bags which each company had carried into action came into their own, providing the wounded with a little warmth. But to get stretcher cases back to the Regimental Aid Post, which was back beyond Goat Ridge at the furthest forward point at which helicopters were prepared to land, involved a 3½-hour carry, and was only done in one case, apart from a number of walking wounded. Desultory artillery fire was still coming down, and there was serious concern that one or two of the Scots Guards wounded might not survive in the severe weather. At this point, an Army Air Corps Gazelle pilot, Captain Sam Drennan, who had been at one time a Non Commissioned Officer in the Regiment, volunteered to fly forward to Tumbledown and take out the more grievous casualties. This he did, flying a number of missions, and for his coolness, bravery and unselfishness, he was later awarded the Distinguished Flying Cross.

The attack on Sapper Hill

It was now the turn of the 'Morgans'—the Welsh Guards. Their order of battle had changed since the tragedy at Fitzroy. The horrific casualties had left them with only one effective rifle company, so men were drafted in from 40 Commando to supplement them. A and C Company were flown in on 10 and 11 June, along with the 40 Commando mortar troop, to bring the battalion up to strength under the command of Lt Colonel Johnny Ricketts.

There were more changes to come, however. The Welsh Guards' Recce platoon had supported 42 Commando's assault on Mount Harriet by securing their start line, while the Milan platoon provided devastating covering fire to support the main assault. The Welshmen felt they were getting their own back—if slowly—and the rest of the battalion, and their attached marines, looked forward to the final battle. Having been cooped up at San Carlos for the duration, they were eager for action.

They were to have a frustrating night. While waiting in their assembly area, they were subjected to both air attack and artillery fire. Then, that night, while waiting as reserve for the Scots Guards, they had a nerve-racking night march through a minefield. For seven hours, they inched along in single file as the sappers went ahead to check for the mines.

The sole Welsh Guards rifle company, 2 Company, had an objective to be taken on the Darwin Road; it had already fallen to the Scots Guards during their diversionary attack before the battle of Mount Tumbledown. Annoyed, they moved on. By this stage all the main objectives had fallen to the British units, and the first white flags had been seen over Port Stanley. Johnny Ricketts thought it was time to get a move on—Sapper Hill must be taken soon, and with the Argentines falling back *en masse*, the quickest way to do it was to get there by helicopter. A company-sized assault was planned, and C Company 40 Commando were sent forward to take the feature.

They fought a brief firefight with the Argentine stragglers, suffering 2 men wounded, before Sapper Hill fell to them, and the rest of the battalion followed on foot. By 1630 hours, the Welsh Guards were firm on Sapper Hill, and they had a grandstand view of the Argentines falling back in disarray.

For the Welsh Guards this was the finish. 40 Commando, who had been champing impatiently at the bit back at San Carlos, were given one more job to keep them happy—a couple of days later they were sent to West Falkland to take the surrender of the Argentine garrison there. It wasn't much of a war for them, to their infinite regret.

Sweeping into Stanley

With the high ground above Port Stanley in British hands, and the streets of the town crammed with dejected Argentine troops, the end was in sight. As their artillery fire began to fall on the airfield, the British now braced themselves for the final push.

THE ARGENTINE SITUATION was now hopeless. 2 Para had moved on to Wireless Ridge, 3 Para were on Mount Longdon, 42 Commando held Mount Harriet, 45 Commando were on Two Sisters. The Scots Guards had Tumbledown. The Gurkhas had taken Mount William, and the Welsh Guards were moving up on Sapper Hill. There was no high ground left in enemy hands.

General Menendez's troops were crammed into the narrow streets of Port Stanley itself. Many of the Argentine conscripts who had retreated cold and hungry from the hardships of their sojourn on the hills saw for the first time the warehouses stuffed to the roof with the food that had never got through to them. The only other position of strategic importance the Argentines held was the airport.

The British forces now steeled themselves to push the enemy into the sea. They had come so far and done so much. There was no doubt in their minds that they could take Port Stanley almost at will. But at what cost? Hand-to-hand fighting in the streets would produce heavy casualties on both sides, and civilians were bound to get hurt. But the British troops had lost many comrades and the prize of the whole campaign was now in sight.

In the streets of Stanley the Argentine soldiers steeled themselves too. But some of the younger conscripts had difficulty in preparing themselves to face the final battle. As one Argentine soldier recalled: 'When the moment of reckoning comes, you feel total crisis. Your whole body, even your face muscles, go amazingly tense. I think one becomes a machine. I felt it most on the last day, when we were ordered to prepare for combat at close quarters. That type of combat is really tough, very difficult. I had already had everything prepared, all my gear was ready, and I went into that crisis. I had ammo all over the place, in my pocket, on the floor. I tried out my Fal [rifle] every so often. It was an incredible crisis. Even now, as I tell you about it, I'm beginning to get hot. Look, my hands are sweating.

'Most of us were in a strange state. Others simply acted quite incoherently. At that moment, an old guy, a major, started pacing round and round the table with his hands in his pockets, in that absolute silence. Each one was going through it in his own way, coping with his own crisis; but the guy's footsteps echoed through the room—tac, tac, tac, tac. If you stopped to look at that scene, you'd go crazy.'

Meanwhile 2 Para were observing movements in Stanley from their position on Wireless Ridge. They were keen to press on and be first into Port Stanley. This, they felt, was their right. But before they were allowed to move in, Brigadier Julian Thompson, officer commanding 3 Commando Brigade, insisted on coming forward by helicopter so that he could see the position for himself.

Order to advance

On his arrival he gave Lieutenant Colonel David Chaundler the green light. The order to advance was given at 1300 hours and B Company moved off Wireless Ridge and down through Moody Brook, past the ruins of the Royal Marine barracks there—the former home of Naval Party 8901, the Falkland Islands garrison—and up onto the higher ground on the other side of the valley.

The Blues and Royals moved along the ridge to give covering fire if neccessary and A Company, followed by D and C, moved on to Port Stanley.

The Argentines saw them coming but their response was confused. 'The kids of the company who'd stayed in Moody Brook had seen the English coming down the hills screaming and yelling like madmen,' says one. 'It seems that the commander of my company hadn't wanted to retreat. He wanted to carry on fighting until the last bullet had been fired. I understand that there was quite a lot of confusion at that time and in many cases the decision to retreat was in the hands of individual officers in each company. That captain wanted to resist but at one point BIM 5 Troops, a marine battalion, passed through Moody Brook. They had fought heroically at one of the fronts. The marines were well equipped and very well trained, but in the end they too had to retreat. When they saw the boys in my company who stayed there they said: "What are you still doing here? We're a whole battalion and we're retreating because the fighting is almost over and you lot, you're crazy, you want to put up a fight. Come on, there are thousands of them, they're coming down screaming their heads off…"

'There were English soldiers all over the place by then. They had lowered the Argentine flags and the English ones were already flying. I felt very bad at that moment, very demoralized. A group of English soldiers passed by and said hello. They were wearing completely waterproof gear with rubber boots. Our Panhard vehicles which had retreated were all on one street, round the corner from the General's house. And a whole load of English soldiers were virtually dismantling them, taking bits home as souvenirs. I stood paralysed watching them, and I began to feel real hate. I didn't like what they were doing. They were part of our equipment, the only ones we had, and they were destroying them. Then I tried to calm myself down and thought, "Sod it, they're just the same as us. They were brought here, too, just as we were." '

As Lt Col Hew Pike of 3 Para up on Mount Longdon gave out orders for an attack on Moody Brook that night, they heard over the radio that 2 Para had already passed through. This irritated the rest of the troops. 2 Para were 'off disobeying orders again'.

As soon as A Company of 2 Para approached Stanley racecourse, off came their helmets and on went their berets. The paras advanced into Stanley and had considerable pride in being the first British troops to enter the town since the beginning of the Argentine occupation.

The CVR(T)s of the Blues and Royals moved off Wireless Ridge and added a slight World War 2 touch as they ferried paras along the road. Lt Robin Innes-Ker produced the magnificent regimental colours and attached them to the radio antenna of his Scorpion.

Halt at the racecourse

As they prepared to enter Port Stanley, the order came that they were not to pass the racecourse. The reason for the halt was that the Argentines had intimated that they were prepared to talk surrender terms. This was the culmination of a four-day 'psyops' campaign which had been waged by Colonel Mike Rose of the SAS and Captain Rod Bell, a Spanish-speaking officer from the Royal Marines. They had broadcast to Port Stanley hospital from the radio room of HMS *Fearless*. Shortly after 1300, along with a radio operator, they flew by helicopter into Port Stanley to meet General Menendez and his staff. While these talks were going on all units were ordered to halt where they were.

The men of 2 Para clattered with full equipment into the grandstand at the racecourse and waited there. But with them was the journalist Max Hastings. Reporting the war for the London *Standard* and *The Daily Express*, he was not subject to military discipline. And the prospect of a scoop was too much for him. He stripped off his rucksack and his camouflage jacket to reinforce his civilian status. Then in a civilian anorak, clutching a walking stick, he strode into the town like a Home Counties dog breeder taking a stroll on the Downs.

'Just around the bend in the road stood a large building fronted with a conservatory that I suddenly realized from memories of photographs was Government House', he says. 'Its approaches were studded with bunkers, whether occupied or not I could not see. Feeling fairly foolish, I stopped, grinned towards them, raised my hands in the air and waited to see what happened.'

Nothing did. Mr Hastings strode off down the road past a group of Argentine soldiers to whom he gave a cheery 'Good morning'. Further down the road he talked to some kelpers who directed him to an officer on the steps of the Argentine administration block. He introduced himself as the correspondent of *The Times*, the only British paper he believed the Argentines would have heard of.

For the 600 civilians who had elected to stay in Port Stanley after the invasion, relief was tinged with sheer exhaustion as the fighting came to an end. The weeks of Argentine occupation had inevitably left the town a shambles.

The shelling which had preceded the Argentine surrender had taken its toll. The racecourse, from which Max Hastings set off on his lone advance into Port Stanley, was reduced to a quagmire reminiscent of a World War 1 landscape. British shelling, which had crept ever closer to the centre of Port Stanley, had put the town's filtration plant out of action, leaving a water supply from low-level tanks that would only have lasted a few more days. At night the inhabitants of Port Stanley had heard the whistle of the Royal Navy's 4.5in shells, as they flew over the town into the Argentine lines. As the British land forces closed in on Stanley, the kelpers became accustomed to the deafening roar of the Argentine heavy artillery sited within the town itself. Now the guns had fallen silent, and the islanders were left to anticipate the aftermath of the conflict.

How the news broke

As the first white flags began to flutter in Port Stanley, radio links sent the news up the chain of command and across the island. At Ajax Bay, the message was transmitted, bounced off a satellite high above the Atlantic and on to Northwood, Middlesex.

ON SATURDAY MORNING, 12 June, when the first reports of the final assault had been relayed to the Prime Minister, she and the Defence Secretary had hastened to the operations room at Northolt to get the news as it came in. In this final stage of the war only a handful of people in Britain were aware of what was happening. They included the Northolt staff, Mrs Thatcher herself, and a small number of senior ministers with whom she kept in constant telephone contact over the weekend.

Fleet Street editors and their analysts were aware that a dramatic stage of the conflict had been reached, but no word was getting through from their men in the South Atlantic for the very good reason that John Nott had issued a special instruction forbidding the filing of any copy by journalists in the Falklands. In vain, reporters who had followed the troops across the islands and into Stanley itself wrote their stories, begged lifts on helicopters to get them to shipboard transmitting facilities, and were foiled at the last fence by the adamant MOD 'minders'.

'I am afraid that there is a complete news blackout. You cannot communicate at all until further notice,' the senior PR man told the first reporter to arrive with the story of the fall of Port Stanley. Eventually the frustrated newsmen were to suffer the ultimate blow of hearing the surrender reported on the BBC World Service.

Back in England, on the morning of Monday 14th, the Prime Minister heard from Northolt that the enemy seemed to be surrendering. The time had come to make the announcement that everyone had been waiting for, but which few believed would come so swiftly. The newsmen's stories has been embargoed specifically so that Mrs Thatcher herself could be the bearer of the triumphant dispatch to Parliament.

That day the House of Commons had plodded dutifully through an endless and uninspiring debate on industrial training. A vote had been taken at 2200, and normally the ranks of MPs would have begun to thin. But there was a buzz in the air. Something was happening. Two hours previously the Prime Minister had received the final confirmation from Northolt that a surrender was under way. She had taken her place in the chamber clutching a small sheaf of hastily hand-written notes, flanked by her war ministers.

At 2212 the Prime Minister rose to her feet to intervene on a point of order. There was an immediate round of encouraging cheers from her own backbenchers, as they sensed triumph in the air. Mrs Thatcher said that she wished to give the House the latest information on the battle of the Falklands. She referred to her notes, and in a slow, clear voice began to read: 'After successful attacks last night, General Moore decided to press forward. The Argentines retreated. Our forces reached the outskirts of Port Stanley. Large numbers of Argentine soldiers threw down their weapons.'

This was what her supporters had come to hear, and a great cheer went up from the Conservative benches. 'They are reported to be flying white flags over Port Stanley.' The cheering broke out again, louder now, and not confined to her own party.

A great cheer went up

'Our troops have been ordered not to fire except in self-defence. Talks are now in progress between General Menendez and our deputy commander, Brigadier Waters, about the surrender of the Argentine forces on East and West Falklands.'

Michael Foot, the leader of the Opposition, had been criticized by many members of the Labour Party for his early support of the Task Force. But there seemed to be no dissenters as he now rose to his feet to congratulate Mrs Thatcher. He thanked her for the good news, congratulated the victorious British forces, and then amidst the cheers of both sides went on: 'We have many matters on which we will have to have discussions and maybe arguments about the origins of this matter and other questions, but I can well understand the anxieties and pressures that must have been upon her during these weeks, and I can understand that at this moment those pressures and anxieties may be relieved, and ...' he paused, ' ... I congratulate her.'

In Portsmouth the wives of the Task Force gathered beneath newly raised flags to rejoice instead of to console new windows as they had done so often over the long weeks. In Plymouth too the news of the ceasefire and surrender brought enormous relief. A spokeswoman for the wives said, 'We can all sleep soundly now. Now there is only one question. Please, when are they coming home?'

Raising the flag

For Marine Sean Egan, lately of Naval Party 8901, it was good to be back in Port Stanley. He and his mates had finished what they began; now it was all over and he could go home with the knowledge of a job well done.

'YOU COULD FEEL the atmosphere in the room when Major Norman was briefing us. Afterwards, we all said goodbye to each other.' Marine Sean Egan was a machine gunner in No 2 Section, Naval Party 8901; on the morning of 2 April 1982, he fired well over 2000 rounds of machine gun ammunition defending Port Stanley from the Argentines. His section destroyed an Argentine Amtrak at White City. Amazingly, they all survived. 'We were all as happy as sand boys to see each other OK after. When we got back to the UK, all we knew was we would be going back down. We didn't know what our job was going to be.'

As part of 'Juliet' Company 42 Commando, their war was quiet. 'We had no real contacts at all. By the time we got to the top of Mt Harriet, it was all over.

'The third phase of the divisional plan was for us to go through Port Stanley. 42 were to be point unit, and 'Juliet' were to be point company— I guess because we knew the town best. In the end, they surrendered, thank God.'

'We moved into Stanley, and the company dossed down in the Beaver hangar. Our job was to vet all the prisoners on the airfield. About three days after the surrender we went to Government House to raise the flag. The flag we put up had been nicked by some officer years and years ago. He gave it to us to put back where it belonged.

'How did it feel? We were just glad it was all over. We'd finished the job and we wanted to go home. The feeling was "Let's get in amongst it, finish it and let's get home." '

Surrender!

It was finally all over. Rod Bell and 'Col Reid' talked Menendez round to a conditional surrender, then Maj Gen Moore moved in formally to sign the document. The British had won; a point had been made and a principle had been upheld.

THE SMOOTH SIGNING of the final surrender document by General Mario Menendez was the outcome of days of patient work by a unique two-man team: a certain 'Col Reid' of 22 SAS and Captain Rod Bell of the Royal Marines.

They had made a series of broadcasts to the Argentine garrison from about 7 June. Both were well qualified. The SAS Colonel's background included negotiations during hostage sieges. Capt Bell was word perfect in South American Spanish and, more importantly, had grown up in Latin America. He was familiar with Argentine social attitudes and values.

One of the enduring beliefs was that the British were men of their word. They were, after all, the tough, efficient engineers who had put the railways in Argentina. Commercial and cultural contacts over centuries had created the old-fashioned idea of the English as honourable, punctual and efficient. In contrast, the Latin American ideal of honour and manly conduct was summed up more by the word 'machismo'.

The purpose of the broadcasts were initially to make contact with the garrison to discuss casualties, prisoners and other related humane topics. The Falkland Islands with their small scattered communities were linked by telephone and by radio. The advantage of using radio was that it would be heard by a wider number of people. But at one stage the telephone link between Estancia House and Stanley was used as an alternative means of communication. Normally the two-man 'psyops' team broadcast from the assault ship *Fearless* twice a day.

In their operation 'Reid' and Bell were assisted by the Air Operations Officer Vice-Commodore Vera who had been captured at Goose Green.

He maintained that Menendez would not respond to the broadcasts and suggested that contact should be made through Brigadier Castelliano of the air force in Stanley, who would speak to Menendez.

Scripts were prepared for Vera and he broadcast, with great sincerity, to the senior commanders in Stanley. Vera was genuinely concerned that civilian casualties should be avoided in Stanley, and the fighting brought to an end.

Fortunately there was an existing common radio frequency that Bell and 'Reid' could break in on. The radio frequency of 45.5 kHz was normally used by the King Edward Memorial Hospital in Stanley for a medical advice line round the islands, and the first contacts were with Dr Alison Bleaney, the acting senior medical officer. It was also heard by an Argentine NCO who summoned an officer, Captain Melbourne Hussey. He maintained a listening brief, but made no contact over the air.

Though 'Reid' and Bell were getting no answer to their appeals, they were convinced that the broadcasts were being monitored. Later they knew they were right when their earlier offers and promises were brought up at the surrender negotiations.

Raising the pressure

As the fighting closed in on Port Stanley it became clear that the destruction of the garrison was now a matter of time. Bell therefore raised the pressure in his twice-daily broadcasts.

'The position of the Argentine forces is now hopeless, you are surrounded by British forces on both sides. If you fail to respond to this message and there is unnecessary bloodshed in Port Stanley the world will judge you accordingly,' he said.

On Sunday 13 June, Dr Bleaney pressed Captain Hussey to respond. On 11 June, Royal Navy gunfire had caused the deaths of three civilians in Stanley—Doreen Bonner, Sue Whitley and Mary Goodwin—who had been living in houses west of the war memorial which British intelligence had reported as unoccupied. These deaths gave a grim new urgency to the British appeals.

Though he did not know of the deaths, Bell urged that a meeting should now take place—a link kept open between the two opposing forces.

Dr Bleaney requested the British to come on the air again at 1200 after she heard their 1000 broadcast. She pressed Hussey to listen but he could take no action until he had contacted his superiors.

Returning to the radio telephone office at John Street, Hussey informed 'Reid' and Bell over the air that Menendez would be prepared to talk three hours later.

A Gazelle helicopter was readied aboard *Fearless* with a white parachute hung beneath its fuselage as a flag of truce, and they set off for Port

Stanley football pitch. In fact, the pilot put the helicopter down 500 yards short of the pitch at 1500 hours and 'Reid', Bell and their signaller had to scramble through some wire fences before they met Captain Hussey. This prompted the now much quoted exchange: 'What happened, you landed in the wrong place?' Bell replied, 'We don't know Stanley as well as you do.'

The group set off up the road, passing the hospital where they exchanged a few words with Dr Bleaney. When they arrived at the Secretariat, General Menendez was outside his office with his two deputies to meet them. To the surprise of the British party, the conference room had been neatly laid out for the meeting. Places were set with paper, pencils and water. Coffee was later produced during the discussion.

'Colonel Reid' saluted General Menendez as the senior officer present, and the talks began with a brief exchange of compliments about the tough but honourable fight that had been put up by both sides.

Menendez had with him officers representing the air force and navy as well as an air force legal advisor. It was clear to everyone that the battle around Stanley was almost at an end—though men were still dying as the talks were going on. The main area of discussion was whether Menendez could, or would, surrender West Falkland.

The Argentines argued that because there was water between them and the garrisons at Fox Bay and Pebble Island they were technically a separate garrison, not under Menendez's command. Consequently, he had no authority to surrender it. Bell countered that though Menendez was quoting correctly from the Geneva Convention, the article he was invoking was meant to apply to islands that were not part of the continental shelf. West Falkland was geographically a part of the Falkland group and therefore under the command and jurisdiction of General Menendez.

The general then asked that the British party could allow them time for more discussion. Meanwhile the British negotiating team kept Whitehall informed by radio satellite link of each of the stages of the negotiations. The Argentine officers were impressed by the fact that they were, in effect, talking direct to London.

The Argentine side said they were now ready for the final meeting. It was time to call in General Moore. But a snow storm delayed his flight, and each side had to wait in separate rooms until he arrived.

The final round of talks began at 2300 and followed the same format as the first round. General Menendez met General Moore outside the conference room. They saluted but did not shake hands. Menendez said that each side had fought well and Moore replied in the same fashion. Then the British General said that they should get on with things and produced the surrender documents.

It would be inaccurate to say that it was an unconditional surrender. Menendez struck the word 'unconditional' out of the documents. He had been promised that the surrender would be with 'dignity and honour' in Bell and 'Reid's' broadcasts.

Menendez also managed to secure the prompt evacuation of his troops as one of the conditions of the surrender. But the British would not let him insert the words 'Islas Malvinas' after 'Falklands'. At 2359 the document was formally signed, and witnessed by Colonel Pennicott.

When it was all over General Menendez asked if he might join his men on the airfield where they were to be grouped prior to repatriation. When this was refused, tears formed in his eyes. He was evacuated to *Fearless* the following morning.

The door closes on Menendez

For the Argentine forces on the islands, bad luck and bad judgement had combined to make defeat inevitable.

The most serious error of all happened on 21 May. It is almost a golden rule of counter-amphibious operations that the defender's best chance of success lies in meeting the invaders on the beach-head. Given that it was a surprise night attack and was unopposed, the nearest Argentine commander should still have rushed troops in great numbers to screen off the beaches. He could have prevented, firstly, the beaches linking up into a perimeter and, secondly, if a perimeter was established, any sort of breakout. Even if that didn't work, the breakout could have been made extremely costly, while Menendez would have still have had enough troops to conduct a stiff defence of Stanley.

A map printed in the Argentine magazine *Gente* showing troops rushing to screen off the beach-head was, in the event, pure fantasy. The Argentines even seemed to ignore the reports of their own OPs, perhaps because they didn't fit their own prediction of the main landing coming in the Port Harriet area. It is reported that the Argentine company on Fanning Head, or another OP, signalled that there were 'thousands of British troops on the beaches'. His report elicited no response from the land forces on the island. It was only after a lone Pucará aircraft overflew San Carlos Water that any action took place, and that was from aircraft based on the mainland.

According to Fleet Air Arm and RAF pilots, it is a mystery why the Argentines spent so much time and effort attacking the warships on the gun line. In a counter-amphibious operation the priority targets are the transports, supply vessels and the command ship. Their intelligence (or possibly a copy of *Jane's Fighting Ships*) should have told them that only HMS *Fearless* was still fitted out as an amphibious command ship, so sinking one of the two LPDs would have given them a 50 per cent chance of destroying local command. The loss of *Canberra* would have been costly both in lives and in political terms; she was almost as good a target as the *QE2*. *Elk* had enough ammunition on board—as did some RFAs—to empty

San Carlos Water, if she had exploded. And the subsequent loss of *Atlantic Conveyor* seriously handicapped the British operation. What if the six naval ships lost had been six of the vital transports? It is probable that the British would have been sufficiently neutralized.

It would appear that the Argentine planners, political leaders and field commanders just did not believe that we would really fight for the islands.

The despatch of the Task Force was seen as a diplomatic move. They even seem to have held to this view after the recapture of South Georgia and the sinking of *General Belgrano*. The attack on HMS *Sheffield* was viewed as making Britain and Argentina quits. Even after the landings at San Carlos, they seem to have thought that the British were merely improving their negotiating position. They did not think that the Brits would go all the way.

In Argentine intelligence reports (such as Special Intelligence Brief No 7/82 prepared by Brigadier General Alfredo Sotero on 17 April 1982), a frontal assault on Port Stanley was reckoned to be the least likely option that the British would take as it would be too costly politically and in casualties to British troops and to the civilian population. It was therefore assumed that the British would try an indirect approach by landing at some more remote place and attacking across country. They considered that the British, therefore, had the choice of a landing on the Fresinet Peninsula (to the north of Port Stanley) which would bring them into a quick confrontation with the Argentine main force. This had the major disadvantages that the Argentines would be most concentrated and that there was a high risk of the civilians suffering casualties. The more likely option was considered to be a landing at an even more remote place. They looked at three 'zones'.

Options

Zone 1 was between the limits of Black Rock House at its south-west extremity and Fitzroy Settlement in the north-east. Zone 2 was the St Louis Peninsula which lies at the end of a narrow isthmus to the north of the Fresinet Peninsula. Zone 3 had the limits of the northern side of San Carlos Water as the north-west extremity and the northern side of Foul Bay as the north-eastern end. No priorities were allocated to these zones to show which was thought to be the most likely British choice.

Part of the less likely Option 1 (the Fresinet Peninsula) was in fact a third option. This was essentially a carbon copy of the Argentines' own invasion of 2 April, and consisted of an attack from the direction of Port Stanley Airport linked to one from the direction of Port Harriet. It was thought that this would be co-ordinated with a 'helicopter assault with up to 500 men, in a general W—E direction (Mount Estancia or Mount Kent—Mount Longdon), ... to conquer key territory and/or disrupt part of our defences'.

It is usually a mistake to assume that the enemy will do what you want or expect him to do. But for some reason in the laying out of his defensive positions Major General Menendez seems to have aimed to cover the threat posed by the British adopting either the Port Harriet or the Zone 1 options, as these had basically the same axis. This choice may have been affected by the road which runs from Darwin to Port Stanley through Fitzroy and which can take Land Rover-type vehicles. It was felt that the British would be heavily reliant on helicopters for moving troops if any other place were chosen. In any case, the British would eventually have to fight in front of Port Stanley. Thus the main Argentine forces were deployed around the town, facing what was assumed to be the main axis of advance: north-east from Fitzroy/Port Harriet. Reserve companies from the major units were located on the hills to the west of the town, and the commander's mobile reserve units were placed on Mounts Kent and Challenger.

In the brief, Brigadier General Sotero stated that 'the reduction of our defensive positions will be slow and costly', with the contingent risk of the operation being interrupted by 'diplomatic pressure from the US and the USSR' and 'they run the risk of an ending of hostilities forced by diplomacy before the conclusion of the operation'. About the options of a remote landing site, he wrote that 'it would take longer to execute the military phase of the operation, with the attendant risk of being unable to achieve the real objective (the capture of Port Stanley) before diplomacy brings an end to hostilities.'

He further thought, probably correctly, that heavy casualties sustained by the British troops or the civilian population would be considered politically unacceptable.

However, if this was their interpretation of the likely sequence of events, the Argentines should have deployed their forces in such a way that the British advance on Port Stanley would be as costly and as long as possible. Essentially this would have meant that each hill and ridge-line would have to be fought for, while the Argentines conducted a withdrawal on a shrinking perimeter towards their main defensive area around Port Stanley. They should have 'held the high ground' in the old military adage. They didn't and, without a fight, relinquished the best ground in the path of the British advance. They chose for their perimeter around Port Stanley ground which was overlooked by Wireless Ridge, Mount Longdon, Two Sisters, Mount Tumbledown, Mount William and Sapper Hill. These hills were at least 'Ground of Tactical Importance', if not 'Vital Ground', and so they should each have been held in very considerable strength; but they weren't. Menendez could have afforded virtually to put a regiment on each, defending in depth.

Wilful blindness

Having assumed that the British axis would be Fitzroy/Port Stanley, the action of 2 Para at Darwin—Goose Green and the later landing of 5 Infantry

Brigade at Bluff Cove seems to have convinced the Argentines of the correctness of their assessment. They seem to have been unwilling to change their minds in spite of all the other activity going on at Douglas, Teal Inlet, Top Malo House, Estancia House, Murrell Heights and Mount Kent. The only relocation which took place was the airlift of the 12th Airmobile Regiment to Goose Green from Mount Kent and Mount Challenger to meet 2 Para.

The hills that Menendez decided to defend gave excellent observation over the approaches. However, the soldiers who garrisoned them received little advice on the best way to prepare their defences.

Though the machine-gun positions at Goose Green were well located and could give interlocking supporting fire, there seems to have been little thought given to the siting of positions on hills nearer Stanley. The artillery however, was well handled with fire falling on positions as they were captured by the British. However, though it fell on likely axes of advance, it did not appear to have been observed and corrected by forward observers. Menendez had a dozen AML 90 Panhard armoured cars which were captured intact and unused in Stanley; had they been moved out onto the hills they could have given direct fire—and even engaged with the CVR(T)s as they supported 2 Para on Wireless Ridge.

General Menendez surrendered with his 'best shot still in the locker'— the prepared defence of Port Stanley—but by then his troops seemed to be unwilling to go on, and by losing the Vital Ground his position was untenable. So he conceded defeat; there was an 18th-century air about the war on both sides. Nevertheless, the conflict could have been won (or lost) on those vital few days on the beaches and in San Carlos Water between 21 and 27 May. The Germans showed how it should be done at Dieppe in 1942, but it was an example the Argentines chose to ignore.

Farewell to the Malvinas

Once the surrender had been signed the Task Force had one pressing concern—what to do with the 11,845 Argentine prisoners. There was plenty of food in the undistributed enemy stockpiles, but precious little shelter against the wintry weather.

THOSE ARGENTINES who had surrendered at Port Stanley were, once they had been disarmed, put initally on the airfield. Although press reports spoke of their being left to fend for themselves in the open in Force 10 winds, there was in fact, plenty of material amongst the wreckage for them to construct rudimentary shelters for themselves. Indeed, this at least gave them something active to do in addition to cleaning up Stanley and its environs, which they did under British direction. Besides, the British troops were little better off. All of the Task Force's tents had been sunk on the *Atlantic Conveyor*, victim of two Exocet missiles on 25 May.

The Argentines were also getting two hot meals a day and, besides this, the majority, especially the conscripts, were relieved that the fighting was over and that they had survived. However, it was immediately clear that the sooner they were repatriated the better, but with no confirmation that hostilities in the South Atlantic were at a permanent end, and a growing feeling that the Junta was not prepared to agree to this, it meant that negotiations for their release might prove difficult. In the event, thanks to the good offices of the International Committee of the Red Cross, agreement was reached remarkably quickly. Perhaps, as far as the Junta was concerned, a major reason was that should they refuse to take them back quickly the British could use this as propaganda against them, which would not only tarnish their image in the world at large, but also cause unrest among the families of the PoWs.

In the meantime, the first task was to bring the PoWs from San Carlos round to Port Stanley, so that as soon as agreement on repatriation had been reached they could be transported back as quickly as possible. This was not just to get them off the Task Force's hands: because of the commitments on troop-carrying shipping, there was no possibility of the Task Force beginning the journey home to Britain until the bulk of the PoWs had been returned. Indeed, *Canberra*, which had spent 14 June, the final day of the fighting, rushing urgent medical stores to HMS *Hermes* for onward transmission to *Uganda*, received orders at 1900 hours to collect the PoWs, most of whom were captured by 2 Para at Goose Green, and bring them round to Port Stanley. She arrived there on the early afternoon of the next day, and took on 1121 PoWs, along with 100 Welsh Guards, who were to be their guards. The experience in processing them on board was to prove invaluable for what was to come. They were brought alongside by LCU and then split into batches of 200. Stripping and searching then followed, and this was proved to be necessary when several assorted weapons were found, including pistols, bayonets and enough parts to make up a complete machine gun, not to mention ammunition.

Early on the 16th, *Canberra* set sail once more, this time for Port Stanley, where she was to take on more prisoners. With the cease-fire confirmation by the Argentines still not clear, she was relieved to have HMS *Andromeda* as an escort. She approached Port William, the official name of the port, cautiously because of reports of Argentine mining—the minesweepers were, however, hard at work. She anchored in the early afternoon, and soon received additional guards in the form of her old friends 3 Para, who contributed one company to reinforce the Welsh Guards. Then the lengthy business of loading more PoWs began, and continued throughout the night. By noon next day, *Canberra* had no less than 4167 PoWs on board and could not take any more. *Norland*, too, had been pressed into service for this task, and she took a further 2,000. The only flaw in the operation was a small riot by some of the PoWs who were waiting to board, and which appears to have been directed at their officers. However, peace was speedily restored, and it was now a question of waiting for the Red Cross negotiations to be satisfactorily concluded.

In the event, arrangements were agreed by Friday, 18 June. The Argentines guaranteed safe conduct for both ships, each of which would have a Red Cross representative on board. In terms of international law, the ships were designated 'cartel ships', which meant that, although a state of war was in theory still considered to exist, they were inviolable, provided they did not carry out any acts of war or, indeed, carry any weapons. Nevertheless, the British government held back 600 PoWs designated 'Special Category', whom they considered as key personnel and were not prepared to release until the Argentines had formally recognized that hostilities were at an end. This in itself was legally questionable, in that Article

118 of the Geneva Convention states that PoWs must be 'repatriated without delay after the cessation of active hostilities'. However, at the time there was no clear proof that active hostilities *were* at an end.

Thus, at 0930 hours on 18 June *Canberra* once again slipped anchor, to be followed by *Norland*, Their destination was Puerto Madryn, some 700 miles south of Buenos Aires. At 1000 hours the next day, *Canberra* entered Argentine territorial waters, and there was a slight nervousness as she was approached by one of Argentina's British-built Type 42 destroyers, *Santissima Trinidad*. However, the latter spoke on the radio in English, stating that she would escort *Canberra* into the harbour. One intriguing coincidence was that the Spanish-speaking Royal Naval Officer put on board *Canberra* in case Spanish was needed happened to have been the liaison officer on board the Argentine ship a few months before, and took the opportunity to ask after her officers.

At 1330 hours the *Canberra* came alongside the jetty, and soon disembarkation of the PoWs began. By now a rapport had been built up with them, and many expressed their gratitude for their treatment on board as they left. There were, however, no civilian crowds there to greet them, only a military reception committee, who saw them on board buses taking them to remote camps in the area.

That evening *Canberra* slipped anchor to return to the Falklands, expecting to collect another load of PoWs as did *Norland*. However, when they arrived back at Port William, and had begun to clean up in preparation, they were told the good news that this plan had been cancelled. Instead, *Canberra* was to embark the three Royal Marine Commando, while *Norland* took the paras, and they were to sail for home.

The balance of PoWs was taken back to Argentina in other merchant ships, apart from the Special Category prisoners who were held until 30 June, when they were put on board MV *St Edmund*. Even then, it was not until 13 July that the United Kingdom announced that she was satisfied that active hostilities were now at an end, and *St Edmund* could sail.

There was, however, one other prisoner of war to be considered, the one British PoW on the mainland, although there were rumours at the time that up to seven SAS men were also being held by the Argentines. The individual in question was Flight Lieutenant Jeffrey Glover, whose Harrier had been shot down by a Blowpipe on 21 May. He had successfully ejected, suffering a broken arm and collar bone, and had been evacuated back to the military hospital at Comodoro Rivadavia. He was, once he was fit enough, released on 8 July.

Wrapping it up in Thule

'Tidying up the back of beyond' was how one commentator described the operation to retake South Thule. The Falklands crisis could be said to have begun here in 1976—and it was to end here, with M Company 42 Commando and Operation Keyhole.

SOUTH THULE ISLAND is a quite exceptionally disagreeable place. Few people have even been there, they do not stay long and even fewer return.

This unpleasant and unlikeable island became the arena for the first and last acts in a rather unlikely war, though these were to be the least warlike of acts since the Antarctic climate demands that the war for survival supersedes all else. In the late 1970s, it is not known exactly when, a small band of Argentines travelled to South Thule on board the icebreaker ARA *General San Martin* (now withdrawn from the fleet). The aim of this group was to set up a meterological and scientific station similar to the several which Argentina has in Antarctica and similar in nature to the stations of the British Antarctic Survey (BAS).

Aside from the value of the meterological information that the Argentine station provided, this small outpost of scientific endeavour had three political benefits for the Junta. Firstly, the base challenged the British claim of having effective government over the Falkland Island Dependencies. Secondly it strengthened the Argentine hand by being a tangible expression of Argentina's interest in developing this part of the world. Thirdly, the base on South Thule established an Argentine presence on a spot which could become strategically important if the Antarctic became an area capable of exploitation.

When the British discovered that their own BAS station in the South Sandwich Islands was not alone on the island chain they faced a problem.

They could either force the Argentines off the island with the possibility that this might cause a violent reaction from Argentina, which was already excitable over the Falklands dispute (and it is well to remember that the fuss created over a similar-sized group landing in South Georgia pushed Argentina into the invasion), or alternatively they could ignore this trifling event and continue with the negotiations. Several years later M Company of 42 Commando were settling down in South Georgia having come to the end of the latter course.

M Company was left on South Georgia to consolidate their position there after the completion of Operation Paraquat, the recapture of the islands. Several parts of the original team involved in Paraquat, including 2 SBS and D Squadron of 22 SAS Regiment were withdrawn for further activity in the Falkland Islands. The remaining Company Group settled down into a weekly cycle of rotating its three Rifle Troops between Administration, Base Defence and Observation as the snowline decended to the shoreline and the South Atlantic winter really set in.

Occasional excitement was caused by 'Stand To's' prompted by belching seals and imaginary periscopes in the harbour, while the unannounced arrival of the tug *Salvageman* one night caused the unamused master of that vessel to suffer a mild blow to the head after being hit by the falling case of a parachute flare.

Leaving a small detachment and HMS *Antrim* to guard South Georgia, Task Group 317–9 set off to complete Operation Keyhole—the capture of Corbeta Uruguay, the Argentine base on South Thule. Corbeta Uruguay had been known to the British since 1976, though it might have been there longer, and was an orderly set of huts with a helicopter hangar, landing strip and several large radio masts. The whole base, which accommodated as many as 40, was set on the Morrell Peninsula, a small spit of land jutting out eastwards from the central volcano (and thus offering some shelter from the westerly winds). There was no real defence possible from such a base and as the Task Group sailed south the Argentines were warned of the impending arrival of the Royal Marines by messages sent on international radio frequencies. Surprise was of no consequence in this matter; what *was* important was protection from the elements, and if the Argentines did not surrender peaceably the frigate *Yarmouth* was on hand to destroy the Argentine huts with her 4.5in guns. On an island where the wind chill factor made the temperature drop to –50°F there was little need for fighting. In addition to HMS *Yarmouth* the Task Group consisted of *Endurance*, the supply ship RAF *Olmeda* and the tug *Salvageman*.

The final, final surrender

A ten-man patrol from the Recce Station was landed on 18 June amid dummy landings to confuse the Argentines. After an extremely uncomfortable night (even for Arctic-trained men) of observation the patrol moved down towards the base, an act which fortunately encouraged the Argentines to surrender only two minutes before *Yarmouth* was due to begin its coastal bombardment.

The Task Group found some ten Argentines in the base, the remainder having been evacuated, with their code books and communications gear destroyed. With the danger of being trapped in the winter pack ice ever present the Task Group rapidly took the prisoners on board and speedily sailed for South Georgia.

Back in relative comfort and order of South Georgia, M Company Group was able to relax. The birth of Prince William in Britain was a chance for festivities which did not go unnoticed, whilst on 25 June, Midsummer's Day (for the norther hemisphere), the Company had a southern 'Christmas' complete with roast turkey and an imitation Christmas tree found intact in the deserted Grytviken Church. After all, if the Marines were to 'enjoy' both the northern and southern hemisphere's winters, who was to stop them from having two Christmases as well?

Homecomings

Scenes like these hadn't been witnessed for years. As the Task Force ships came home one by one, they berthed on a tide of emotion unrivalled since World War 2. For the men and women who served in the Falklands, it was no less than they deserved.

WITH THE FIGHTING at an end, the Task Force's aim achieved and the immediate euphoria of victory having waned, the thoughts of all in the Task Force were on home. However, there were the immediate tasks of clearing up Port Stanley, especially the airfield, seeing to the 11,845 Argentine PoWs and planning the defences of the Falklands so that any possible future Argentine attempts at invasion could be thwarted. Quite clearly to revert to the size of the original garrison, Naval Party 8901, was unacceptable, and a considerably larger force would be needed. However, until this could be sent south from the United Kingdom, it was clear that at least part of the Land Forces Falkland Islands (LFFI) would have to remain. In any event, there was also the problem of the PoWs, and there were simply not the resources available to be able to look after them for more than a short time.

Thus, while LFFI began the mammoth task of clearing and cleaning up, as well as trying as best they could to cope with the PoWs, negotiations were opened for the return of the latter. By 19 June, satisfactory arrangements had been worked out and the first 6,200 POWs set sail for Port Stanley bound for Puerto Madryn in *Canberra* and *Norland* with Argentine promises of safe conduct. In the meantime Rex Hunt returned to the Falklands to his new job as Civil Commissioner, while Major General Jeremy Moore was made Military Commissioner. Within a week, there were ships available and the first units could begin the long voyage home.

Airborne Forces Day

When they had sailed south two and a half months before, the time on board did not seem long enough with the very full programme of training and the knowledge that they were likely to have a fight. Now there was a feeling of anti-climax and reaction to the intense excitement of the past few weeks. In spite of a training programme to keep them occupied, the days dragged sluggishly past. Perhaps an indication of all this was the celebration of Airborne Forces Day on 4 July in *Norland*. It ended up in a pitched battle between 2 and 3 Para. Yet, next morning, the two battalions apologized to one another and resumed their previous good relations—the chance to 'let off steam' had done everyone some good.

For 5 Brigade who were left on the Falklands, again it was a question of keeping people occupied and, because it seemed at the time that they would not be home until September at the earliest, the maintenance of motivation was that much more difficult. On 30 June, they saw the last batch of Argentine prisoners off on board MV *St Edmund*. They were 519 of the so-called 'Special Category' which included key personnel, including the Commander of West Falkland and the naval Exocet commander at Port Stanley, and had been retained until last in case the Argentines caused any difficulties over the repatriation of the bulk of the prisoners. The day before this, 2nd Bn Scots Guards, less Right Flank Company which remained at Ajax Bay, were deployed to West Falkland as the garrison there, with the rest of 5 Brigade remaining on East Falkland. Besides remaining on the alert for any possible Argentine incursion, the task of clearing up continued. Parties also 'walked the ground' of the campaign, and post mortems were held at all levels. This was especially important as there was a need to assimilate all possible lessons while the events were still fresh in everyone's minds, and the Ministry of Defence in London was bombarding the Task Force with questions. Cemeteries were built and memorials erected. Expeditions were sent out to observe the wildlife, and help given to the kelpers. Sports pitches were laid out as well as firing ranges, and naval and military parties made exchange visits.

On arrival at Ascension, the paras were honoured with a visit from the Chief of the General Staff, Sir Edwin Bramall, who, accompanied by Lt General Sir Richard Trant, Commander South-East District and Land Deputy to C-in-C Fleet, had flown out to meet them, as well as pay tribute to those who had played such a vital part in the Ascension Island back-up to the Task Force. Then, it was by RAF and RN helicopter to Wideawake Airfield, where they boarded RAF VC10s to fly them back to Brize Norton. Here, they were met by the Colonel-in-Chief of the Parachute Regiment, Prince Charles, Admiral Sir John Fieldhouse, C-in-C Fleet, General Sir Anthony Farrar-Hockley, Colonel Commandant of the Parachute Regiment and, not least, their families and loved ones. Led by the two commanding officers, David Chaundler and Hew Pike, they disembarked to the strains of 'Congratulations', played by the Regimental Band, then through customs and they were reunited at last with their families, and the emotion poured out.

However, the most spectacular welcomes were reserved for the returning ships, mainly because the quayside enabled more spectators to be there, and there was also something very romantic in the eyes of the public about a ship rather than an aircraft returning from the wars. An indication of what those returning by sea might expect was given when *QE2* docked at Southampton on 12 June with survivors from HMS *Antelope, Ardent* and *Coventry*. The quayside was lined with friends and relatives of those on board, and The Royal Marines Band of Commander-in-Chief Naval Home Command marched and counter-marched. It was a fitting welcome, but perhaps nothing to match the scenes of *Canberra*'s return.

The 'Great White Whale' had earned the special affection of both the Task Force and those at home, and the latter were determined to display this in full. Sunday 11 July started misty. As *Canberra* passed the Isle of Wight, small boats began to appear and join her. Then, as the early mist cleared, aircraft began to circle overhead. More boats appeared, and soon large groups of people could be seen on the shore. Then at 0900 hours the Prince of Wales arrived on board by helicopter, accompanied by Admiral Sir John Fieldhouse and Lt Gen Sir Stuart Pringle, Commandant General Royal Marines. They spent an hour on board and then departed to allow her and those on board to savour the welcome awaiting them on their own. No less than 50,000 people turned up to greet her as she came alongside, and to those on board they had the appearance of a sea of Union Jacks and banners. The Royal Marines Band on the quayside played 'Hearts of Oak', 'Rule Britannia' and the Royal Marines regimental quick march 'A Life on the Ocean Wave' over and over again and a host of red, white and blue balloons was released. It was an expression of emotional patriotism that the British had long felt they had lost, and there were few present who remained dry-eyed. For the rust-stained *Canberra*, her crew and the Royal Marines it was a fitting welcome after her 94 days at sea.

Back home

And so it went on. As every ship returned to her home port, the welcome to *Canberra* was repeated. *Fearless* and *Intrepid* arrived back on the 14th. *Hermes*, the flagship of the Task Force, was home on 21 July, Mrs Thatcher and Admiral of the Fleet Sir Terence Lewin having visited her off Spithead. On the same day arrived HMS *Herald*, a hospital ship which had endured the dangers of Bomb Alley and ferried casualties from San Carlos to Montevideo. On 13 July, the frigate *Brilliant* came home to be followed eight days later by her sister ship *Broadsword*. It was the same with the supporting ships RFA *Blue Rover* and *Stromness* which docked at Portsmouth on 17 and 19 July respectively—and the many others, large and small.

There were, too, other odd parties coming in by air. Thus M Company 42 Commando, which had recaptured South Georgia and then gone on to expel the Argentines from South Thule, flew into RAF St Mawgan in Cornwall on 18 July and the Royal Naval helicopters of 824, 826 and 846 Squadrons flew into their peacetime bases at Culdrose and Yeovilton.

However, for all the troops and ships coming home, some replacements were needed. In terms of ships, a number set sail for the South Atlantic immediately after the end of hostilities. Thus, only four months after completing a major refit, HMS *Birmingham*, sister ship to *Sheffield*, left Portsmouth on 18 June, and on the same day the destroyer *Southampton* and frigates *Rhyl, Danae* and *Apollo* also left. Fresh Harriers arrived to take over from their battle-worn confrères, and finally, on 2 August, the Royal Navy's newest carrier, *Illustrious*, left.

At the end of the month, the new garrison troops took over from 5 Brigade, who embarked in the hard-working *Norland* and the hospital ship *Uganda*. Before they left, however, there was one unusual occurrence, when Gdsm Williams of the Scots Guards, who had been posted missing after the battle for Tumbledown, appeared out of nowhere to rejoin the battalion. Finding himself on his own during the battle, he had hidden for six weeks not knowing that the victory had been won. The Scots and Welsh Guards did as the paras did before them, and transferred to VC10s at Ascension, flying into Brize Norton to the same welcome as their predecessors, while 1/7 Gurkha Rifles went the whole way by sea in *Uganda*. For them, the joy at coming home was not quite the same. Home to them is Nepal, where their families were awaiting the end of their two-year tour in England. Nevertheless, on arrival back in Church Crookham, the local people, who felt themselves the adopted families of the Gurkhas, made certain that the latter did have their own special celebration, when the battalion marched back through the streets of the little town to their barracks.

OPERATION CORPORATE

WAR DEAD

ROYAL NAVY

HMS *Coventry*
MEM(M)1 F O ARMES
ACWEA J D L CADDY
MEM(M)1 P B CALLUS
APOCA S R DAWSON
AWEM(R)1 J K DOBSON
PO(S) M G FOWLER
WEM(O)1 I P HALL
LT R R HEATH
AWEM(N)1 D J A OZBIRN
LT CDR G S ROBINSON-
MOLTKE
LRO(W) B J STILL
MEA2 G L J STOCKWELL
AWEA1 D A STRICKLAND
AAB(EW) A D SUNDERLAND
MEM(M)2 S TONKIN
ACK I E TURNBULL
AWEA2 P P WHITE
WEA/APP I R WILLIAMS

HMS *Fearless*
MEA(P) A S JAMES
ALMEM(M) D MILLER

HMS *Glamorgan*
POAEM(L) M J ADCOCK
CK B EASTON
AEM(M) M HENDERSON

AEM(R)1 B P HINGE
LACAEMN D LEE
AEA(M)2 K I McCALLUM
CK B J MALCOLM
MEM(M)2 T W PERKINS
L/CK M SAMBLES
L/CK A E SILLENCE
STD J D STROUD
LT D H R TINKER
POACMN C P VICKERS

HMS *Sheffield*
LT CDR D I BALFOUR
POMEM(M) D R BRIGGS
CA D COPE
WEA1 A C EGGINGTON
S/LT R C EMLY
POCK R FAGAN
CK N A GOODALL
LMEM(M) A J KNOWLES
LCK A MARSHALL
POWEM A R NORMAN
CK D E OSBORNE
WEA1 K R F SULLIVAN
CK A C SWALLOW
ACWEMN M TILL
WEMN2 B J WALLIS
LCK A K WELLSTEAD
MAA B WELSH

CK K J WILLIAMS
LT CDR J S WOODHEAD

HMS Hermes
LT CDR G W J BATT
POACMN K S CASEY
LT N TAYLOR

HMS Invincible
LT W A CURTIS
LT CDR J E EYTON-JONES
NA(AH)1 B MARSDEN

HMS Ardent
AB(S) D D ARMSTRONG
LT CDR R W BANFIELD
AB(S) A R BARR
POAEM(M) P BROUARD
CK R J S DUNKERLEY
ALCK M P FOOTE
MEM(M)2 S H FORD
ASTD S HANSON
AB(S) S K HAYWARD
AB(EW) S HEYES

WEM(R)1 S J LAWSON
MEM(M)2 A R LEIGHTON
AEMN(1) A McAULEY
ALS(R) M S MULLEN
LT B MURPHY
LPT G T NELSON
APOWEM(R) A K PALMER
CK J R ROBERTS
LT CDR J M SEPHTON
ALMEM(M) S J WHITE
ALMEM(L) G WHITFORD
MEM(M)1 G S WILLIAMS

HMS Argonaut
AB(R) I M BOLDY
S(M) M J STUART

HMS Antelope
STD M R STEPHENS

Atlantic Conveyor
AEM(R)1 A U ANSLOW
CPOWTR E FLANAGAN
LAEM(L) D L PRYCE

ROYAL MARINES

CPL J G BROWNING
MNE P D CALLAN
MNE C DAVISON
SGT R ENEFER
SGT A P EVANS
CPL K EVANS
CPL P R FITTON
LT K D FRANCIS
L/CPL B P GIFFIN
MNE R D GRIFFIN
A/SGT I N HUNT
C/SGT B R JOHNSTON
SGT R A LEEMING
CPL M D LOVE

MNE S G McANDREWS
MNE G C MacPHERSON
L/CPL P B McKAY
MNE M J NOWAK
LT R J NUNN
MNE K PHILLIPS
SGT R J ROTHERHAM
MNE A J RUNDLE
CPL J SMITH
CPL I F SPENCER
CPL A B UREN
CPL L G WATTS
MNE D WILSON

ARMY

22 Special Air Service
A/CPL R E ARMSTRONG
A/SGT J L ARTHY
A/WO1 I M ATKINSON
A/CPL W J BEGLEY
A/SGT P A BUNKER
A/CPL BURNS
SGT P P CURRASS
A/SGT S A I DAVIDSON
WO11 L GALLAGHER
CAPTAIN G J HAMILTON
A/SGT W C HATTON
A/SGT W J HUGHES
A/SGT P JONES
L/CPL P N LIGHTFOOT
A/CPL M V McHUGH
A/CPL J NEWTON
A/WO11 P O'CONNOR
CPL S J G SYKES
CPL E T WALPOLE

Army Air Corps
L/CPL S J COCKTON
S/SGT C A GRIFFIN

Scots Guards
GDSM D J DENHOLM
GDSM D MALCOLMSON
L/SGT C MITCHELL
GDSM J B C REYNOLDS
SGT J SIMEON
GDSM A G STIRLING
GDSM R TANBINI
WO11 D WIGHT

Royal Signals
S/SGT J I BAKER
MAJOR M L FORGE
CPL D F McCORMACK

Royal Electrical and Mechanical Engineers
CFN M W ROLLINS
CFN A SHAW
L/CPL A R STREATFIELD

Royal Engineers
SPR P K GHANDI
SPR C A JONES
CPL A G McILVENNY
CPL M MELIA
L/CPL J B PASHLEY
S/SGT J PRESCOTT
SPR W D TARBARD
CPL S WILSON

Army Catering Corps
L/CPL B C BULLERS
PTE A M CONNETT
PTE M A JONES
PTE P W MIDDLEWICK

Royal Army Medical Corps
L/CPL I R FARRELL
MAJOR R NUTBEEM
PTE K PRESTON

Gurkha Rifles
L/CPL BUDHAPARSAD LIMBU

2nd Battalion, The Parachute Regiment
LT J A BARRY
L/CPL G D BINGLEY
L/CPL A CORK
CAPTAIN C DENT
PTE S J DIXON
C/SGT G P M FINDLAY
PTE M W FLETCHER
CPL D HARDMAN
PTE M HOLMAN-SMITH

PTE S ILLINGSWORTH
LT COL H JONES
PTE T MECHAN
PTE D A PARR
CPL S R PRIOR
PTE F SLOUGH
L/CPL N R SMITH
CPL P S SULLIVAN
CAPTAIN D A WOOD

3rd Battalion,
The Parachute Regiment
PTE R J ABSOLON
PTE G BULL
PTE J S BURT
PTE J D CROW
PTE M S DODSWORTH
PTE A D GREENWOOD
PTE N GROSE
PTE P J HEDICKER
L/CPL P D HIGGS
CPL S HOPE
PTE T R JENKINS
PTE C D JONES
PTE S I LAING
L/CPL C K LOVETT
CPL S P F McLAUGHLIN
CPL K J McCARTHY
C/SGT I J McKAY
L/CPL J H MURDOCH
L/CPL D E SCOTT
PTE I P SCRIVENS
PTE P A WEST

Welsh Guards
L/CPL A BURKE
L/SGT J R CARLYLE
GDSM I A DALE
GDSM M J DUNPHY
GDSM P EDWARDS
SGT C ELLEY
GDSM M GIBBY
GDSM G C GRACE
GDSM P GREEN
GDSM G M GRIFFITHS
GDSM D N HUGHES
GDSM G HUGHES
GDSM B JASPER
GDSM A KEEBLE
L/SGT K KEOGHANE
GDSM M J MARKS
GDSM C MORDECAI
L/CPL S J NEWBURY
GDSM G D NICHOLSON
GDSM C C PARSONS
GDSM E J PHILLIPS
GDSM G W POOLE
GDSM N A ROWBERRY
L/CPL P A SWEET
GDSM C C THOMAS
GDSM G K THOMAS
L/CPL N D M THOMAS
GDSM R G THOMAS
GDSM A WALKER
L/CPL C F WARD
GDSM J F WEAVER
SGT M WIGLEY
GDSM D R WILLIAMS

ROYAL AIR FORCE
RAF Upavon
FLT LT G W HAWKINS

CHINESE

RFA *Sir Tristram*
YU SIK CHEE
YEUNG SWI KAMI

RFA *Sir Galahad*
LEUNG CHAU
SUNG YUK FAI

Atlantic Conveyor
NG POR
CHAN CHI SING
HMS *Sheffield*
LAI CHI KEUNG

HMS *Coventry*
KYE BEN KWO

ROYAL FLEET AUXILIARY

RFA *Fort Grange*
QM WS FRASER
RFA *Sir Galahad*
3RD ENG C HAILWOOD
2ND ENG P HENRY
3RD ENG A MORRIS
Atlantic Conveyor
1ST RADIO OFFR R HOOLE

MERCHANT NAVY

Atlantic Conveyor
BOSUN J DOBSON
MECHANIC F FOULKES
STD D HAWKINS
MECHANIC J HUGHES
CAPT I NORTH
MECHANIC E VICKERS

FALKLANDS CIVILIANS

DOREEN BONNER
MARY GOODWIN
SUE WHITLEY

ROLL OF HONOUR

ROYAL NAVY, ROYAL MARINES, ROYAL FLEET AUXILIARY AND MERCHANT NAVY

Distinguished Service Order

Commodore Samuel Clark DUNLOP CBE, Royal Fleet Auxiliary; Captain Michael Ernest BARROW, Royal Navy; Captain John Jeremy BLACK MBE, Royal Navy; Captain William Robert CANNING, Royal Navy; Captain John Francis COWARD, Royal Navy; Captain Peter George Valentine DINGEMANS, Royal Navy;

From the citation for Captain E S J Larken's DSO

'During air attacks, he conducted his ship's defence personally from the exposed gun direction platform and, in so doing, was an inspiring example of personal bravery to his men'.

Captain Edmund Shackleton Jeremy LARKEN, Royal Navy; Captain Christopher Hope LAYMAN MVO, Royal Navy; Captain Linley Eric MIDDLETON ADC, Royal Navy; Captain Philip Jeremy George ROBERTS, Royal Fleet Auxiliary; Captain B G Y YOUNG, Royal Navy; Lieutenant Colonel Nicholas Francis VAUX, Royal Marines; Lieutenant Colonel Andrew Francis WHITEHEAD, Royal Marines; Commander Christopher Louis WREFORD-BROWN, Royal Navy; Lieutenant Commander Brian Frederick DUTTON QGM, Royal Navy; Lieutenant Commander Ian STANLEY, Royal Navy.

Captain Brian Young, DSO, of HMS Antrim

Distinguished Service Cross, Posthumous

Captain Ian Harry NORTH, Merchant Navy; Lieutenant Commander Gordon Walter James BATT, Royal Navy; Lieutenant Commander John Stuart WOODHEAD, Royal Navy; Lieutenant Commander John Murray SEPHTON, Royal Navy.

Distinguished Service Cross

Captain George Robert GREEN, Royal Fleet Auxiliary; Captain David Everett LAWRENCE, Royal Fleet Auxiliary; Captain Anthony Francis PITT, Royal Fleet Auxiliary; Commander Paul Jeffrey

---

ROLL OF HONOUR

In practice, medals and decorations awarded to British armed service personnel for gallantry on active service fall into a number of grades. Each includes decorations for roughly comparable acts by men of the different services; and each includes two parallel sequences of awards, one for officers and one for enlisted ranks: traditionally separate sequences which do not, however, imply any difference in merit: the RAF officer's Distinguished Flying Cross for instance, and the RAF sergeant's Distinguished Flying Medal denote no difference in bravery whatsoever.

The grades are first and foremost, the Victoria Cross; second, the Distinguished Service Order, Distinguished Conduct Medal and Conspicuous Gallantry Medal; third, the Military Cross, Distinguished Service Cross, Distinguished Flying Cross, Military Medal, Distinguished Service Medal and Distinguished Flying Medal; fourth, the Air Force Cross and Air Force Medal. A fifth category comprises awards and honours such as Mention in Dispatches which are not gallantry medals as such, but carry special insignia. Two further categories, outside this sequence, include the George Medal and the civil and military divisions of the Order of the British Empire.

BOOTHERSTONE, Royal Navy; Commander Christopher John Sinclair CRAIG, Royal Navy; Commander Anthony MORTON, Royal Navy; Commander Nicholas John TOBIN, Royal Navy; Commander Nigel David WARD AFC, Royal Navy; Commander Alan William John West, Royal Navy; Lieutenant Commander Andrew Donaldson AULD, Royal Navy; Lieutenant Commander Michael Dennison BOOTH, Royal Navy; Lieutenant Commander Hugh Sinclair CLARK, Royal Navy; Lieutenant Commander John Anthony ELLERBECK, Royal Navy;

From the citation for Lieutenant Commander N W Thomas's DSC

'On one occasion, he shot down one of a wave of four Skyhawks and in the ensuing dog-fight in cloud and when his remaining missile indicated that it had acquired a target, he showed great coolness in holding his fire until he was able to confirm that it had in fact detected his wingman rather than the enemy, so preventing a tragic accident'.

VICTORIA CROSS

Instituted in the Crimean War, the VC is awarded to officers and men alike as the supreme decoration for gallantry under fire. The simple bronze cross—originally cast from the metal of captured Russian cannon—is awarded only for a specific act in battle, performed in complete disregard for personal safety. About a quarter of all awards have been posthumous; and between 1945 and April 1982 only four awards had been made to British service personnel. The claret-coloured ribbon is unique and unmistakable.

Lieutenant Commander Hugh John LOMAS, Royal Navy; Lieutenant Commander Neil Wynell THOMAS, Royal Navy; Lieutenant Commander Simon Clive THORNEWILL, Royal Navy; Lieutenant Alan Reginald Courtenay BENNET, Royal Navy; Lieutenant Nigel Arthur BRUEN, Royal Navy; Lieutenant Richard HUTCHINGS, Royal Marines; Acting Lieutenant Keith Paul MILLS, Royal

Lt Richard Hutchings, DSC, his wife and two sons

From the citation for Sub Lieutenant P T Morgan's DSC

'On two occasions he dived into the flooded forward magazine, in the knowledge that in addition to the hazards posed by twisted and jagged metal, there was an unexploded bomb in the compartment amongst damaged ordnance'.

Marines; Lieutenant Nigel John NORTH, Royal Navy; Lieutenant Stephen Robert THOMAS, Royal Navy; Sub Lieutenant Peter Thomas MORGAN, Royal Navy; Fleet Chief Petty Officer (Diver) Michael George FELLOWS BEM.

Military Cross

Major Charles Peter CAMERON, Royal Marines; Captain Peter Murray BABBINGTON, Royal Marines; Lieutenant Clive Idris DYTOR, Royal Marines; Lieutenant Christopher FOX, Royal Marines; Lieutenant David James STEWART, Royal Marines.

Distinguished Flying Cross, Posthumous

Lieutenant Richard James NUNN, Royal Marines.

Distinguished Flying Cross

Captain Jeffrey Peter NIBLETT, Royal Marines.

Air Force Cross

Lieutenant Commander Douglas John Smiley SQUIER, Royal Navy; Lieutenant Commander Ralph John Stuart WYKES-SNEYD, Royal Navy.

Distinguished Conduct Medal

Corporal Julian BURDETT, Royal Marines.

George Medal, Posthumous

Second Engineer Officer Paul Anderson HENRY, Royal Fleet Auxiliary.

George Medal

Able Seaman (Radar) John Edward DILLON.

From the citation for Able seaman (Radar) J E Dillon's GM

'He extricated himself and despite pain from a large shrapnel wound in his back attempted unsuccessfully to free a man pinned down by a girder across his neck. He then made his way through the 'smoke towards a further man calling for help, whom he found trapped under heavy metal girders, bleeding from head and face wounds and with his left hand severely damaged. After several attempts between which he had to drop to the deck to get breathable air, AB(R) Dillon succeeded in raising the debris sufficiently to allow the man to drag himself free. AB(R) Dillon's antiflash hood had been ripped off in the explosion; so afforded him no protection from the heat, and his left ear was burned'.

Distinguished Service Medal, Posthumous

Petty Officer Marine Engineering Mechanic (M) David Richard BRIGGS; Acting Corporal Aircrewman Michael David LOVE, Royal Marines.

Distinguished Service Medal

Colour Sergeant Michael James FRANCIS, Royal Marines; Sergeant Peter James LEACH, Royal Marines; Chief Marine Engineering Mechanic (M) Michael David TOWNSEND; Chief Petty Officer (Diver) Graham Michael TROTTER; Chief Petty Officer Aircrewman Malcolm John TUPPER; Petty Officer John Steven LEAKE; Sergeant William John LESLIE, Royal Marines; Acting Petty Officer (Sonar) (SM) Graham John Robert LIBBY; Leading Aircrewman Peter Blair IMRIE; Leading Seaman (Radar) Jeffrey David WARREN.

Military Medal

Sergeant Thomas COLLINGS, Royal Marines; Sergeant Michael COLLINS, Royal Marines; Sergeant Joseph Desmond WASSELL, Royal Marines; Corporal Michael ECCLES, Royal Marines; Corporal David HUNT, Royal Marines; Corporal Stephen Charles NEWLAND, Royal Marines; Corporal Harry SIDDALL, Royal Marines; Corporal Chrystie Nigel Hanslip WARD, Royal Marines; Acting Corporal Andrew Ronald BISHOP, Royal Marines; Marine Gary William MARSHAL, Royal Marines.

Distinguished Flying Medal

Sergeant William Christopher O'BRIEN, Royal Marines.

Queen's Gallantry Medal, Posthumous

Acting Colour Sergeant Brian JOHNSTON, Royal Marines.

The Department for National Savings

1 DISTINGUISHED CONDUCT MEDAL

2 CONSPICUOUS GALLANTRY MEDAL

These are the equivalent decorations, for enlisted ranks, of the officers' DSO. They date from the Crimean War. The DCM is for Army personnel, the CGM and more recent CGM (Flying) for Royal Navy, Royal Marines, Merchant Navy and Royal Air Force personnel. They are rarely awarded and highly prized, and many awards have been for acts which were 'borderline' VC recommendations. The ribbons are in the traditional colours of the three services: red and blue, white and blue, and light and dark blue.

Queen's Gallantry Medal

Chief Engineer Officer Charles Kenneth Arthur ADAMS, Royal Fleet Auxiliary; Lieutenant John Kenneth BOUGHTON, Royal Navy; Lieutenant Philip James SHELDON, Royal Navy; Third Officer Andrew GUDGEON, Royal Fleet Auxiliary; Third Engineer Brian Robert WILLIAMS, Merchand Navy; Marine Engineering Artificer (M) 1st Class Kenneth ENTICKNAPP; Petty Officer Medical Assistant Gerald Andrew MEAGER.

From the citation for Third Officer A Gudgeon's QGM

'On two occasions during this time [the campaign] he showed great courage in risking his life in order to save others. When HMS Antelope blew up and caught fire in San Carlos Water, he volunteered to cox the crash boat to pick up survivors. This he did knowing that HMS Antelope had a second unexploded bomb on board. Despite the fire spreading rapidly, he carried out the rescue of several survivors.'

The Press Association

DISTINGUISHED SERVICE ORDER

Instituted in 1886, for officers 'who had rendered meritorious or distinguished service in war', this honour is awarded only to officers who have been mentioned in despatches for their conduct of active operations. Typically, it is the reward for a unit commander of one of the fighting services who shows especially skilled and courageous leadership qualities in action. The blue-edged red ribbon of the beautiful enamelled cross recalls the ribbons of the Army Gold Cross and other medals of the Napoleonic Wars.

Chief Officer Peter Hill, Mention in Dispatches

Mention in Despatches

Chief Officer John Keith BROCKLEHURST, Merchant Navy; Commander Robert Duncan FERGUSON, Royal Navy; Chief Officer Peter Ferris HILL, Royal Fleet Auxiliary; Major Peter Ralph LAMB, Royal Marines; Commander Roger Charles LANE-NOTT, Royal Navy; Commander Thomas Maitland Le MARCHAND, Royal Navy; Major Michael John NORMAN, Royal Marines; Major David Anthony PENNEFATHER, Royal Marines; Chief Engineer James Mailer STEWART, Merchant Navy; Commander James Bradley TAYLOR, Royal Navy; Commander Bryan Geoffrey TELFER, Royal Navy; Major Rupert Cornelius VAN DER HORST, Royal Marines; Lieutenant Commander Michael Stephen BLISSETT, Royal Navy; Lieutenant Commander Barry William BRYANT, Royal Navy; Lieutenant Commander Robert Gerwyn BURROWS, Royal Navy; Lieutenant Commander John Sydney Maurice CHANDLER, Royal Navy; Lieutenant Commander John Normanton CLARK, Royal Navy; Lieutenant Commander William Edgar HURST, Royal Navy; Lieutenant Commander John PARRY, Royal Navy; Captain Michael Anthoy Falle COLE, Royal Marines; Lieutenant Commander Gervais Richard Arthur CORYTON, Royal Navy; Lieutenant Commander Rodney Vincent FREDERIKSEN, Royal Navy; Lieutenant Commander David Gordon GARWOOD, Royal Navy; Lieutenant Commander Andrew Clive GWILLIAM, Royal Navy; Lieutenant Commander Lon Stuart Grant HULME, Royal Navy; Lieutenant Commander Ian INSKIP, Royal Navy; Lieutenant Commander Robin Sean Gerald KENT, Royal Navy; Lieutenant Commander John Andrew LISTER, Royal Navy; Lieutenant Commander Iain Bruce MACKAY, Royal Navy; Lieutenant Commander Clive Ronald WELLESLEY MORRELL, Royal Navy; Lieutenant Commander Kenneth Maclean NAPIER, Royal Navy; Captain Andew Bennett NEWCOMBE, Royal Marines; Lieutenant Commander Michael John O'CONNELL, Royal Navy; Captain Eugene Joseph O'KANE, Royal Marines; Captain Andrew Robert PILLAR, Royal Marines; Captain Nicholas Ernest POUNDS, Royal Marines; Lieutenant Commander Alvin Arnold RICH, Royal Navy; Lieutenant Commander Robert Ernald WILKINSON, Royal Navy; Lieutenant Philip James BARBER, Royal Navy; Lieutenant Nicholas Abraham Marsh BUTLER, Royal Navy; Lieutenant Christian Thomas Gordon CAROE, Royal Marines; Lieutenant Christopher Hugh Trevor CLAYTON, Royal Navy; Lieutenant Ronald Lindsay CRAWFORD, Royal Marines; Lieutenant William Alan CURTIS, Royal Navy (Posthumous); Lieutenant Andrew John EBBENS, Royal Marines; Lieutenant William James Truman FEWTRELL, Royal Navy; Lieutenant Fraser HADDOW, Royal Marines; Lieutenant Robert Ian HORTON, Royal Navy; Lieutenant Herbert John LEDINGHAM, Royal Navy; Lieutenant David Anthony LORD, Royal Navy; Lieutenant Peter Charles MANLEY, Royal Navy; Lieutenant Andrew Nevill McHARG, Royal Navy; Lieutenant John Andrew Gordon MILLER, Royal Navy; Lieutenant Paul Graham MILLER, Royal Navy; Lieutenant Andrew Gerald MOLL, Royal Navy; Lieutenant Richard John ORMSHAW, Royal Navy; Lieutenant Christopher Laurence PALMER, Royal Navy; Lieutenant Roland Frederick

PLAYFORD, Royal Marines; Lieutenant Christopher James POLLARD, Royal Navy; Lieutenant Anthony PRINGLE, Royal Navy; Lieutenant Peter Iain Mackay RAINEY, Royal Navy; Lieutenant Frederick William ROBERTSON, Royal Navy; Lieutenant Robin Edgar John SLEEMAN, Royal Navy; Lieutenant David Alexander Bereton SMITH, Royal Navy; Lieutenant Nicholas TAYLOR, Royal Navy (Posthumous); Lieutenant Christopher TODHUNTER, Royal Navy; Lieutenant D A H WELLS, Royal Navy; Sub Lieutenant Richard John BARKER, Royal Navy; Sub Lieutenant Stewart Greig COOPER, Royal Navy; Sub Lieutenant Richard Charles EMLY, Royal Navy (Posthumous); Sub Lieutenant David Edgar GRAHAM, Royal Navy; Sub Lieutenant Paul John HUMPHREYS, Royal Navy; Midshipman Mark Thomas FLETCHER, Royal Navy; Fleet Chief Marine Engineer Artificer (P) Ernest Malcolm UREN; Warrant Officer Class 2 Robert John BROWN, Royal Marines; Warrant Officer Class 2 Adrian Spencer ROBINSON, Royal Marines; Chief Air Engineering Artificer (M) Richard John BENTLEY; Marine Engineering Artificer (H) 1st Class Derek Adrian BUGDEN; Colour Sergeant Barrie DAVIES, Royal Marines; Weapon Engineering Artificer 1st Class Anthony Charles EDDINGTON (Posthumous); Chief Marine Engineering Artificer (H) Keith William GOLDIE; Chief Petty Officer (Ops) (M) Eric GRAHAM; Chief Petty Officer (Diver) Brian Thomas GUNNELL; Marine Engineering Artificer (H) 1st Class peter Gerhard JAKEMAN; Marine Engineering Artificer (H) 1st Class Peter Gerhard JAKEMAN; Marine Engineering Artificer (M) 1st Class Kevin MARTIN; Marine Engineering Mechanician (M) 1st Class Timothy MILES; Marine Engineering Artificer (M) 1st Class Stephen Derek MITCHELL; Weapon Engineering Mechanician 1st Class Peter Robert MOIR; Marine Engineering Mechanician (M) 1st Class Hugh Bromley PORTER; Marine Engineering Mechanician 1st Class Alan Gordon SIDDLE; Chief Marine Engineering Mechanic Tyrone George SMITH; Marine Engineering Artificer (M) 1st Class Simon Patrick TARABELLA; Acting Chief Weapon Engineering Mechanician Michael Gordon TILL (Posthumous); Marine Engineering Mechanician (L) 1st Class William Geoffrey WADDINGTON; Colour Sergeant Everett YOUNG, Royal Marines; Petty Officer Aircrewman Alan ASHDOWN; Petty Officer Aircrewman John Arthur BALLS, BEM; Petty Officer Aircrewman David Brian FITZGERALD; Sergeant Peter BEEVERS, Royal Marines; Sergeant Ian William BRICE, Royal Marines; Sergeant Edward Lindsay BUCKLEY, Royal Marines; Sergeant Brian Gordon BURGESS, Royal Marines; Petty Officer Aircrewman Richard BURNETT; Sergeant Edgar Robert CANDLISH, Royal Marines; Sergeant Robert Terence COOPER, Royal Marines; Sergeant Graham DANCE, Royal Marines; Sergeant Colin Charles DE LA COUR, QGM, Royal Marines; Sergeant Brian DOLIVERA, Royal Marines; Petty Officer Marine Engineering Mechanic (M) John Richard ELLIS; Sergeant Andrew Peter EVANS, Royal Marines (Posthumous); Sergeant Ian David FISK,

1 **MILITARY CROSS**
2 **DISTINGUISHED SERVICE CROSS**
3 **DISTINGUISHED FLYING CROSS**

These decorations were instituted during World War 1 for junior officers of the Army, Royal Navy and Marines and Royal Air Force respectively. The MC and DSC are reserved for officers up to the rank of major

and commander respectively. The awards are for 'gallant and distinguished services in action' and in the case of the DFC it is only awarded for acts performed while flying on active operations against the enemy. The typical award is to a junior officer who leads his men in battle with exceptional courage and resourcefulness. Aircrew officers

may be awarded the DFC either for consistent skill and courage over a number of missions, or for single missions. The purple and white of the MC ribbon are repeated in that of the DFC, in the multi-striped arrangement traditional for the RAF; the DSC retains the Royal Navy's austere blue and white.

1 **MILITARY MEDAL**
2 **DISTINGUISHED SERVICE MEDAL**
3 **DISTINGUISHED FLYING MEDAL**

These are the equivalent decorations to the MC, DSC and DFC for enlisted ranks, and also date from World War 1. The

memorandum instituting the DSM in 1914 best sums up the conditions of award of all three medals: it was for men who '... show themselves to the fore in action, and set an example of bravery and resource under fire'. Awards are made both for

individual acts of courage, and for leadership in battle by NCOs. The MM ribbon is in national colours; both the DSM and DFM ribbons are slight variations on the design of the equivalent officers' awards.

Royal Marines; Weapons Engineering Artificer 2nd Class Jonathan Martin Charles FOY; Sergeant David Keith HADLOW, Royal Marines; Sergeant Kevin Michael JAMES QGM, Royal Marines; Petty Officer (Missile) Hugh JONES; Marine Engineering Artificer 2nd Class David John LEANING; Sergeant William David Paul LEWIS, Royal Marines; Sergeant Mitchell McINTYRE, Royal Marines; Sergeant Henry Frederick NAPIER, Royal Marines; Petty Officer (Rader) Jack PEARSON; Petty Officer Air Engineering Mechanic (M) Stuart RAINSBURY; Acting Petty Officer Marine Engineering Mechanic (M) David Morgan Kerlin ROSS; Sergeant Thomas Arthur SANDS, Royal Marines; Sergeant William John STOCKS, Royal Marines; Sergeant Christopher Ralph STONE, Royal Marines; Petty Officer Aircrewman

Colin William TATTERSALL; Weapon Engineering Mechanician 2nd Class Barry James WALLIS (Posthumous); Sergeant Robert David WRIGHT, Royal Marines; Acting Leading Medical Assistant George BLACK; Acting Leading Marine Engineering Mechanic (M) Craig Robert BOSWELL; Corporal Christopher John Graham BROWN, Royal Marines; Corporal Gordon COOKE, Royal Marines; Leading Seaman (Missile) Robert Marshall GOULD; Leading Aircrewman James Andrew HARPER; Acting Leading Marine Engineering Mechanic (M) Stanley William HATHAWAY; Leading Radio Operator (Tactical) Roderick John HUTCHESON; Leading Seaman (Diver) Phillip Martin KEARNS; Corporal Thomas William McMAHON, Royal Marines; Leading Aircrewman Ian

ROBERTSON; Leading Seaman (Diver) Charles Anthony SMITHARD; Leading Seaman (Diver) Anthony Savour THOMPSON; Leading Aircrewman Stephen William WRIGHT; Leading Medical Assistant Paul YOUNGMAN; Radio Operator (Tactical) 1st Class Richard John ASH; Lance Corporal Peter William BOORN, Royal Marines; Able Seaman (Missile) Nicholas Scott BROTHERTON; Marine Engineering Mechanic (M) 1st Class Lee CARTWRIGHT; Marine Engineering Mechanic (M) 1st Class Michael Lindsay CHIPLEN; Able Seaman (Missile) Andrew COPPELL; Marine Engineering Mechanic (M) 1st Class Christopher CROWLEY; Marine Engineering Mechanic (M) 1st Class David John EDWARDS; Lance Corporal Barry GILBERT, Royal Marines; Able Seaman (Missile)

Stephen INGLEBY; Able Seaman (Radar) Mark Stanley LEACH; Medical Assistant Michael NICELY; Marine Engineering Mechanic (M) 1st Class David John SERRELL; Marine Engineering Mechanic (M) 1st Class Alan STEWART; Able Seaman (Diver) David WALTON; Marine Robert BAINBRIDGE, Royal Marines; Marine Nicholas John BARNETT, Royal Marines; Marine David Stanley COMBES, Royal Marines; Marine Gary CUTHELL, Royal Marines; Marine Leslie DANIELS, Royal Marines; Marine Stephen DUGGAN, Royal Marines; Marine Leonard John GOLDSMITH, Royal Marines; Marine Graham HODKINSON, Royal Marines; Marine Mark Andrew NEAT, Royal Marines; Marine Geoffrey NORDASS, Royal Marines; Marine David Lloyd O'CONNOR, Royal Marines; Marine Christopher James SCRIVENER, Royal Marines; Marine John STONESTREET, Royal Marines; Marine Ricky Shaun STRANGE, Royal Marines; Marine Perry THOMASON, Royal Marines; Seaman (OPS) Douglas James WHILD; Marine Paul Kevin WILSON, Royal Marines.

Queen's Commendation for Brave Conduct

Second Officer Ian POVEY, Royal Fleet Auxiliary; Chief Marine Engineering Mechanic (L) Alan Frank FAZACKERLEY; Chief Weapon Engineering Mechanic (R) William RUMSEY; Weapon Engineering Mechanic (R) 1st Class John Richard JESSON; Marine Engineering Mechanician (M) 1st Class Thomas Arthur SUTTON; Acting Colour Sergeant David Alfred WATKINS, Royal Marines; Petty Officer Class 2 Boleslaw CZARNECKI, Merchant Navy; Petty Officer Weapon Engineering Mechanic (R) Graeme John LOWDEN; Radio Operator (Tactical) 1st Class David Frederick SULLIVAN; Marine Paul Anthony CRUDEN, Royal Marines.

ARMY

Victoria Cross (Posthumous)

Lieutenant Colonel Herbert JONES OBE, The Parachute Regiment; Sergeant Ian John McKAY, The Parachute Regiment.

Distinguished Service Order

Major Cedric Norman George DELVES, The Devonshire and Dorset Regiment; Major Christopher Patrick Benedict KEEBLE, The Parachute Regiment; Lieutenant Colonel Hew William Royston PIKE MBE, The Parachute Regiment; Lieutenant Colonel Michael Ian Eldon SCOTT, Scots Guards.

From the citation for Major C N G Delves's DSO

'Following the successful establishment of the beachhead in San Carlos Water, Major Delves took his SAS Squadron 40 miles behind the enemy lines and established a position overlooking the main enemy stronghold in Port Stanley where at least 7000 troops were known to be based. By a series of swift operations, skilful concealment and lightning attacks against patrols sent out to find him, he was able to secure a sufficiently firm hold on the area after ten days for the conventional forces to be brought in'.

Distinguished Service Cross

Warrant Officer Class 2 John Henry PHILLIPS, Corps of Royal Engineers.

Military Cross, Posthumous

Captain Gavin John HAMILTON, The Green Howards (Alexandra, Princess of Wales' own Yorkshire Regiment).

Military Cross

Major Michael Hugh ARGUE, The Parachute Regiment; Captain Timothy William BURLS, The Parachute Regiment; Major David Alan COLLETT, The Parachute Regiment; Lieutenant Colin Spencer CONNOR, The Parachute Regiment; Major John Harry CROSLAND, The Parachute Regiment; Major Charles Dair FARRAR-HOCKLEY, The Parachute Regiment; Major John Panton KISZELY, Scots Guards; Lieutenant Robert Alasdair Davidson LAWRENCE, Scots Guards; Captain William Andrew McCRACKEN, Royal Regiment of Artillery; Captain Aldwin James Glendinning WIGHT, Welsh Guards.

From the citation for Major J P Kiszely's MC

'Under fire and with a complete disregard for his own safety, he led a group of his men up a gully towards the enemy. Despite men falling wounded beside him he continued his charge, throwing grenades as he went. Arriving on the enemy position, he killed two enemy with his rifle and a third with his bayonet. His courageous action forced the surrender of the remainder. His was the culminating action in the Battalion successfully seizing its objective'.

Distinguished Flying Cross

Captain Samuel Murray DRENNAN, Army Air Corps; Captain John Gordon GREENHALGH, Royal Corps of Transport.

Distinguished Conduct Medal, Posthumous

Private Stephen ILLINGSWORTH, The Parachute Regiment; Guardsman James Boyle Curran REYNOLDS, Scots Guards.

Distinguished Conduct Medal

Corporal David ABOLS, The Parachute Regiment; Staff Sergeant Brian FAULKNER, The Parachute Regiment; Sergeant John Clifford MEREDITH, The Parachute Regiment; Warrant Officer Class 2 William NICOL, Scots Guards; Sergeant John Stuart PETTINGER, The Parachute Regiment.

From the citation for Staff Sergeant B Faulkner's DCM

'He never faltered, setting a magnificent personal example of courage and competence, that was well beyond anything that could reasonably be expected. One burst of shellfire left him concussed, but he swiftly returned to his duties. One minute he could be seen consoling young soldiers, severely distressed by the experience of losing their comrades... then yet again tending for the casualties themselves'.

Conspicuous Gallantry Medal, Posthumous

Staff Sergeant James PRESCOTT, Corps of Royal Engineers.

Military Medal, Posthumous

Private Richard John de Mansfield ABSOLON, The Parachute Regiment; Lance Corporal Gary David BINGLEY, The Parachute Regiment.

Left to right: L/cpl Bentley, Sgt Barrett, Pte Grayling and MMs

Military Medal

Corporal Ian Phillip BAILEY, The Parachute Regiment; Lance Corporal Stephen Alan BARDSLEY, The Parachute Regiment; Sergeant Terence Irving BARRETT, The Parachute Regiment; Lance Corporal Martin William Lester BENTLEY, The Parachute Regiment; Sergeant Derrick Sidney BOULTBY, Royal Corps of Transport; Corporal Trevor BROOKES, Royal Corps of Signals; Corporal Thomas James CAMP, The Parachute Regiment; Private Graham Stuart CARTER, The Parachute Regiment; Guardsman Stephen Mark CHAPMAN, Welsh Guards; Corporal John Anthony FORAN, Corps of

From the citation for Corporal J A Foran's MM

'During the assault, Corporal Foran, Royal Engineers, led a patrol through an unmarked enemy minefield to assault an enemy position. The patrol came under heavy fire, a burst from a machine gun killing two men. A further two men were wounded by exploding mines.

Without hesitation and completely disregarding his own safety, Corporal Foran re-entered the minefield and cleared a path to his injured colleagues. Having treated them he cleared a route back out of the minefield, enabling the casualties to be evacuated'.

L/Cpl Dale Loveridge, MM, and his fiancée Barbara

Royal Engineers; Sergeant Desmond FULLER, The Parachute Regiment; Private Barry James GRAYLING, The Parachute Regiment; Corporal Thomas William HARLEY, The Parachute Regiment; Bombardier Edward Morris HOLT, Royal Regiment of Artillery; Sergeant Robert White JACKSON, Scots Guards; Lance Corporal Dale John LOVERIDGE, Welsh Guards; Sergeant Joseph Gordon MATHER, Special Air Service Regiment; Sergeant Peter Hurcliche Rene NAYA, Royal Army Medical Corps; Warrant Officer Class 2 Brian Thomas NECK, Welsh Guards; Guardsman Andrew Samuel PENGELLY, Scots Guards; Lance Corporal Leslie James Leonard STANDISH, The Parachute Regiment; Sergeant Roman Hugh WREGA, Corps of Royal Engineers.

Mention in Despatches

Sergeant Ian AIRD, The Parachute Regiment; Private Simon John ALEXANDER, The Parachute Regiment; Lieutenant Colonel James ANDERSON, Royal Army Medical Corps; Corporal Raymond Ernest ARMSTRONG, The Royal Green Jackets (Posthumous); Major The Honourable Richard Nicholas BETHEL MBE, Scots Guards; Captain Anthony Peter BOURNE, Royal Regiment of Artillery; Private Andrew Ernest BROOKE, The Parachute Regiment; Driver Mark BROUGH, Royal Corps of Transport; Captain Christopher Charles BROWN, Royal

AIR FORCE CROSS

Given the hazards of all military flying, whether or not in the presence of the enemy, this decoration, along with the Air Force Medal, was instituted late in World War I for officers and enlisted personnel respectively for acts of courage or devotion to duty while flying but not actually in combat. They are typically awarded to aircrew who show such qualities in the face of, for example, extreme weather conditions, severe physical exhaustion, or in damaged aircraft. The ribbons reflect those of the DFC and DFM. One DFM was awarded.

Regiment of Artillery; Guardsman Gary BROWN, Scots Guards; Captain Ian Anderson BRYDEN, Scots Guards; Major William Keith BUTLER, Royal Corps of Signals; Staff Sergeant William Henry CARPENTER, Special Air Service Regiment; Lance Corporal Leonard Allan CARVER, The Parachute Regiment; Lieutenant (Queen's Gurkha Officer) CHANDRAKUMAR PRADHAN, 7th Duke of Edinburgh's Own Gurkha Rifles; Staff Sergeant Trevor COLLINS, Corps of Royal Engineers; Private Kevin Patrick CONNERY, The Parachute Regiment; Chaplain to the Forces Third Class David COOPER, Royal Army Chaplains Department; Lieutenant Mark Rudolph CORETH, The Blues and Royals (Royal Horse Guards and 1st Dragoons); Private Adam Michael CORNEILLE, The Parachute Regi-

Regiment (Posthumous); Corporal David FORD, Corps of Royal Engineers; Warrant Officer Class 2 John FRANCIS, Royal Regiment of Artillery; Lieutenant David Peart FRANKLAND, Royal Corps of Transport; Lance Corporal Roy GILLON, Corps of Royal Engineers; Private (now Lance Corporal) Darren John GOUGH, The Parachute Regiment; Lance Sergeant David GRAHAM, The Parachute Regiment; Major Patrick Hector GULLAN MBE, MC, The Parachute Regiment; (Acting Corporal) Joseph Edward HAND, The Parachute Regiment; Lance Corporal (Acting Corporal) Stephen Paul HARDING-DEMPSTER, The Parachute Regiment; Corporal David HARDMAN, The Parachute Regiment (Posthumous); Private Patrick John HARLEY, The Para-

Richard Ryszad KALINSKI, The Parachute Regiment; Captain Simon James KNAPPER, The Staffordshire Regiment (The Prince of Wales's) Staff Sergeant (Acting Warrant Officer Class 2) Anthony LA FRENAIS, Special Air Service Regiment; Major Brendan Charles LAMBE, Royal Regiment of Artillery; Lieutenant Clive Ralph LIVINGSTONE, Corps of Royal Engineers; Lance Corporal Christopher Keith LOVETT, The Parachute Regiment, (Posthumous); Lieutenant Jonathan George Ormsby LOWE, Royal Corps of Transport; Staff Sergeant Clive Dennis LOWTHER, Special Air Service Regiment; Lance Corporal Duncan MACCOLL, Scots Guards; Major Roderick MACDONALD, Corps of Royal Engineers; Piper Peter Alexander MACINNES, Scots Guards; Lance Corporal John Daniel MAHER, Corps of Royal Engineers; Captain Robin John MAKEIG-JONES, Royal Regiment of Artillery; Private Andrew MANSFIELD, The Parachute Regiment; Major Tymothy Alastair MARSH, The Parachute Regiment; Sergeant Peter James MARSHALL, Army Catering Corps; Lance Sergeant Thomas McGUINNESS, Scots Guards; Captain Joseph Hugh McMANNERS, Royal Regiment of Artillery; Lieutenant Alasdair Macfarlane MITCHELL, Scots Guards; Lance Sergeant Clark MITCHELL, Scots Guards (Posthumous); 2nd Lieutenant Ian Charles MOORE, The Parachute Regiment; Private Richard Peter George MORRELL, The Parachute Regiment; Major Philip NEAME, The Parachute Regiment; Corporal Thomas Kiernan NOBLE, The Parachute Regiment; Private Emmanuel O'ROURKE, The Parachute Regiment; Lieutenant Jonathan David PAGE, The Parachute Regiment; Private (Acting Corporal) David John PEARCY, Intelligence Corps; Corporal Jeremy Frank PHILLIPS, The Parachute Regiment; Private (Acting Sergeant) Brian William PITCHFORTH, The Queen's Regiment; Private Anthony POTTER, Royal Army Ordnance Corps; Lance Corporal Barry John RANDALL, Corps of Royal Engineers; Sergeant Peter RATCLIFFE, Special Air Service Regiment; Lance Corporal Graham RENNIE, Scots Guards; Warrant Officer Class 2 Malcolm Douglas RICHARDS, Royal Regiment of Artillery; Lance Corporal Julian Jon RIGG, Army Air Corps; Lieutenant Colonel John David Arthur ROBERTS, Royal Army Medical Corps; Major Barnaby Peter Stuart ROLFE-SMITH, The Parachute Regiment; Captain Christopher Roy ROMBERG, Royal Regiment of Artillery; Lieutenant Colonel Hugh Michael ROSE, OBE, Coldstream Guards; Sergeant Ian ROY, Corps of Royal Engineers; Captain Julian David Gurney SAYERS, Welsh Guards; Lieutenant (Acting Captain) Matthew Rodgers SELFRIDGE, The Parachute Regiment (Posthumous); Warrant Officer Class 2 Michael John SHARP, Army Air Corps; Corporal John William SIBLEY, The Parachute Regiment; Major Colin Stewart SIBUN, Army Air Corps; Sapper (Acting Lance Corporal) William Austen SKINNER, Corps of Royal Engineers; Major Graham Frederick William SMITH, Royal Regiment of Artillery; Captain Royston John SOUTHWORTH, Royal Army Ord-

nance Corps; Corporal of Horse Paul STRETTON, The Blues and Royals (Royal Horse Guards and 1st Dragoons); 2nd Lieutenant James Douglas STUART, Scots Guards; Lieutenant William John SYMS, Welsh Guards; Corporal (Acting Sergeant) Robert Clive TAYLOR, Royal Corps of Signals; Major Anthony TODD, Royal Corps of Transport; Lance Corporal Gary TYTLER, Scots Guards; Private (Acting Corporal) Peter Andrew WALKER, The Staffordshire Regiment (The Prince of Wales's); Sergeant Richard John WALKER, Army Air Corps; 2nd Lieutenant Guy WALLIS, The Parachute Regiment; Lieutenant Mark Evan WARING, Royal Regiment of Artillery; Captain James Nicholas Edward WATSON, Royal Regiment of Artillery; Lieutenant Geoffrey Ronald WEIGHELL, The Parachute Regiment; Lieutenant (now Captain) Mark Graham WILLIAMS, Royal Regiment of Artillery; Lieutenant (now Captain) Maldwyn Stephen Henry WORSLEY-TONKS, The Parachute Regiment.

ROYAL AIR FORCE

Distinguished Service Cross

Flight Lieutenant David Henry Spencer MORGAN, Royal Air Force, 899 Naval Air Squadron.

Distinguished Flying Cross

Wing Commander Peter Ted SQUIRE AFC, Royal Air Force; Squadron Leader Richard Ulric LANGWORTHY AFC, Royal Air Force; Squadron Leader Calum Neil McDOUGALL, Royal Air Force; Squadron Leader Jeremy John POOK, Royal Air Force; Flight Lieutenant William Francis Martin WITHERS, Royal Air Force.

From the citation for Wing Commander P T Squire's DFC

'Wing Commander Squire led his Squadron with great courage from the front, flying 24 attack sorties. He flew many daring missions, but of particular note was an attack at low level with rockets on targets at Port Stanley Airfield in the face of heavy anti-aircraft fire when both he and his wing man returned damaged. Also a bombing attack on an HQ position when, on approach, a bullet passed through his cockpit which temporarily distracted him, but he quickly found an alternative target and bombed that instead'.

Air Force Cross

Wing Commander David EMMERSON, Royal Air Force; Squadron Leader Arthur Max ROBERTS, Royal Air Force; Squadron Leader Robert TUXFORD, Royal Air Force; Flight Lieutenant Harold Currie BURGOYNE, Royal Air Force.

Queen's Gallantry Medal

Flight Lieutenant Alan James SWAN, Royal Air Force; Flight Sergeant Brian William JOPLING, Royal Air Force.

ment; Corporal Ian Clifford CORRIGAN, Corps of Royal Electrical and Mechanical Engineers; Lieutenant Mark Townsend COX, The Parachute Regiment; Staff Sergeant Phillip Preston CURRASS, QGM, Royal Army Medical Corps (Posthumous); Lance Sergeant Alan Charles Ewing DALGLEISH, Scots Guards; Lance Corporal Neal John DANCE, The Parachute Regiment; Lance Sergeant Ian DAVIDSON, Scots Guards; Major Peter Eastaway DENNISON, The Parachute Regiment; Staff Sergeant George Kenneth DIXON, Royal Regiment of Artillery; Piper Steven William DUFFY, Scots Guards; Lance Corporal Kevin Peter DUNBAR, The Parachute Regiment; Gunner Gary ECCLESTON, Royal Regiment of Artillery; Captain Martin Patrick ENTWISTLE, Royal Army Medical Corps; Lieutenant Colonel Keith Richard Hubert EVE, Royal Regiment of Artillery; Captain Paul Raymond FARRAR, The Parachute Regiment; Private Mark William FLETCHER, The Parachute

chute Regiment; Major Richard Bruce HAWKEN, Corps of Royal Engineers; Lieutenant Robert Charles HENDICOTT, Corps of Royal Engineers; Corporal (Acting Sergeant) Joseph HILL, The Parachute Regiment; Lieutenant Colonel George Anthony HOLT, Royal Regiment of Artillery; Warrant Officer Class 2 Graham HOUGH, Welsh Guards; Captain (now Major) Euan Henry HOUSTOUN MBE, Grenadier Guards; Lance Bombardier (Acting Bombardier) Owain Dyfnallt HUGHES, Royal Regiment of Artillery; Captain Stephen James HUGHES, Royal Army Medical Corps; Corporal Stephen Darryl ILES, Corps of royal Engineers; Lieutenant The Lord Robert Anthony INNESKER, The Blues and Royals (Royal Horse Guards and 1st Dragoons); Bombardier John Rodney JACKSON, Royal Regiment of Artillery; Gunner Jeffrey JONES, Royal Regiment of Artillery; Lance Corporal Kenneth Bryan JONES, Royal Corps of Transport; Sergeant

MENTION IN DISPATCHES

QUEEN'S COMMENDATION FOR BRAVE CONDUCT

QUEEN'S COMMENDATION FOR VALUABLE SERVICE IN THE AIR

Servicemen of all ranks who distinguish themselves by some act of courage or skill which is not held to qualify them for the

award of a higher honour receive these commendations. Like all other decorations they are awarded on the recommendation of unit commanders—though once again, like all other decorations, far fewer are awarded than are recommended. The visible mark of this class of honour is an oak leaf insignia, which is worn by service personnel sewn to the ribbon of the campaign medal relevant to the award, or directly to the tunic if no campaign is involved.

Although most of these medals and decorations are specific to one or other of the fighting services, officers and men of other services may receive them if their duties qualify them. For instance, in these days of combined operations, a Royal Marine officer or pilot might be awarded a DFC or DFM; and naval or air personnel serving on the ground as specialist or liaison personnel attached to an Army unit might be awarded Army decorations for their conduct during ground combat.

Flt Lt Alan Swann, QGM

Knight Batchelor

Rex Masterman HUNT CMG, HM Civil Commissioner, Falkland Islands.

CB (Civil Division)

Kenneth John PRITCHARD, Assistant Under Secretary, Ministry of Defence.

CMG

David Heywood ANDERSON, Foreign and Commonwealth Office.

Order of the Bath (Military Division)

KCB

Major General John Jeremy MOORE, CB, OBE, MC; Rear Admiral John Forster WOODWARD.

CB

Air Vice-Marshal George Arthur CHESWORTH, OBE, DFC, Royal Air Force; Commodore Michael Cecil CLAPP, Royal Navy; Air Vice-Marshal Kenneth William HAYR, CBE, AFC, Royal Air Force; Brigadier Julian Howard Atherden THOMPSON, OBE, ADC, Royal Marines; Rear Admiral Anthony John WHETSTONE;

Order of the British Empire (Military Division) GBE

Admiral Sir John David Elliott FIELDHOUSE, GCB

KBE

Air Marshal Sir John Bagot CURTISS, KCB, Royal Air Force; Vice Admiral David John HALLIFAX

CBE

Captain Paul BADCOCK, Royal Navy; Captain Nicholas John BARKER, Royal Navy; Colonel Ian Stuart BAXTER, MBE, late Royal Corps of Transport; Colonel John David BIDMEAD, OBE, late Royal Corps of Transport; Captain Christopher Peter Oldbury BURNE, Royal Navy; Colonel (Now Brigadier) David Bryan Hall COLLEY OBE, late Royal Corps of Transport; Group Captain Clive Ernest EVANS, Royal Air Force; Captain Raymnd Hunter FOX, Royal Navy; Captain John GARNIER, MVO, Royal Navy; Group Captain Alexander Freeland Cairns HUNTER, OBE, AFC, Royal Air Force; Group Captain Patrick KING, OBE, Royal Air Force; Captain Michael Henry Gordon LAYARD, Royal Navy; Colonel Bruce Christopher McDERMOTT, OBE, late Royal Army Medical Corps; Captain Robert McQueen, Royal Navy; Group Captain Jeremy Simon Blake PRICE, ADC, Royal Air Force; Captain Jonathan James Richard TOD, Royal Navy; Captain John Peter WRIGLEY, Royal Navy.

OBE

Commander Thomas Anthony ALLEN, Royal Navy; Wing Commander Anthony John Crowther BAGNALL, Royal Air Force; Commander Lional Stuart Joseph BARRY, Royal Navy; Wing Commander David Llewellyn BAUGH, Royal Air Force; Lieutenant Colonel Anthony Edward BERRY, The Royal Green Jackets; Commander Peter Stanley BIRCH, Royal Navy; Major Robert James BRUCE, Royal Marines; Major John Shane CHESTER, Royal

Marines; Commander Michael CUDMORE, Royal Navy; Captain John Barrie DICKINSON, Royal Fleet Auxiliary; Wing Commander Peter FRY, MBE, Royal Air Force; Commander Frederick Brian GOODSON, Royal Navy; Lieutenant Colonel Ivar Jack HELLBERG, Royal Corps of Transport; Commander Lister Theodore HICKSON, Royal Navy; Major (Now Lieutenant Colonel) Peter John HUBERT MBE, The Queen's Regiment; Surgeon Lieutenant Commander (Acting Surgeon Commander) Richard Tadeusz JOLLY, Royal Navy; Commander Christopher John ESPLIN-JONES, Royal Navy; Captain John Stuart KELLY, MBE, Royal Navy; Commander David Arthur Henry KERR, Royal Navy; Commander Martin Leonard LADD, Royal Navy; Captain Peter James McCARTHY, Royal Fleet Auxiliary; Commander Peter John McGREGOR, Royal Navy; Lieutenant Colonel William Stewart Petrie McGREGOR, Royal Army Medical Corps; Major David John MINORDS, Royal Marines; Lieutenant Colonel David Patrick de Courcy MORGAN, 7th Duke of Edinburgh's Own Gurkha Rifles; Squadron Leader Brian Sydney MORRIS, AFC, Royal Air Force; Commander Andrew William NETHERCLIFT, Royal Navy; Commander (Acting Captain) Anthony James OGLESBY, Royal Navy; Captain Gilbert Paul OVERBURY, Royal Fleet Auxiliary; Commander George Sheddon PEARSON, Royal Navy; Captain Shane REDMOND, Royal Fleet Auxiliary, Lieutenant Colonel John Francis RICKETT, MBE, Welsh Guards; Commander Andrew Stephen RITCHIE, Royal Navy; The Reverend Anthony McPherson ROSS, Royal Navy; Commander Robert Austin ROWLEY, Royal Navy; Commander

Jeremy Thomas SANDERS, Royal Navy; Commander Ronald James SANDFORD, Royal Navy; Lieutenant Colonel (Quartermaster) Patrick John SAUNDERS, Corps of Royal Engineers; Major James Maurice Guy SHERIDAN, Royal Marines; Commander Donald William SHRUBB, Royal Navy; Wing Commander Joseph KERR, AFC, Royal Air Force; Wing Commander Anthony Peter SLINGER, Royal Air Force; Lieutenant Colonel Michael John HOLROYD SMITH, Royal Regiment of Artillery; Wing Commander Charles Julian STURT, Royal Air Force; Major Simon Ewen SOUTHBY-TAILYOUR, Royal Marines; Major Jonathan James THOMSON, Royal Marines; Wing Commander Brian James WEAVER, Royal Air Force; Lieutenant Colonel Ronald WELSH, Royal Army Medical Corps; Commander Christopher Watkin WILLIAMS, Royal Navy; Commander George Anthony Charles WOODS, Royal Navy; Captain Christopher Anthony PURTCHER-WYDENBRUCK, Royal Fleet Auxiliary.

Warrant Officer Daniel Philmore BARKER, Royal Air Force; Major Edward Leo BARRETT, Royal Corps of Transport; Major Charles Gordon BATTY, Royal Army Medical Corps; Lieutenant Commander Michael John Douglas BROUGHAM, Royal Navy; Lieutenant Commander Roger Charles CAESLEY, Royal Navy; Flight Lieutenant Edna May CLINTON, Women's Royal Air Force; Lieutenant Roger Stephen COLLINS, Royal Navy; Warrant Officer Class 1 (Regimental Sergeant Major) Anthony James DAVIES, Welsh Guards; Major Christopher Matthew DAVIES, Corps of Royal Engineers; Lieutenant Alan David DUMMER, Royal Navy; Flight Lieu-

---

Flt Lt Alan Swann, QGM

Queen's Commendation for Valuable Service in the Air

Squadron Leader Timothy Newell ALLEN, Royal Air Force; Squadron Leader Anthony Frank BANFIELD, Royal Air Force; Squadron Leader Geoffrey Roger BARRELL, Royal Air force; Flight Lieutenant John Allin BROWN, Royal Air Force; Flight Lieutenant Peter Alfred STANDING, Royal Air Force; Squadron Leader (now Wing Commander) Martin Donald TODD, Royal Air Force; Squadron Leader Ernest Frederick WALLIS, MBE Royal Air Force; Flight Lieutenant Michael Ernest BEER, Royal Air Force; Flight Lieutenant James Dalrymple CUNNINGHAM, Royal Air Force; Flight Lieutenant John Norman KEABLE, Royal Air Force; Flight Lieutenant Murdo MacDonald MacLEOD, Royal Air Force; Flight Lieutenant Glyn David REES, Royal Air Force; Flight Lieutenant Robert Leslie ROWLEY, Royal Air Force; Flight Sergeant Stephen Edward SLOAN, Royal Air Force.

Mention in Despatches

Squadron Leader John Geoffrey ELLIOTT, Royal Air Force; Squadron Leader Robert Douglas IVESON, Royal Air Force; Flight Lieutenant Edward Henry BALL, Royal Air Force; Flight Lieutenant Mark William James HARE, Royal Air Force; Flight Lieutenant Gordon Carnie GRAHAM, Royal Air Force; Flight Lieutenant Alan Tom JONES, Royal Air Force; Flight Lieutenant Ian MORTIMER, Royal Air Force; Flight Lieutenant Hugh PRIOR, Royal Air Force; Flight Lieutenant Richard John RUSSELL, AFC Royal Air Force; Flight Lieutenant Robert Dennis WRIGHT, Royal Air Force; Flying Officer Peter Lewis TAYLOR, Royal Air Force; Flying Officer Colin MILLER, Royal Air Force; Flight Sergeant Derek William KNIGHTS, Royal Air Force; Corporal Alan David TOMLINSON, Royal Air Force

Queens's Commendation for Brave Conduct

Junior Technician Adrian THORNE, Royal Air Force; Senior Aircraft man Kenneth James SOPPETT-MOSS, Royal Air Force.

CIVILIAN
Life Peer

Admiral of the Fleet Sir Terence Thornton LEWIN GCB, MVO, DSC, lately Chief of the Defence Staff.

GEORGE MEDAL
QUEEN'S GALLANTRY MEDAL

These two medals, together with the George Cross (not in fact awarded in the Falklands War), are outside the normal sequence of awards for behaviour in combat on land, sea and air.

The GM is awarded to both civilian and service personnel for acts of exceptional bravery in circumstances not covered by the award of strictly military honours. It may, for example, be given for extraordinary bravery in bomb disposal work. The GC can be described as a civilian VC.

Instituted in 1974, the Queen's Gallantry Medal replaces the previous award of the British Empire Medal for acts of gallantry. It is primarily a civilian honour but, like the GC and GM, can be awarded to service personnel for acts which do not meet the criteria for specifically military decorations. It is listed after the DFM in order of precedence, and is often awarded in peacetime, as well as for suitable acts in war but not in the course of active operations.

tenant John DUNGATE, AFM, Royal Air Force; Major John Anthony EAST, Royal Army Medical Corps; Lieutenant Commander Colin John EDWARDS, Royal Navy; Fleet Chief Radio Supervisor David John EGGERS; Warrant Officer Class 1 Leslie ELLSON, Welsh Guards; Lieutenant Simon Jonathan BRANCH-EVANS, Royal Navy; Major Andrew Roger GALE, Royal Corps of Signals; Lieutenant Commander Richard GOODENOUGH, Royal Navy; Lieutenant Commander Michael GOODMAN, Royal Navy; Major Charles GRIFFITHS, Royal Army Medical Corps; Major (Quartermaster) Gerald Norman GROOM, Royal Corps of Transport; Warrant Officer Class 2 (Acting Warrant Officer Class 1) Thomas HAIG, Special Air Service Regiment; Lieutenant Commander Robert William HAMILTON, Royal Navy; Major Laurence HOLLINGWORTH, Royal Army Ordnance Corps; Captain Colin Francis HOWARD, Royal Marines; Lieutenant Commander Gerard Martin John IRVINE, Royal Navy; Lieutenant Commander Peter John JAMES, Royal Naval Reserve; Squadron Leader Clive Graham JEFFORD, Royal Air Force; Fleet ChiefWriter Christopher Geoffrey LAMB; Fleet Chief Petty Officer (OPs) (S) Michael John LEGG; Squadron Leader William Frederick LLOYD, Royal Air Force; Lieutenant Commander James Hutcheon LOUDON, Royal Navy; Captain Ronald MARSHALL, Intelligence Corps; Flight Lieutenant Brian Thomas MASON, Royal Air Force; Lieutenant Commander Horace Alfred MAYERS, Royal Navy; Captain Terence Gerald McCABE, Royal Army Medical Corps; Warrant Officer Class 1 Michael John McHALE, Royal Army Medical Corps; Lieutenant Commander Ian Scott McKENZIE, Royal Navy; Lieutenant Commander James Murdoch MILNE, Royal Navy; Captain (Quartermaster) Norman Edward MENZIES, The Parachute Regiment; Lieutenant (Now Captain) Frederick James MOODY, Scots Guards; Warrant Officer Class 2 Derek MOORE, Royal Corps of Transport; Fleet Chief Marine Engineering Artificer (H) Peter William MULLER; Acting Flight Lieutenant Anthony NEALE, Royal Air Force; Fleet Chief Petty Officer (OPS) (S) Robert John NICHOLLS; Squadron Leader David Miller NIVEN, Royal Air Force; Lieutenant David Charles Winston O'CONNELL, Royal Navy; Lieutenant Commander Lawrence David POOLE, Royal Navy; Lieutenant Brian PURNELL, Royal Navy; Warrant Officer Class 1 Robin Glen RANDALL, Royal Corps of Engineers; Major (Ordnance Executive Officer) John Moorby RIDDING; Royal Army Ordnance Corps; Flight Lieutenant Paul Anthony ROOM, Royal Air Force; Captain Michael Jeremy SHARLAND, Royal Marines; Surgeon Lieutenant Commander Philip James SHOULER, Royal Navy; Squadron Leader Trevor SITCH, Royal Air Force; Master Air Loadmaster Alan David SMITH, Royal Air Force; Lieutenant David Fielding SMITH, Royal Navy; Lieutenant Commander David John Robert WILMOT-SMITH, Royal Navy; Captain Dennis SPARKS, Royal Marines; Squadron Leader John Edward STOKES, Royal Air Force; Major John Ronaldson STUART, Royal

Spink and Son Ltd

ORDER OF THE BATH
ORDER OF THE BRITISH EMPIRE
ORDER OF ST MICHAEL AND ST GEORGE

1 CB (military); 2 OBE (military); 3 CMG; 4 MBE (civilian); 5 CBE (military)

These awards complete the Falklands honours picture. The first two are awarded both to military personnel and civilians.

The Most Honourable Order of the Bath, tracing a tenuous ancestry back to a court appointment instituted in 1399, was revived in 1725 as an award for senior officers for service in action. There are three classes:

Knight Grand Cross (GCB); Knight (GCB) and Companion (CB). The senior two classes carry knighthoods as the titles imply. The KCB has traditionally been the reward for the commander-in-chief of victorious British forces. The CB can only be conferred on an officer of the equivalent rank of major, commander or higher.

The Most Excellent Order of the British Empire was instituted in 1917, and a military division was created the following year. It is primarily a civilian award, conferred for a wide range of services to the nation, in five grades: GBE, KBE (both grades carrying knighthoods), CBE, OBE, and MBE. It is conferred in the various grades on military personnel of all ranks for valuable service which does not qualify, by reason of circumstance, for any specifically military decoration. In honours lists such awards are usually described as being in the 'military division'.

The Most Distinguished Order of St Michael and St George was instituted in 1818 and is awarded, in four classes, traditionally but not exclusively, for overseas service. As such it is the principal award for diplomats.

Corps of Signals; Major Michael Gordon TAYLOR, Royal Corps of Signals; Lieutenant Commander John Nicholas Owen WILLIAMS, Royal Navy; Warrant Officer Class 2 Philip Michael WILLIAMS, Royal Corps of Transport; Major Timothy James WILTON, Royal Regiment of Artillery; Major Guy Justin YEOMAN, Royal Corps of Transport; Warrant Officer Class 2 Robert Charles YEOMANS, Royal Corps of Signals.

British Empire Medal (Military Division)

Petty Officer Medical Assistant Keith ADAMS; Air Engineering Mechanician (R) 1st Class John Leslie BAILEY; Chief Air Engineering Mechanic (M) Norman Ronald BARWICK; Flight Sergeant John Harry BELL, Royal Air Force; Marine Engineering Artificer (H) 1st Class Thomas James BENNETTO; Staff Sergeant William Frank BLYTH, Royal Corps of Transport; Staff Sergeant Edward George BRADBURY, Corps of Royal Engineers; Sergeant Roger Joseph BROWN, Corps of Royal Engineers; Chief Air Engineering Artificer (R) 1st Class David Martine CHILDS; Master-at-Arms Anthony Francis COLES; Sergeant James McMillan COLEMAN, Royal Air Force; Chief Marine Engineering Mechanician (P) Geoffrey Stuart COX; Staff Sergeant Michael John DENT, Corps of Royal Engineers; Chief Air Engineering Mechanic (L) William David EATON; Staff Sergeant James FENWICK, Corps of Royal Electrical and Mechanical Engineers; Air Engineering Artificer (M) 1st Class Stuart GOODALL; Staff Sergeant Robert Leonard GRIFFITHS, Royal Corps of Signals; Corporal Norman John HALL, Corps of Royal Engineers; Sergeant David HARVEY, Royal Army Ordnance Corps; Staff Sergeant Colin Lee HENDERSON, Army Catering Corps; Chief Air Engineering Aritificer, (M) David John HERITIER; Corporal Graham John HERRINGTON, Royal Pioneer Corps; Chief Petty Officer (D) Leonard Brian HEWETT; Staff Sergeant John Duncan HOLMES, Royal Army Ordnance Corps; Corporal William Henry HOPKINS, Royal Army Ordnance Corps; Private David John HUNT, Army Catering Corps; Chief Petty Officer Caterer John Arthur JACKSON; Air Engineering Aritificer (H) 1st Class David Eric JONES; Flight Sergeant Kenneth KENNY, Royal Air Force; Chief Technician Thomas Joseph KINSELLA, Royal Air Force; Air Engineering Artificer (L) 1st Class Robert Anthony John MASON; Medical Technician 1st Class Stuart McKINLAY; Chief Petty Officer Cook Michael Gerald MERCER; Leading Wren Stores Accountant Jacqueline MITTON, Women's Royal Naval Service; Chief Wren Education Assistant Anne MONCTON, Women's Royal Naval Service; Sergeant Denis Ronald PASFIELD, Corps of Royal Engineers; Staff Sergeant Paul RAYNER, Corps of Royal Engineers; Staff Sergeant (Acting Warrant Officer Class 2) Malachi REID, Royal Army Medical Corps; Air Engineering Artificer (L) 2nd Class Alan John SMITH; Chief Petty Officer (OPS) (M) Owen Gwyn STOCKHAM; Air Engineering Aritificer (L) 1st Class Roger James Edward STRONG; Staff Sergeant Christopher Glyn TAYLOR,

Corps of Royal Electrical and Mechanical Engineers; Chief Air Engineering Mechanician (L) 1st Class Thomas Lowen TEMPLE; Leading Wren Dental Hygienist Kim TOMS, Women's Royal Naval Service; Chief Wren Family Services Barbara Marion TRAVERS, Women's Royal Naval Service; Sergeant Peter TUXFORD, Royal Air Force; Chief Technician Richard Keith VERNON, Royal Air Force; Sergeant John Charles VICKERS, Royal Air Force; Corporal David John VIVIAN, Royal Air Force; Acting Leading Stores Accountant Gerard John WALSH; Petty Officer (Missile) John James Trevor WATERFIELD; Petty Officer (Missile) Edward Lee WELLS; Air Engineering Mechanician (M) 1st Class David John WILLIAMS; Sergeant Brian WINTER, Royal Marines; Corporal (Acting Sergeant) Anthony WORTHINGTON, Corps of Royal Engineers.

CBE (Civil Division)

Captain Donald Arthur ELLERBY, Master m.v. NORLAND; Ian McLeod FAIRFIELD, Chairman and Chief Executive, Chemring plc; Miss Patricia Margaret HUTCHINSON, CMG HM Ambassador, Montevideo; Roger Tustin JACKLING, Assistant Secretary, Ministry of Defence; Captain Dennis John SCOTT-MASSON, Master SS CANBERRA; Captain John Penny MORTON, Master, m.v. ELK; Nigel Hamilton NICHOLLS, Assistant Secretary, Ministry of Defence; Eric John RISNESS, Deputy Chief Scientific Officer, Ministry of Defence; William Bell SLATER, Managing Director, The Cunard Steam-Ship Company plc; John Robert Christopher THOMAS, Deputy Chief Scientific Officer, Ministry of Defence.

OBE

Peter Derek ADAMS, Principal Scientific Officer, Ministry of Defence; Russell George ALGAR, Senior Principal, Ministry of Defence; The Reverend Harry BAGNALL, Dean of Christchurch, Falkland Islands; Michael John BEYNON, Chief Map Research Officer, Ministry of Defence; Alison Ann, Mrs BLEANEY, Acting Senior Medical Officer, Falkland Islands; Margaret Janet, Mrs BOURNE, Senior Principal Scientific Officer, Ministry of Defence; Reginald BUTCHER, Managing Director, Wimpey Marine Ltd; David William CHALMERS, Constructor (C), Ministry of Defence; Captain William James Christopher CLARKE, Master, m.v. EUROPIC FERRY; Captain Alan FULTON, Master, Cable Ship IRIS; Roderick Owen GATES, Executive Director, Aircraft Engineering, Marshall of Cambridge (Engineering) Ltd; Andrew John GLASGOW, Projects Director, Marconi Underwater Systems Ltd; Edgar James HARVEY, Principal Professional and Technology Officer, Ministry of Defence; Stanley Stephen HOLNESS, Senior Principal, Department of Trade; Vernon Edward HORSFIELD, Works Manager, Woodford Aircraft Group, British Aerospace plc; Christopher HULSE, Foreign and Commonwealth Office; Miss Maureen Mary JONES, Foreign and Commonwealth Office; Derek LEWIS, Professional and Technology Superintendent, Ministry of Defence; Arthur Frederick George MOSS, Divisional Manager,

HM Dockyard, Gibralter; John Patrick RABY, Projects Director, Humber Graving Dock and Engineering Company Ltd; Captain David Michael RUNDLE, Master, m.v. BRITISH WYE; Captain Michael John SLACK, Master, m.s. WIMPEY SEAHORSE; The Right Reverend Monsignor Daniel Martin SPRAGGON, MBE, Prefect Apostolic, Falkland Islands; Raymond Sydney TEE, Principal Professional and Technology Officer (Constructor), Ministry of Defence; Peter VARNISH, Principal Scientific Officer, Ministry of Defence; Ronale WATSON, Local Director, Quality Assurance, Swan Hunter Shipbuilders Ltd; Robert WEATHERBURN, Senior Principal Scientific Officer, Ministry of Defence; John Anthony WELDON, Principal Professional and Technology Officer, Ministry of Defence.

SOUTH ATLANTIC MEDAL
The ribbon of the campaign medal, awarded to all who took part, bears a rosette if the recipient entered the combat zone.

The Royal Mint

MBE

Valerie Elizabeth, Mrs BENNETT, Acting Matron, Stanley Hospital, Falkland Islands; Jane Hunter, Mrs BOLTON, Clerical Officer, Ministry of Defence; Colin Michael BOYNE, Senior Scientific Officer, Ministry of Defence; David Laing BREEN, Radar Systems Engineer, Marconi Radar Systems Ltd; Ronald Arthur BROWN, Marine Services Officer II (Engineer), Ministry of Defence; Terence James CAREY, Electrical Superintendent, Falkland Islands; Edgar Dennis CARR, Regional Manager, Southampton, General Council of British Shipping; Anthony Martin CLEAVER, Photographer, Press Association; Albert Frederick George COLLINS, Steelwork Production Manager, Vosper Ship Repairers Ltd; Arthur John COLLMAN, Professional and Technology Officer II, Ministry of Defence; Peter Merlyn John COOK, Professional and Technology Officer II, Ministry of Defence; Frederick Joseph COOPER, Passenger and Cargo Manager's Assistant, British Transport Docks Board, Southampton; David John CORMICK, Senior Field Engineer, Marconi Space and Defence Systems Ltd; Richard Arthur DREW, Foreign and Commonwealth Office; Miss Patricia DURLING, Higher Executive Officer, Ministry of Defence; Stuart EARNSHAW, Chief Marine Superintendent, Thoresen Car Ferries Ltd; Miss Mary Georgiana ELPHINSTONE, Volunteer Medical Officer, Falkland Islands; Miss Rosemary Margaret ELSDON, Senior Nursing Sister, SS CANBERRA; James Robert Rutherford FOX, Radio News Reporter, British Broadcasting Corporation; John Aubrey FRENCH, Senior Scientific Officer, Ministry of

Defence; Brian Arthur GORRINGE, Catering Manager Grade II, Staff Restaurant, Ministry of Defence; Eric Miller GOSS, Manager, Goose Green Farm, Falkland Islands; Michael John Stephen HATTON, Professional and Technology Officer II, Department of Trade; Miss Sybil Matilda HILL, Clerical Assistant, Department of Trade; Gerald William Tom HODGE, Professional and Technology Officer II, Ministry of Defence; William HUNTER, Professional and Technology Officer II, Ministry of Defence; Ronald Daniel LAWRENCE, Higher Executive Officer, Cabinet Office; Robert Graham John LLOYD, Assistant Manager, Warehouse and Distribution Services, Navy, Army and Air Force Institutes; David McALPIN, Flight Trials Engineer, Ferranti plc; William Robert McQUEEN, Senior Scientific Officer, Meteorological Office; David MONUMENT, Maintenance Superintendent, P&O Steam Navigation Company; Thomas Ronald MORSE, Foreign and Commonwealth Office; Valerie Ann, Mrs MOTHERSHAW, Executive Officer, Ministry of Defence; Dawn Barbara Mavis, Mrs MURRAY, Senior Scientific Officer, Ministry of Defence; Patricia Margaret, Mrs NUTBEEM, Chairwoman, 16 Field Ambulance RAMC Wives' Club, Aldershot; Squadron Leader Thomas James PALMER, RAF (Retd), Headquarters, United Kingdom Land Forces, Ministry of Defence; Miss Elizabeth PATTEN, Senior Welfare Officer, St John and Red Cross Service Hospitals Welfare; Terence John PECK CPM, Councillor, Legislative Council, Falkland Islands; Denis PLACE, Water Supervisor, Falkland Islands; Jonathan Trevor PRICE, Executive Officer, Ministry of Defence; James Frederick QUIRK, Senior Executive Officer, Royal Naval Supply and Transport Service; Paul ROBINSON, Higher Scientific Officer, Ministry of Defence; John Robertson Page RODIGAN, Professional and Technology Officer II, Ministry of Defence; Kevin William SHACKLETON, Contract Engineer, Ames Crosta Babcock Ltd; Michael Sydney SHEARS, Production Manager, Vosper Thornycroft (UK) Ltd; Captain Derek SIMS, Senior Cargo Surveyor, Hogg Robinson (GFA) Ltd; Miss Angela SLAYMAKER, Clerical Officer, Ministry of Defence; Squadron Leader John Michael SMITH, RAF (Retd), Senior Operations Manager, Dynamics Group, British Aerospace plc; Rodney Lorraine START, Senior Executive Officer, Department of Trade; Angela Elizabeth, Mrs THORNE, Executive Officer, Ministry of Defence; John TURNER, Senior Scientific Officer, Meteorological Office; Patrick James WATTS, Director, Broadcasting Service, Falkland Islands; Richard Stephen WHITLEY, Veterinary Officer, Falkland Islands.

British Empire Medal (Civil Division)

Arthur James ALDRED, Process and General Supervisory Grade D, Ministry of Defence; Malcolm ASHWORTH, Dairyman, Falkland Islands; Garry BALES, Able Seaman, Tug IRISHMAN; Irene Ingeborg, Mrs BARDSLEY, Club Manageress, Excellent Steps, Portsmouth, Navy, Army and Air Force Institutes; Richard Sydney BARRETT, Chief Steward,

Cable Ship IRIS; Dennis Paul BETTS, Able Seaman, Tug IRISHMAN; Roy Samuel BLANCHARD, Foreman Shipwright, Vosper Ship Repairers Ltd; Michael Harfield BOYES, Laboratory Mechanic, Ministry of Defence; Najla Dorothy, Mrs BUCKETT, Housewife, Falkland Islands; Tim DOBBYNS, Farmer, Falkland Islands; Eric Christopher EMERY, Professional and Technology Officer III, Department of Trade; Luis ESTELLA, Process and General Supervisory Grade E, HM Dockyard, Gibraltar; James Stephen FAIRFIELD, lately Corporal, Royal Marines, Falkland Islands; Robert James FORD, Senior Storeman, Ministry of Defence; James Anderson GOLDIE, Stores Officer Grade C, Royal Fleet Auxiliary RESOURCE; Leslie Sydney HARRIS, Senior Electrician, Falkland Islands; Ronald John HATCH, Marine Services Officer IV (Deck), Ministry of Defence; John HAYWOOD, Progressman Planner Technical (Shipwright), Ministry of Defence; Jack JOHNSTON, Senior Storekeeper, Royal Fleet Auxiliary FORT AUSTIN; James Frederick JONES, Professional and Technology Officer III, Ministry of Defence; Bernard ORAM-JONES, Shipwright, Ministry of Defence; Brian John JOSHUA, Catering Manager, Pan American Airways, United States Air Force Base, Ascension Island; KANG, SHIK-MING, Laundryman, HMS BRILLIANT; Gordon James LANE, Laboratory Mechanic, Ministry of Defence; Alan John LEONARD, Chief Cook, SS ATLANTIC CAUSEWAY; Joseph Anthony LYNCH, Stores Officer Grade C, Ministry of Defence; Paul McEWAN, Stores Officer Grade C, Royal Fleet Auxiliary REGENT; Michael McKAY, Farmer, Falkland Islands; Philip MILLER, Tractor Driver, Falkland Islands; Edwin George MORGAN, Professional and Technology Officer III, Ministry of Defence; Andrew James Graham NISBET, Professional and Technology Officer III, Ministry of Defence; Hilda Blanche, Mrs PERRY, Telephone Superintendent, Falkland Islands; Peter Richard PETERSON, Mechanical Fitter, David Brown Gear Industries; Raymond Arthur ROBJOHN, Superintendent, Experimental Flight Shed, Westland Helicopters; Derek Robert Thomas ROZEE, Plumber, Falkland Islands; Ellis Walton SAMPSON, Stores Officer Grade C, Ministry of Defence; Victor SEOGALUTZE, Assistant Chief Inspector, Bridport Gundry plc; David Albert SMERDON, Professional and Technology Officer IV, Ministry of Defence; Vernon STEEN, Guide, Falkland Islands; SUEN, Ling-Kan, Laundryman, HMS ANTRIM; Donald Victor THREADGOLD, Telecommunications Technical Officer Grade II, Ministry of Defence; Miss Karen Lois TIMBERLAKE, Nursing Sister, Falkland Islands; Roland TODD, Professional and Technology Officer III, Ministry of Defence; Frank John TOUGH, Professional and Technology Officer III, Ministry of Defence; Eileen, Mrs VIDAL, Radio Telephonist, Falkland Islands; Miss Bronwen Vaughan WILLIAMS, Nursing Sister, Falkland Islands; Colin Walter WILSON, Foreman, Repair Support Area, Marconi Radar Systems; Christopher John WINDER, Professional and Technology Officer III, Ministry of Defence.